THE
RORKE'S
DRIFT
COMMANDERS

THE
RORKE'S
DRIFT
COMMANDERS

Gonville Bromhead and
John Chard

James W. Bancroft

FRONTLINE
BOOKS

THE RORKE'S DRIFT COMMANDERS
Gonville Bromhead and John Chard

First published in Great Britain in 2022 by

Frontline Books
An imprint of
Pen & Sword Books Ltd
Yorkshire – Philadelphia

ISBN 978 1 39900 996 6

A CIP catalogue record for this book is
available from the British Library

Typeset in 10.5/13 pt Palatino by SJmagic DESIGN SERVICES, India.

Printed and bound by CPI Group (UK) Ltd, Croydon, CR0 4YY

Pen & Sword Books Ltd incorporates the imprints of Pen & Sword Archaeology, Atlas,
Aviation, Battleground, Discovery, Family History, History, Maritime, Military, Naval,
Politics, Social History, Transport, True Crime, Claymore Press, Frontline Books, Praetorian
Press, Seaforth Publishing and White Owl

For a complete list of Pen & Sword titles please contact

PEN & SWORD BOOKS LTD
47 Church Street, Barnsley, South Yorkshire, S70 2AS, England
E-mail: enquiries@pen-and-sword.co.uk
Website: www.pen-and-sword.co.uk

Or

PEN AND SWORD BOOKS
1950 Lawrence Rd, Havertown, PA 19083, USA
E-mail: Uspen-and-sword@casematepublishers.com
Website: www.penandswordbooks.com

Contents

Introduction

Lieutenants Gonville Bromhead and John Chard knew each other for less than a month. They were brought together by fate, and they had fame thrust upon them. As did the place known as Rorke's Drift, which prior to 1879 was a peaceful homestead situated a long way from any large town on the South African veldt. Although they both came from families whose various members were highly distinguished for their military service and for their service to the Church, they became reluctant heroes after being awarded Britain's highest decoration for valour, the Victoria Cross, for showing staunch leadership during the immortal defence of Rorke's Drift.

A British invasion force had crossed the Buffalo River into Zululand on 11 January 1879, and advanced into enemy territory towards a rock feature known as Isandlwana, where they established a base camp. Men of B Company, 2nd Battalion, 24th Regiment, under Lieutenant Bromhead had been assigned to the duty of garrisoning the field hospital and store house which had been established at Rorke's Drift, on the Natal side of the river. Lieutenant Chard of the Royal Engineers was ordered to

John Rouse Merriott Chard VC.

move up from Durban to Rorke's Drift to work on fixing and maintaining one of the ponts at the river and arrived there on 19 January. Thus was the situation that fate had handed the two young officers.

On 22 January 1879, the camp at Isandlwana was attacked by an overwhelming army (*impi*) of Zulu warriors and most of the British force was cut to pieces – literally. A mass of warriors eager to shed more blood moved on to attack the garrison at Rorke's Drift, where only about 150 men were stationed, some of whom were wounded or too ill to fight. However, 'Unity is Strength' and the two commanders and their fellow officers supervised the building of barricades to turn the post into a reasonably effective defensive position and placed their men at the ready to hold their ground.

It must have seemed that it was time for them to 'Learn to Die' as about 3,000 Zulus made ferocious attacks and spontaneous assaults on the garrison throughout the night. 'Never Despairing', the cool leadership of the commanders and the discipline, courage and stamina of the soldiers present was such that the warriors could not overcome them, and they eventually lost heart and moved off back into Zululand. When a relief force arrived, the hospital had been practically destroyed but most of the remainder of the fort was intact and the British had suffered relatively few casualties.

Part of the official citation for the Victoria Cross stated: 'Had it not been for the fine example and excellent behaviour of these two Officers under the most trying circumstances, the defence of Rorke's Drift post would not have been conducted with that intelligence and tenacity which so essentially characterised it.' Eleven defenders were awarded the Victoria Cross, a total that had been surpassed previously but has never been equalled since. Lieutenants Chard and Bromhead received the medal,

Gonville Bromhead VC.

and the seven presented to the 24th Regiment is the most awarded to one regiment for a single action.

The two officers came to be known as the 'Heroes of Rorke's Drift'. They received accelerated promotions, the thanks of both Houses of the British Parliament and were invited to audiences with Queen Victoria, who became very fond of Chard in particular. They were also showered with civilian awards, and coming from families with strong

The defenders of the garrison at Rorke's Drift expected no mercy from the Zulu warriors, and they fought with great gallantry, vowing to sell their lives dearly. Men who were wounded helped at the barricades by distributing ammunition and shouting encouragement. They held off the ferocious onslaughts even when they suffered most of their casualties before nightfall. Their steadfast determination disheartened the Zulus and forced them to give up the fight. *(Illustration by Geoff Dickson)*

religious beliefs, perhaps the greatest tribute was when stained-glass church memorial windows were dedicated to them.

Unfortunately, the awards caused bad feeling among their superior officers, who recorded detrimental remarks towards them. However, the glowing testimonies provided by Gonville Bromhead's comrades within his regiment and the expressions of great admiration for John Chard shown by the people of Devon and Somerset for the rest of his life outshone any jealous criticisms they had to suffer.

Some of their family and friends were of the opinion that they were too modest for their own good, and that they had failed to take full advantage of their new-found fame. However, it would seem that John Chard developed a notable ability to make the acquaintance of influential people throughout his relatively short life.

A member of the Chard family remembered him as a man who never seemed to come to terms with what he had done and never considered his deed to have been as heroic as people thought. Indeed, both Bromhead and Chard slipped happily back into their career lives, which they carried out with great competence and devotion to duty. They both died of particularly dreadful diseases, even for those days. Bromhead from typhoid fever in India in 1891, in his 46th year, and Chard from cancer in Somerset in 1897, aged 50.

However, the exceptional courage of Bromhead and Chard and the small band of heroes struck a chord with the British public which has echoed down the years. In 1964 the defence of Rorke's Drift was brought to the public's attention once again with the screening of the epic motion picture *Zulu!* – Chard being portrayed by Sir Stanley Baker, and Bromhead providing Sir Michael Caine with his first starring role. Since then, a steady flow of books and television programmes, and even study groups, have perpetuated the memory of that fateful day.

For the narrative of the defence of Rorke's Drift every effort has been made to tell the events with the words of those who were there, and when more than one defender witnessed or took part in an incident the account of the person who seems to have been in the best position to see it has been used, especially the most relevant to the commanding officers.

Most of the information for this publication comes from the JWB Historical Archive, which the author has compiled over five decades, and another book would be required to annotate each statement made. However, in addition to the Bibliography and Main Research Sources, some notes are included within the text and the main research sources relevant to each chapter listed separately.

Chapter 1

Ancestry

Gonville became the most famous Bromhead, but several members of his distinguished family gave great service to the Church, and the heritage of their military prowess dates back to the Jacobite Rebellion, Wolfe's campaign at Quebec, the American War of Independence, the Peninsular War and the Battle of Waterloo, the Crimean War, several of Britain's colonial campaigns during the reign of Queen Victoria and the two world wars. Members of the family are serving with the armed forces to this day. An inscription on one of the Bromhead graves in the family's historic home village of Thurlby says: '*Disce Mori*' – 'Learn to Die' – and they are a family who have learned to fight and die for their country with great honour.

The family of Bromhead has been established in Lincolnshire since the beginning of the twelfth century, and it is said that the name derives from the old English word 'brom' – meaning a broom or gorse, and 'heafod' – meaning a head of land, and the name was indeed usually given to someone who was a landowner or even a lord of the manor.

The family motto is '*Concordia Res Crescunt*', which can be interpreted in various ways, but usually as 'Unity is Strength' – appropriate for a defender of Rorke's Drift. The family crest is officially described as: 'Azure on a Bend Argent between two Leopard's Faces, or a Mural Crown Gules between two Fleurs-de-lis-Sables. Out of a Mural Crown gules a Unicorn's Head Argent homed, or in the Mouth a Rose Gules slipped and leave proper.'

Gonville was born on 29 August 1845, at Versailles in the Yvelines department of Paris, the youngest of four sons in a family of ten children to Edmund de Gonville Bromhead, who lived at Thurlby Hall near Lincoln, a country house built in the early eighteenth century.*

_____

* The memorial window at Thurlby displays the year of his birth as 1844.

1

CONCORDIA RES CRESCUNT

The Bromhead coat of arms and crest. The motto in English is 'Unity is Strength'.

On 15 September 1823 Edmund married Judith Christine Cahill (born in Sligo on 11 September 1803), who was thirteen years younger than him. She was the youngest daughter of the pioneering archaeologist Captain James Wood, of Woodville House in County Sligo, Ireland (which still exists), and his wife Anne, who was the eldest daughter of Abraham Martin of Cleveragh in County Sligo. Captain Wood was the High Sheriff of County Sligo in 1826. On their marriage Edmund built a house named Cairnsfoot in St John's Parish in Sligo, where they made their home. However, on the outbreak of the terrible Irish potato famine in the mid-1840s, they spent some time at Versailles near Paris, and then they returned permanently to Thurlby Hall. They retained the house in Sligo for letting out and about 100 acres of land in the area.

Gonville was deaf to some degree, although it has not been possible to confirm how severe his hearing problem was, or indeed the actual cause. Some medical journals suggest a link between being conceived when the mother is older than average, and Judith was 41 when Gonville was born. However, she did have a daughter even later than Gonville. His deafness was mentioned by several people, who included Colonel Farquhar Glennie of the 1st South Wales Borderers, although the statement by Lieutenant Henry Curling of the Royal Artillery that

The village of Thurlby near Lincoln is mentioned in the Domesday Book, and Thurlby Hall, the home of the Baron Bromheads, is a country house built in the early eighteenth century. It is now a Grade II listed building.

he was 'deaf as a post' is almost certainly exaggerated. His brother Charles was a favourite of General Wolseley and other high-ranking officers, so if it was an issue, they may have been able to get officials to overlook it if he was only partially deaf.

A recruitment Act from the middle period of the Napoleonic Wars included the following guidance (a medical may not necessarily have taken place): 'Recruits had to sign that they had no rupture (hernia), they were not troubled with fits, in no way disabled by lameness, have perfect use of all limbs, and that they were not a runaway.' There was a height requirement of 5ft 6in, but there is no comment about hearing. It is important to note that right into the nineteenth century each regiment had its own interpretation of what constituted 'Fit to Serve' – and the rules were certainly bent, especially when recruits were scarce. There was a battalion on active service inspected by the military hospital surgeon during the Seven Years War that had all of the problems mentioned, as well as men with fingers, toes, ears, an eye and 'other extremities' missing, the latter being somewhat disconcerting. Consequently, at that time it would seem that deafness was not officially an impediment to joining or serving.

Close to Thurlby Hall, among trees just off the beaten track, is the medieval Norman Church of St Germain, which was founded in 1133 by William, the Constable of Bishop Alexander of Lincoln. It was re-built in 1820. The Bromhead family worshipped at the church, and Edmund donated £1,000 of his own money for restoration in 1842. The old thatch was replaced by slates, the floor was newly cemented and he had the pews, choir stalls and the south door replaced by Thurlby oak, although the original ancient ironwork was retained on the door. The church contains many memorials to the Bromhead family, including all five Baron Bromheads. The earliest memorial dedicated to a Bromhead states: 'Bromhead Benjamin 1702/03/07 – Here lies the body of Benjamin Bromhead esq'r of Thurlby who died March 7th 1702.'

The graves of Gonville's great-grandparents, Boardman (or Bordman) (born 17 September 1728) and Frances (born in 1730), are also in the church. His great-grandfather's name is spelled both ways depending on which source is consulted. He was baptised in 1728, at St Margaret's Church in King's Lynn, Norfolk. Frances was a descendant of the family of Edmund Gonville, who founded Gonville Hall in Cambridge in 1348. On its enlargement by Dr John Caius in 1557 it became Gonville and Caius College, the fourth oldest college in the city. Former pupils include Dr Edward Adrian Wilson, who died with Captain Scott in the Antarctic in 1912; Lawrence Beesley, who survived the sinking of the *Titanic* in the same year; Harold Abrahams, who won the 100m gold medal at the 1924 Olympic Games; and Sir Francis Crick, who discovered and

The Church of St Germain at Thurlby, where many of the Bromhead family are buried, including the five Baron Bromheads who have passed away.

4

developed the structure of DNA for which he was awarded the Nobel Prize in Physiology and Medicine in 1969. The college is also famous for entering the Football Association's Challenge Cup for the 1880–1 and 1881–2 seasons.

Boardman and Frances married at the Church of St Mary Magdelene in Bailgate, Lincoln, on 18 May 1756. They had a daughter named Elizabeth, but she died as a baby in 1764.

Boardman served as ensign with the 62nd (Wiltshire) Regiment under General James Wolfe at Quebec in 1759, and, according to local legend in Lincolnshire, he is believed to have been the officer who assured the general of the French retreat. He transferred to the 28th (North Gloucestershire) Regiment and gained the rank of general. Frances died on 9 January 1801, and Boardman died on 7 December 1804, aged 76.

Boardman had four brothers in the army, one of whom, Edward, was serving as a Dragoon when he was killed at the Battle of Falkirk Muir in 1746, during the Jacobite Rising. His brother James (1738–1804) was a captain with the 34th (Cumberland) Regiment and is said to have taken part in the Seven Years War (1756–63), including the Battle of Minden in 1759, although the 34th Regiment do not have it as a battle honour.

The family's connection with the 24th Regiment began when two other brothers, Benjamin and John, served as officers with the 2nd Battalion, and transferred after it was re-designated as the 69th (South Lincolnshire) Regiment in 1758.

The military achievements of Boardman's son, Gonville, resulted in him being created the 1st Baron Bromhead. He was born at Lincoln on 20 September 1758. He was educated under Dr Joseph Wharton at Winchester College, and then under the famed Master Lewis Lochée at the Military Academy in Little Chelsea. Lochée was a specialist in the study of fortifications, and one wonders if the baron passed any of his knowledge down the family to his grandson.

Possibly because of his father's influence, Gonville was appointed staff officer and quartermaster of the 62nd Regiment when he was very young. However, he proved his worth on several occasions. When he came of age he was commissioned as ensign in the 62nd Regiment in 1774, and was appointed lieutenant two years later. He served with the regiment during General John Burgoyne's campaign of 1777 in North America. According to *The Annual Biography and Obituary for the Year 1823*, his military service entailed the following:

In the ensuing campaign (1777), being with the advance in taking possession of Mount Independence, he narrowly escaped the

5

explosion of several mines, which the enemy left on evacuating the place. Shortly afterwards, on the 19th of September, 1777, at the battle of Freeman's Farm, nearly the whole of his regiment was destroyed, himself and two privates being the only two persons of the company to which he belonged, that were not either killed or wounded. On this occasion he was attached by Sir Francis Clerke, to the colours of the 9th (Norfolk) Regiment, which was then advancing. He was also present at the disastrous affair of the 7th of October, after which the army retired to Saratoga; and at Fort Hardy, near that place, he was wounded. At this time also General Burgoyne, the commander-in-chief, being anxious to recover stores to a great amount which had fallen into the hands of the enemy, he volunteered to ascend the river in the night, and succeeded, amidst a heavy fire, in cutting the cables of the bateaux, which drifted down with a large quantity of provisions to the royal army: for this service he was honoured with his Excellency's thanks. Being with the army at Saratoga, he was detained prisoner of war upwards of three years.

On his return to the regiment in England after his exchange in 1781, Gonville served as lieutenant in Captain William Hall's Company, and was appointed captain in 1786.

The grave of Lieutenant General, Sir Gonville Bromhead and his wife, Frances, in Thurlby churchyard. His distinguished military service earned him the appointment of 1st Baron Bromhead in 1806.

On 18 July 1787, Gonville married Lady Jane, the daughter of Sir Charles, 1st Baron Ffrench, and they had three sons – Sir Edward Thomas Ffrench, 2nd Baronet; Sir Edmund de Gonville, 3rd Baronet; and the Revd Charles Ffrench, who was born on 18 May 1795. He became the vicar of Cardington in Bedfordshire, and he died unmarried on 2 August 1855. It is not recorded that Gonville and Jane also had a daughter named Catherine Ffrench, who died on 15 December 1796, aged 5 years, and is buried at Thurlby.

The Annual Biography and Obituary continued:

Arthur Annersley, 1st Earl of Mountnorris, raised the 126th Regiment in 1794, known as the Lochaber (Cameron's) Fencible Infantry, and Gonville became lieutenant-colonel of the new regiment. During the Irish rebellion of 1796–1798 he actively assisted his brother-in-law, Lord Thomas Hamilton Ffrench, in organizing the yeomanry cavalry, and served himself as a volunteer. Lord Carhampton, the commander-in-chief in Ireland, at that period, expressing himself sensible of his zeal, recommended him for more efficient service, and he was immediately appointed to the lieutenant-colonelcy of the Lochaber Highlanders, who were stationed on the coast, in expectation of the descent of a large French force. When the volunteer levy in England was made, on the threatened invasion, he was appointed brigadier-general on the staff, and by indefatigable exertions, rendered the great body of his different corps fully competent to act with the line.

The Lochaber Highlanders were a fencible corps raised by the Campbell clan, and assembled at Falkirk in 1799, ironically where Gonville's Uncle Edward had been killed in action. The unit was moved to Ireland in 1800 and was disbanded after arriving back in Scotland in 1802.

The Bromhead baronetcy was announced in the *London Gazette* for 19 February 1806, in recognition of his military service. He was placed on half-pay six years later. He became colonel in 1801, major general in 1808 and lieutenant general in 1813. Gonville died at Thurlby on 18 May 1822 and is buried there. Lady Jane died on 2 September 1837 and is also buried at Thurlby.

Gonville was succeeded on his death by his eldest son, later Sir Edward Thomas Ffrench. Edward was born in Dublin on 26 March 1789. He was educated at Halifax, and at the University of Glasgow from 1806–8. He then went up to Caius College, Cambridge, gaining his Bachelor of Arts in 1812 and his Master of Arts in 1815.

The ante-room at Thurlby Hall, where the Bromheads waited to receive visitors. There are various interesting items on view. The wooden seat is known as a settle, a form of domestic furniture of the time. The Zulu shield is of the regimental *isihlangu* pattern. According to a Zulu specialist, it looks to be from the uThulwana regiment, so it was possibly retrieved from Rorke's Drift. The slightly crumpled 1870s forage cap above the bugle is probably Gonville's as his family are known to have it. The other two forage caps are of a later period. The Afghan knives on the far wall were probably brought back by Benjamin Parnell. The lead water cistern containing ski gear looks somewhat out of place.

As a prominent mathematician, he was a founder member of the Analytical Society of Cambridge, and was associated with some of the great names in the philosophical and mathematical circles in Lincoln, and contributed many articles to their journals. He was also a founder and sometime president of the local mechanics' institute, a forerunner of the modern working men's club. He was George Green's patron, and he was a friend of George Boole. He was also a contemporary of Charles Babbage, who became a lifelong friend. He was appointed Fellow of the Royal Society (FRS) in 1817, and Fellow of the Royal Society of Edinburgh (FRSE). He was admitted to the Inner Temple and was entitled to practise as a barrister. He held the office of High Steward of Lincolnshire, and as such was a Justice of the Peace for Kesteven in Lincolnshire. He was dogged by ill-health throughout his life, and suffered failing sight when he was older. He died unmarried at Thurlby Hall on 14 March 1855, and is buried at Thurlby.

Gonville's parents are commemorated with a stone in the church and they are buried in the churchyard. Major Sir Edmund de Gonville Bromhead was born at Thurlby on 22 January 1791. He entered the 54th (West Norfolk) Regiment, and served in the Walcheren Expedition to the Netherlands in 1809, when disease among the British army forced them to withdraw. He served in the Peninsular War, and his gravestone at Thurlby records that he fought at Waterloo. His regiment was part of the extreme right of the line Wellington drew up and as such was several miles to the north of the main battle area. However, he later performed an extremely gallant act when he led the 'Forlorn Hope' at the storming of the French town of Cambrai, and in so doing lost an eye. He succeeded as the 3rd Baron Bromhead on 14 March 1855 and died on 25 October 1870.

Born in 1775, Gonville's Uncle John is arguably the most distinguished member of the family. He was commissioned as ensign in the 24th Regiment in 1793. He transferred as major in the 2nd Battalion, 34th (Cumberland) Regiment on 16 May 1805, and then he transferred to the 77th (East Middlesex) Regiment as lieutenant colonel on 3 August 1809. The 77th was also present during the Walcheren Expedition. He commanded the 77th and the 2nd/5th (Northumberland) Fusiliers in the 3rd Division of the army during the retreat from El Bodon in 1811, formed them into a square and marched through the French cavalry to rejoin Wellington. In early 1812 he commanded them in the siege and storming of Ciudad Rodrigo, and the siege and storming of Badajoz. For his service he received a gold medal and was appointed CB (Companion of the Order of the Bath), and he was promoted colonel by brevet on 12 August 1819. He died in Lincoln in 1837, and his Peninsular gold medal is retained by the family.

The Baron Bromheads

Name	Place and Date of Birth	In Office	Age at Death
1st Gonville	Lincoln, 1758	1806–22	64
2nd Edward Thomas Ffrench	Dublin, 1789	1822–55	66
3rd Edmund de Gonville	Thurlby, 1791	1855–70	79
4th Benjamin Parnell	Sligo, 1838	1870–1935	96
5th Benjamin Dennis	Bengal, 1900	1935–81	81

* * *

John Rouse Merriott Chard was born at Boxhill House in the Plymouth district of Pennycross on 21 December 1847. The area was originally known as Weston Peverell, but most locals referred to it as Pennycross by the end of the nineteenth century. The house in which he was born was on what is now known as Honicknowle Lane, in the area taken over by the Plymouth YMCA building. There is a plaque commemorating his birthplace high up on the wall of the building just to the left of the entrance.

John was just over two years younger than Gonville, and like him he came from a large family, being the middle son of three in the family of eight children of Dr William Wheaton Chard and his wife Jane.

In 1779, members of John's family obtained a licence to dig clay on 2 acres of land at Pathe, south-west of Othery near Bridgwater in Somerset, to build kilns to make brick and tile, in return for providing

Boxhill House, 1956. It was the birthplace and family home of John Rouse Merriott Chard. Plymouth City Council let the property to the local YMCA, who had it demolished to build a sports centre in 1974. A blue plaque at the entrance to the centre commemorates the Rorke's Drift hero's birthplace.

the lord of the manor with good brick for his house. The Chard family also used the materials to build Pathe House on land called Stone Quarry at Pathe. The operation was ceased in 1841 and the land was filled and levelled; the house remained and is now a Grade II listed building.

John's paternal grandparents were a landowner named William Chard (born at Othery on 2 March 1770) and his wife, Charlotte Maria (formerly Rouse, born at Othery in 1779), who had married at St Michael's Church on 22 December 1817. Charlotte was one of seven children, and her father, the Revd Ezekiel Athanasius Rouse, performed the ceremony. Charlotte died at Othery on 26 July 1839. The Rouse family still have connections with the area.

In John's obituary it was stated:

The Chard family is a very interesting one, being descended from Cerdic, King of the West Saxons (467–534). This became corrupt into Chard, and will be so-found in the Domesday Book. From old records still extant it can be seen that the line included Thomas Chard, the last Abbott of Forde Abbey, who was despoiled by Henry VIII, and who died in 1554.

Forde Abbey in Dorset was founded in the twelfth century, and Thomas Chard is remembered as its greatest abbot. He succeeded in 1521, and the monastery flourished under his guidance. However, his work was interrupted in 1539 by the dissolution of the larger monasteries. Knowing the reputation of King Henry VIII, he handed the abbey over to the Crown without much protest. He became vicar of St Mary's Church in Thorncombe, Dorset, until his death in 1543. The name Rouse is taken from his mother's family name, and it is presumed that the name Merriott refers to the town in south Somerset.

Dr William Wheaton Chard was born on 22 October 1818, at Othery, and was baptised at St Michael's Church. He was described as a landed proprietor of Pathe House in Othery. He matriculated at Emmanuel College in Cambridge in 1837. At the time of John Chard's funeral the then vicar of St Michael's Church in Othery related that in the church there was a memorial window to his father, and that the Revd Rouse was vicar at Othery church for forty-six years, from 1776 until his death in 1822. William and Jane married at St Michael's Church on 20 November 1839.

Jane was born at Stoke Climsland in the valley of the River Tamar in Cornwall on 10 July 1815. She was the daughter of a solicitor named

John Chard's father was born at Pathe House in Othery near Bridgwater in Somerset, and the family worshipped at St Michael's Church, seen here. His parents married in the church and his oldest sibling, Charlotte Maria Herring Chard, was also born at Othery.

John Hart Brimacombe (born in 1786, died at Stoke Climsland on 7 September 1851) and his wife Mary (formerly Harvey, 1791–1848). They were married at All Saints Church in Stoke Climsland on 8 September 1811. Jane had a brother named William Hart Brimacombe (1812–56), who was an attorney at law.

William Wheaton is said to have devised the Chard motto of '*Nil Desperandum*' – 'Never Despairing' – and also the predominantly blue family crest and coat of arms. It is described as: 'Argent, on a chevron azure between two partridges proper, in chief and in base a greyhound courant sable, a garb between two bugle-horns stringed gold. The Crest being a silver eagle rising, with the dexter claw resting on an azure escutcheon and holding in the beak an oak branch slipped proper.'

Chapter 2

Siblings

Of his own generation, Gonville's oldest sibling, Frances Judith, was born at Sligo in 1824. She married the Revd Arthur Coates BA, on 5 April 1847, who was the rector of St John the Divine's Church at Pemberton in Wigan from 1849 to 1872. The second daughter, Helen Morrison, was born at Sligo in 1826.*

Edward was born at Sligo on 21 March 1832. He was commissioned into the 4th (King's Own) Regiment as ensign on 15 February 1855, and joined the unit while it was on active service at Sebastopol in the Crimea, where they were joined by their sister unit the 34th Border Regiment. During the Siege of Sebastopol the 4th Regiment took part in the two disastrous assaults on the Great Redan on 18 June and 8 September 1855. The first assault was so severe that it resulted in the award of twenty Victoria Crosses, the most ever given for a single action in the history of the coveted award. The second assault proved to be the last land engagement of the campaign and the Russians evacuated the town the following day. Edward was promoted lieutenant on 21 December 1855. He was promoted captain in 1866, and he left the regiment in 1867. He joined the 76th (West Riding) Regiment and went with them to Burma in January 1868. Captain Edward Bromhead died at Thyetmyo in Burma, on 9 January 1869, aged 37, and he is buried there. A memorial stone was erected at his grave '. . . by his brother officers'.

Alice Margaret was born at Sligo on 12 March 1834, and Janette Gonville was born at Sligo on 4 July 1836.

Benjamin Parnell was born in Sligo on 22 October 1838. Following the death of Edward he succeeded as the 4th Baron Bromhead on 25 October 1870. He was commissioned as ensign in the 30th (Cambridgeshire)

---

* Margaret Judith Coates, who died aged 2 months, was buried at St John the Divine's in 1851.

13

Above left: Gonville's oldest brother, Edward, saw service with the 4th (King's Own) Regiment in the Crimea. During the Siege of Sebastopol, the 4th Regiment took part in the two disastrous assaults on the Great Redan. His death in 1869 deprived him of becoming the 4th Baron Bromhead.

Above right: Captain Charles Bromhead highly distinguished himself during his service against the Ashanti in the disease-ridden jungle of West Africa, before taking part in the Anglo-Zulu War. He gained great favour with the officers who were known as the Ashanti Ring.

Regiment at Delhi in 1859, and was appointed captain with the 40th Bengal Native Infantry, in the Indian Staff Corps. He married Hannah 'Annie' Franklin (born in India in 1848), the daughter of the Revd James Smith. Their marriage took place at Meerut in India on 24 October 1866. They had eight children, mostly born in Bengal between 1867 and 1878.

Charles James was born at Versailles on 15 September 1840, and served with the 2nd Battalion, 24th Regiment. He was commissioned as ensign on 30 August 1859, became lieutenant on 20 February 1863, captain on 19 February 1872 and brevet major on 1 April 1874. He was adjutant of the 2nd Battalion from 29 May 1863 to 16 December 1869.

Victoria Gonville was born in London in 1844, and she married Dr Warren Hastings Diamond on 15 September 1863. After Gonville in 1845 came the tenth and last child, Elizabeth Frances, who was born at Versailles in 1847. She married Dr Evelyn Henry Frederick Pocklington on 5 September 1870. Their only child, Mary de Gonville, was born in Wimbledon in 1872.

Dr Pocklington was registered at the Royal College of Surgeons and, as chief medical officer for the area, held his surgery at the Wimbledon Cottage Hospital. He had worked as medical officer in the prison service, and as 'a magnificent shot' he was medical officer with the East Surrey Regiment Volunteers. He specialised in the treatment of infectious diseases, and established the fever hospital in Wimbledon. Through his efficient work he managed to get several epidemics under control and save many lives. While he was in practice the number of illnesses through infectious diseases was half the national average. In 1887 it was reported that an outbreak of scarlet fever had infected 600 people. Acting swiftly, he tracked down the source to one particular dairy and stopped the milk supply. As a result, there were only five fatalities, and one of those was a monkey which was partial to a glass of milk. It is still remembered to this day as the 'Wimbledon Monkey'.

It was something of a bitter-sweet time for this generation of the Bromhead family. Benjamin Parnell's first child, Gonville James, died as a baby in 1868, and his second son, Edward Gonville, was born in 1869, not long after his brother Edward had died. Their youngest sister, Elizabeth Frances, married in 1870, just a month before their father died, and their mother died less than three years later.

On 7 March 1879, the *Daily Telegraph* published a letter from the Revd Henry Calverley, the rector of nearby Bassingham church. John Prebble, who wrote the screenplay for the film *Zulu!*, used the remarks in his letter as background information. Mrs K. Preston, a descendant of Charles James Bromhead, wrote to Prebble from Llandudno expressing scepticism about both claims. Seemingly accepting Mrs Preston's doubts, in his reply Prebble listed those officers and men known to have attended Wolfe as he died and speculated that the Revd Calverley may have become mixed up with Lieutenant Brown, a relation to the Bromheads on the maternal side of the family.

The letter stated:

Whatever may be the merits or demerits, from a political or military point of view of the Zulu War, England in general and Lincolnshire in particular, may well be proud of the Bromheads of Thurlby Hall. They are certainly a 'fighting family', soldiers 'to the manner [sic] born', and they deserve well of their country. Ensign Boardman [sic] Bromhead fought at Quebec against the French in 1759, under General Wolfe, and was the man who told him as he lay dying in the arms of victory: 'They run!' His grandson, Sir Edmund de Gonville Bromhead fought at Waterloo. Of his four sons three are living and long may they live. The eldest, Captain Bromhead of the 76th died at Burmah [sic]; the second son, and present baronet, Sir Benjamin Bromhead of the 22nd Bengal Native Infantry, is now serving with Sir Sam Browne at Kandahar. If he has not fought and won, it is his misfortune and not his fault. The third son, Major Charles Bromhead, of the 24th is a very distinguished officer, and won glory and his majority in the Ashantee campaign. The fourth son, Lieutenant (now presumably Major) Gonville Bromhead, also of the 24th, has proved himself, though last, not least, of the gallant brotherhood, by his brilliant feat of arms at Rorke's Drift. Of such stuff heroes are made. All honour to the brave, whether alive or dead, who 'count their lives not dear' at the call of duty, and who make the name of England a terror and praise throughout the world. Such men as these, though deed yet speak, and will speak, through future ages. This is rather a warlike trumpet for a minister of peace to blow. But we must take things, not as they ought to be but as they are. And I am not sure if things were called by their right names, whether the foreign battles of the State Militant of the present day are not more useful as well as more creditable than the home battles about doctrine and discipline, conformity or unconformity, which occupy so much of the time and energies of her clerical sister, the Church Militant.

A guide for visitors to the Church of St Germain in Thurlby states:

It would be impossible for the visitor to be unaware of the contribution to the life of the church, the local community and to the nation made by the Bromhead family, who have lived at Thurlby Hall since the 17th Century. The family crest is over the vestry door and on the windows of the north aisle, and their distinguished service in their country's armed forces is commemorated in numerous plaques and particularly in the East Window in memory of Gonville Bromhead VC, the hero of Rorke's Drift. The initials E Ff B, 1842, in so many places show how

16

thorough and extensive was the restoration of St Germain's which Sir Edward Bromhead undertook in 1842–43. There are indications everywhere of the family's love for the church and concern for its fabric. The parishioners of Thurlby are very conscious of the debt they owe to the Bromhead family, a debt which can only be repaid with love and respect for its members with loyalty to the church whose continuing witness the family has done much to ensure.

A letter received by the author from one of Gonville Bromhead's descendants states: '. . . you refer to Lieutenant Bromhead as "Gonny" taken presumably from Gonville, his first name. He himself pronounced his first and surname as if the "O" was replaced by "U" – Gunville Brumhead – as it were; as told to me by my Grannie.'

Gonville's older brothers, Edward, Benjamin Parnell and Charles James, were educated at St John's Diocesan School in Lincoln, and he began his education at the Thomas Magnus Grammar School in Newark-on-Trent in 1860. It is now a listed building known as Magnus Church of England Academy. At the time of his death, the *Newark Advertiser*

Gonville began his education at the Thomas Magnus Grammar School in Newark-on-Trent in 1860. The site of the school is now a listed building and known as Magnus Church of England Academy. A local newspaper recorded that it was where he was 'actively participating alike in sport and study, and developing that sound mind in a sound body'.

17

stated: 'Those of our readers who will remember the days when Major Bromhead was a boy at the Newark Grammar School actively participating alike in sport and study, and developing that sound mind in a sound body of which he gave so memorable an illustration by his gallantry at Rorke's Drift . . .'.

Indeed, he excelled at various activities, including combat sports such as boxing, wrestling and singlestick, and he was a good cricketer. The team was coached by county professionals, and was apparently taken to away matches by 'a coach and four spanking greys'. The 'Newark Magnus' publication described him as a member of the cricket eleven: 'Gonville Bromhead, afterwards famous as in command at Rorke's Drift, a left-hand medium bowler. Mention of it [Rorke's Drift] could still bring cheers at Magnus gatherings many years afterwards. Bromhead became the fourth old boy to give his name to a House.' At the time of the 1861 census Gonville was the only boy left at home in Thurlby Hall, and he left the school in 1864.

Several weeks after the defence of Rorke's Drift on 5 March 1879 a letter appeared in a newspaper known as the *Guardian*, which was a weekly Church magazine. It was written by William John Humble of Clayton-cum-Frickley Vicarage in Doncaster. He is likely to have known Gonville quite well as he was born in the year after him, attended Thomas Magnus Grammar School and played cricket. Under the title 'Lt Bromhead of the 24th', he stated:

Sir, There is a name present on the lips of Englishmen which will live for all time in the brightest annals of English history. As one who was bound to Gonville Bromhead by the closest ties of that intimate friendship which can only exist once in a lifetime, will you allow me to state that it was not of his Queen only that he became a 'good soldier'. Beneath that reserve which often conceals so much that is of sterling worth in the English character lay hid a deep and loyal love for all that is great and noble in life. Like many others he owed most of what was dear to him in opinion to the higher influence and teaching of the headmaster at Newark Grammar School. An earnest, simple-hearted Churchman, when Bromhead joined his regiment, he was not ashamed to carry his Christianity with him into the army.

At school he was ever among the foremost on the river and on the cricket field and excelled in all those sports which demand the qualities so necessary for a soldier – quickness of eye and readiness of hand. Gentle, modest, unassuming, he was a boy for boys to

Gonville Bromhead, standing far right in this photograph, with the 1862 Magnus School cricket eleven, with whom he was a good left-hand medium bowler. He was a stocky young man who also excelled at boxing, wrestling and fighting with sticks, known as singlestick.

love and for all to esteem. He has 'become a name' and yet the very last person to realise the fact will be himself.

The school was named after a local landowner who became chaplain to Henry VIII. It produced several men who became prominent in their fields of expertise. They included Godfrey Hounsfield (1919–2004), who, in 1979, received the Nobel Prize for Physiology and Medicine for creating the first X-ray Computed Tomography (CT Scanner). Dusty Hare MBE was born in Newark and played rugby union for Newark RUFC and Nottingham RFC. Like Gonville, he was also a good cricketer and played at county level for Nottinghamshire. However, he is best remembered as the England and the British Lions goal-kicking full-back, who still holds the world record for most first-class points scored.

* * *

John Chard's oldest sibling, Charlotte Maria Herring, was born at Othery on 25 April 1840. It seems that William and Jane and baby Charlotte

19

went to live with Jane's family at Stoke Climsland in Cornwall, where they employed six servants. William Wheaton had acquired his first game certificate on 26 September 1844.

They then moved to Pennycross, where William Wheaton junior was born on 24 December 1841, Mary Jane was born in 1845 and after John was born in 1847, Jane Brimacombe was born on 16 March 1850, but she was baptised at St Budeaux.

At the time of the 1851 census they lived at Mount Tamar House (now part of Mount Tamar School) in the Higher St Budeaux district of Plymouth. There is a Rorke's Close and a Chard Road close by. Florence was born there in 1854, Charles Edward was born there on 4 December 1856 and Margaret Edith was born there in 1858.

Mount Tamar House had originally been the home of the famous captain Sir Thomas Bayard (1743–98) of the Royal Navy. He took part in the American Revolutionary Wars and led the British fleets when they defeated the Dutch at the Battle of Camperdown in 1797 and the French at the Battle of Tory Island in 1798.

The family worshipped at St Budeaux church, and a plaque at the church entrance states: 'St Budeaux Church: Constructed in 1563

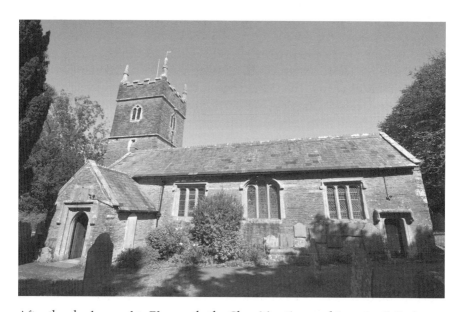

After they had moved to Plymouth, the Chard family worshipped at St Budeaux church, where Sir Francis Drake had married. John Chard's parents and one of his sisters, Jane Brimacombe, are buried in the churchyard. *(Courtesy of Stephen Luscombe)*

and containing relics from the previous chapel built before 1066. In 1569 Sir Francis Drake here married Mary Newman. The site of two battles during the Civil War when the church was almost destroyed. Restored in 1655.'

The 1861 census records that the family had moved further into the city and resided at 19 Portland Villas, a property which is now owned by the University of Plymouth.

William Wheaton Chard followed family tradition and joined the 1st Battalion, 7th Royal Fusiliers. He served in India, including the Umbeyla Expedition in 1863. This was considered to be one of the fiercest and most difficult campaigns ever fought on the North-West Frontier of India. A British expeditionary force was sent out to deal with the tribesmen of Sitana, who had been constantly marauding into British-held territory. In order to reach Sitana the troops had to march through the Umbeyla Pass, where they were ambushed by Bunerwel tribesmen from the heights above them. In order to counter this, the troops had to assault two peaks known as the Crag Piquet and the Eagle's Nest. They had to capture and re-capture the peaks at least three times, which incurred heavy fighting and dreadful losses. For instance, the 71st Highlanders suffered more casualties than they did in the Crimean War and Indian Mutiny combined. During the fighting on Crag Picquet the 7th Regiment was besieged in a small camp overnight by a large enemy force, and two officers of the Indian army gained the Victoria Cross as they launched a rescue operation. For his service William received the Indian General Service Medal, 1854, with *Umbeyla* clasp. Charles Edward followed his father to Emmanuel College on 1 June 1875.

In 1861 at St Mary's Church in Plympton, Plymouth, Charlotte Maria Herring married Major William Barrett of the 2nd West Somerset Militia, who was born at Chard on 5 February 1823. They lived at Moredon House in North Curry, Somerset, and they had four children. The Barrett family were very wealthy, and as cricket was becoming an extremely popular sport in the county they became well-known in Somerset cricketing circles. Having been founded at Taunton in 1875, the Somerset County Cricket Club was admitted to First Class status in 1891 and finished third the following season. The Somerset and Devon Wanderers were established at Castle Cary and on representing Great Britain at the 1900 Olympic Games they are the only team ever to become Olympic champions at cricket.

On 15 August 1865 Mary Jane married Charles Hensman (1841–1912), the son of the Revd Charles Heycock of Owston Abbey near Melton

A photograph of the Chard family taken on 8 October 1879, soon after Major Chard returned from South Africa. Major Chard is seated on the ground on the right of picture, and Driver Robson is standing far right in the white helmet. The occasion is the marriage of his sister Florence to the Revd Robert Charles Lathom-Browne, the vicar of North Curry. The family celebrated two weddings that year. William Wheaton Chard married Fanny Alexandrina Augusta Yule.

Mowbray in Leicestershire, who was appointed captain of the 75th (Stirlingshire) Highlanders on 14 October 1868.

John Chard was educated at the Plymouth New Grammar School, which had been established as the Plymouth Subscription Classical and Mathematical School in 1822, and later became the Plymouth Corporation Grammar School. In an article published in *Life* magazine, a fellow student recalled him as 'a quiet boy, not much-over given to games, and with the peculiarity of wearing the largest hat in school'.

Chapter 3

Military Service

The unit which became the 24th (2nd Warwickshire) Regiment, was originally raised in Kent in 1689 as Sir Edward Dering's Regiment of Foot, and did its first of many tours of Ireland serving in that troubled country until 1692. John Churchill, Duke of Marlborough, one of England's greatest commanders, took over as colonel in 1702, and the regiment took part in the War of the Spanish Succession, 1702–13, gaining many famous battle honours. It became known as the 24th Regiment of Foot in 1751.

A 2nd Battalion was raised in 1756, for service in the Seven Years War, and was re-numbered as the 69th (South Lincolnshire) Regiment, in 1758. Two of Gonville's great uncles, Benjamin and John, were commissioned into the 2nd Battalion in 1756, and they both transferred to the 69th in 1758. Benjamin rose to the rank of colonel, and John became a captain.

In 1776 the 24th Regiment was in North America, and after Quebec had been relieved, they were in frequent action as part of the advance guard during the British army's march south for the American War of Independence. Through lack of provisions and reinforcements, the campaign was a disaster, and the 24th Regiment were part of the outnumbered British force which had to surrender at Saratoga in 1777.

In 1782 the unit was instructed to style itself the 24th (2nd Warwickshire) Regiment, and in 1801 it was sent to Egypt. It took part in the capture of Alexandria, for which it was awarded its first battle honour 'Egypt', and adopted the 'sphinx' as insignia on the regimental colour and the collar badge. They then saw their first tour of service at the Cape of Good Hope, 1805–10. In 1804 a 2nd Battalion was raised at Warwick, and the regiment took part in the Duke of Wellington's campaigns. It served with distinction in the Peninsular War, gaining nine battle honours – Talaveras, 1809, Fuentes D'Onors, the storming

An impressive commemorative plaque prepared as a memorial to the soldiers of the 24th Regiment who were killed in action at Isandlwana. It displays the eighteen battle honours gained by the regiment up to and including the Zulu War.

and siege of Badajoz, 1812 (in which Gonville's Uncle John took part), Salamanca, 1812, Pyrenees, 1813, Nivelle, 1813, Orthes, 181; and Peninsula, 1808–14. The unit was disbanded at the end of the campaign.

The regiment then served in India, 1846–61, during which time it took part in the Sikh Wars, and during the Battle of Chillianwallah in 1849 it succeeded in breaking through enemy lines and capturing guns, but suffered heavy losses. For this campaign it received the battle honours Chillianwallah, 1849, Goojerat, 1849 and Punjaub, 1848–9.

In 1858 a 2nd Battalion was raised in Sheffield, and it was this unit which gained the regiment's first Victoria Crosses. On 21 March 1867, the frigate *Assam Valley* dropped anchor off the southern tip of Little Andaman Island, known to be inhabited by the Onge natives, and the commander and seven of his men rowed ashore to forage for firewood. They landed near a large rock, and on getting over the reef they were seen to make their way into the jungle. The *Assam Valley* waited for two days, and when they did not return the ship sailed back to Rangoon to report the incident.

A contingent of men from the 24th Regiment arrived at the place where the men had last been seen, and when they went ashore they came under a hail of spears from hostile natives and as they could not get off the beach because of bad weather they had become stranded and in peril of their lives.

A steamer named the *Arracan* then arrived with more soldiers of the 24th Regiment. Seeing the perilous situation, Surgeon Campbell Douglas and Privates David Bell, William Cooper, William Griffiths and Thomas Murphy – 'in a very gallant and daring manner' – volunteered to man a gig and risked their lives as they made strenuous efforts to proceed through the dangerous surf to attempt a rescue, Surgeon Douglas having had some experience of sailing. However, the weather worsened and the boat began to fill up with water, so they had no choice but to return to their ship.

The Victoria Cross set belonging to Surgeon Campbell Mellis Douglas (1845–1909), which was one of the first five ever to be awarded to Bromhead's 24th Regiment. In the same year he had joined the 2nd/24th Regiment, five men of the same battalion risked their lives in trying to save comrades from the clutches of hostile natives in dangerous water at Little Andaman Island in the Indian Ocean. It was one of the very few to be awarded to servicemen for action not considered to be in the face of the enemy.

They could see the men on the beach fighting for their lives, so they decided to make an even more determined second attempt. The doctor guided the boat with superb skill, as the four privates rowed with great exertion through the surf in constant peril of being swamped as the waves smashed into it or lifted it high into the air. This time they reached the shore, where five of the men scrambled aboard. They assured the men left stranded that they would be back as quickly as possible, as they turned the craft around and braved the rough waters again to ferry their load back to the ship.

They made a third perilous journey back to the shore, where they picked up the remainder of the men and got them safely away from the beach. Their gallantry saved seventeen of their comrades from the virtual certainty of being massacred and cut up by the savages. With all the men safely accounted for they returned to Rangoon.

When the incident was reported to the commanding officer in India, he recommended that all five gallant rescuers should receive the Victoria Cross, and the awards were announced in the *London Gazette* for 17 December 1867, they being the first awards to the 24th Regiment.

In 1872 the 1st Battalion returned to South Africa to deal with inter tribal fighting in the Transkei, and in 1873 the regiment moved their depot from Warley in Birmingham to Brecon in Wales.

Less than three weeks before the Little Andaman affair, Gonville Bromhead entered the 2nd Battalion, 24th (2nd Warwickshire) Regiment of Foot on 20 April 1867, as ensign by purchase, and was trained at Croydon, where he gained popularity among his fellow officers as one who was a helpful senior to new recruits. At nearly 6ft tall and with a powerful frame, he became a champion at any sport he cared to put his hand to. He made a good impression, and an article about him published in the *Hartlepool Mail* of 26 February 1879, stated:

> I was with him for some time at the army tutors at Croydon some twelve years ago, and it is interesting to look back upon him as he appeared to us at the time. About five feet ten inches in height, so well-built that he did not look as tall, he seemed to me to be quite the bean ideal of an English officer. It was our custom of an evening, as soon as 'study' was over, to indulge in bouts of wrestling, boxing and singlestick in the gymnasium outside, and Bromhead was so expert in all of these that he invariably beat everyone opposed to him. With all this he was so kind and genial that the youngsters among us could chaff him and play tricks on him with impunity, and without fear of retaliation. Quiet and most unassuming in his

demeanour, he nevertheless often showed friendliness to those who happened to be unpopular. By kindness to newcomers, and in a thousand other ways, the thorough worth and goodness were with him.

He was promoted by selection to the rank of lieutenant on 28 October 1871. At the time of the defence of Rorke's Drift a lieutenant in an infantry regiment was paid 6s. 6d. a day.

At this time his brother Charles was making a name for himself among senior officers of the British army, including none other than the brilliant General Garnet Wolseley, a colonial wars specialist. Charles had been commissioned as ensign in the 2nd Battalion, 24th Regiment in 1859, becoming lieutenant and adjutant in 1863 and reaching the rank of captain by 1872.

In the year Gonville had entered the army, on the West Coast of Africa Kofi Karikari, who came to be known as King Koffee, acceded to the Ashanti throne. On taking power he is supposed to have said: 'My business is war!' His reputation for dreadful savagery was such that to be threatened with the coming of this frightful 'bogeyman' was enough to terrify any child in Britain to do exactly as they were told.

During the Ashanti War Captain Charles Bromhead took charge of hundreds of native labourers as they built the road to Kumasi through disease-ridden jungle. When it was completed, it included 237 bridges.

The Ashanti were a fierce race. In 1824 they had destroyed a British force under Sir Charles Macarthy and took his skull back to their capital at Kumasi to be used as a royal drinking cup. When the Dutch sold the British some territory in 1872, including Elmina Castle which the Ashanti coveted as a slave emporium, King Koffee drank a toast to war from the skull of Sir Charles and mobilised his warriors across the Prah River to provoke what was to become the Third Ashanti War.

General Wolseley was instructed to deal with the situation and to try to achieve a swift victory before the March rains made the already fever-ridden terrain impassable. Dosed with quinine and leading African and West Indian troops, Captain Bromhead played a leading part in preparing the way for the regular troops to arrive. They cleared a road all the way to Kumasi which included 237 bridges, and they established supply bases all along it. Among the newspaper correspondents who were sent to report on the war was Henry Morton Stanley, who had recently returned from his legendary meeting with Dr David Livingstone.

Captain Bromhead was sent as a special commissioner to negotiate with the King of Eastern Assin and then to the King of Abra. He was a staff officer to Colonel Festing during the operations at Dunquah from 26 October to 1 November 1873 and commanded Abra warriors at the repulse of the Ashanti army at Abrakrampa from 5 to 6 November 1873. He commanded the reconnaissance in force on 8 November 1873. Afterwards he was second in command at Russell's Fort, and at the capture and destruction of Abdubrassie.

On the arrival of the regular British force, which included the Black Watch, the Rifle Brigade and the Royal Welsh Fusiliers, he was present at the Battle of Amoaful on 31 January 1874, and in the capture and destruction of Becquah in February 1874, during which operation Major Lord Edric Gifford of the 24th Regiment gained the Victoria Cross. He was with the advance guard engagement at Jarbinah, took part in the skirmish at Ambuscade and the operation between Adwabin and the River Ordah. He took part in the battles at Ordashu on 4 February 1874 and was with the triumphant troops as they swept into Kumasi on 5 February 1874. The capital is said to have stunk of blood, and the soldiers were appalled to find the remains of thousands of sacrificial victims, the sight of which made Wolseley physically sick.

Having become short on supplies and fearing disease and the oncoming March rains, Wolseley ordered Kumasi to be burnt to the ground and rushed his men back to the coast. He later described the campaign as '. . . the most horrible war I ever took part in'.

A collection of tropical exotic insects collected by Captain Charles Bromhead while on active service in West Africa and mounted in a glass case. *(Courtesy of Spencer Braithwaite)*

Captain Bromhead returned to England on 26 February 1874, where the troops were feted with invitations to balls and banquets to celebrate the victory. For his service he was Mentioned in Dispatches, was promoted brevet major dated 1 April 1874 and received the Ashanti Medal with *Coomassie* clasp.

Bromhead arrived in South Africa in February 1879 with the reinforcements, where he took command of detachments at Dundee, Landman's Drift and Koppie Alleen. When Sir Garnet Wolseley assumed command he appointed Charles to command his escort of mounted infantry, including on his visit to Ulundi.

Benjamin Parnell was a colonel with the Indian Staff Corps, and served with the 22nd (Punjab) Bengal Native Infantry during the Afghanistan War of 1878–80, being involved in the operations around Kandahar.

Colonel Bromhead's signature from the back of the case. The item came into the possession of the Braithwaite family when they and Charles Bromhead's branch of the family owned properties at Ruthin in North Wales. *(Courtesy of Spencer Braithwaite)*

Lieutenant Gonville Bromhead was stationed at The Citadel in the Western Heights in Dover from 26 July 1874 to 21 June 1877, when he is reported to have taken part in local battalion cricket matches in the area. He was then posted to Chatham, and in the following year he was the officer in command of B Company, 2nd Battalion, 24th Regiment, when the unit received orders for active service in South Africa, and they embarked aboard the troopship *Himalaya* at Portsmouth on 1 February 1878, to set sail for the Cape of Good Hope. When the 2nd Battalion arrived in South Africa to assist in the 9th Cape Frontier War the two battalions of the regiment operated in the same country for the first time. This campaign consisted mainly of sweeping skirmishes to flush rebel natives out of the bush, and it was over by mid-1878.

* * *

John Chard entered the Royal Military Academy at Woolwich. The course lasted two-and-a-half years and was designed to produce competent technicians rather than leaders of troops. The main subjects

Chard would have studied were artillery (practical and theoretical), fortification and bridging, mathematics, natural and experimental philosophy, landscape drawing, mechanics and French and Hindustani (with German an alternative). He was also able to attend lectures in astronomy, mineralogy, geology and metallurgy. A course on military history and the art of war was started a few months before he left. When he passed-out eighteenth from a batch of nineteen in 1868, he was remembered for always being late for breakfast. He was commissioned as lieutenant in the Corps of Royal Engineers on 15 July 1868. One of the men who passed out and was commissioned into the Royal Engineers with him was Adam Bogle, who later took part in the first Football Association Cup Final in 1872; the first ever final of its kind in the history of the game.

The Corps of Royal Engineers has one battle honour 'Ubique', meaning 'Everywhere', which sums up their role perfectly. Most of the earliest applications of engineering were for military purposes, in the building of fortifications, bridges and roads, and drawing maps to guide the infantry troops.

Before 1855, as war raged in the Crimea, the technical elements of the British army, such as artillery and engineering, were provided by the Board of Ordnance. Artillery and engineer officers formed part of the early 'artillery trains', and the ancestor of the Corps of Royal Engineers emerged from the Board of Ordnance in 1717. Before 1782 the officers of the Royal Engineers did not have a military title, but in that year they were first granted commissions. It was not until 1787 that the military officers of the engineer department were constituted the Corps of Royal Engineers; the men being regimented into the Corps of Royal Military Artificers.

When Napoleon invaded Egypt in 1798, a detachment was sent to Constantinople to train the Turkish army, other companies performing good service in Malta, Italy, Sicily and the West Indies. In 1813 the title Corps of Royal Sappers and Miners replaced that of the Military Artificers and did effective work under the Duke of Wellington in the Peninsular and Waterloo campaigns.

The Crimean War was the scene of manifold activities by the engineers in the construction of trenches to get closer to the Sebastopol fortifications, during which time they gained the unit's first eight Victoria Crosses, and afterwards the officers and men were united to form one Corps under the title Royal Engineers. After the Indian Mutiny in 1857–8 the Bengal, Madras and Bombay Corps of Engineers was transferred to the Royal Engineers.

As the Corps developed in a progressive world it became responsible for such things as the construction and repair of ports and airfields and the operation of railways. When an army is advancing, they are occupied in repairing bridges and roads blown up by the enemy; and when retreating they are responsible for the demolition of roads and bridges behind them.

The uniform worn by a lieutenant of the Royal Engineers was a scarlet single-breasted jacket with nine brass buttons at equal distance down the front of the tunic from collar to waist seam. The collar was 2in high, rounded in front, the edge and collar seam being furnished with round back and gold cord. The collar and cuffs were of garter blue velvet, and the cuffs did not exceed 10½in in circumference at the wrists. The trousers, which were usually tucked into brown leather riding boots, were of dark-blue Oxford mixture and had a scarlet stripe, 1¾in wide down the outer seam. When on active service they wore a brown leather shoulder belt with buckle, tip and slide in engraved gilt. The sword belt was of the same materials, which was worn under his jacket. It was usual for an engineer officer to have a sketching case attached to the belt by three narrow slings.

After two years at Chatham, John Chard sailed to Bermuda in October 1870, being employed in the building of fortifications at the Hamilton Dockyard. The British government had begun to view Bermuda more as a base than a colony, and in 1869 work began on a floating dry-dock, and it is likely that Lieutenant Chard was employed on this work.

Sadly, while John was away his father died on 22 July 1873, aged 54, and he was buried at St Budeaux church. He returned to England in January 1874. He was posted to Malta in February 1874, where he was again employed in the construction of defences. A programme to improve Malta's defences was under way, to protect the dockyard and harbour from attack. He returned to England in April 1876, and after a short stay at Chatham, was appointed to the Western District at Exeter.

The St George's Lodge of Freemasons 112 had moved to their present premises at Freemasons Hall, 27 Gandy Street, Exeter, on St George's Day in 1877, and the history of the lodge outlined under the heading 'A National Hero': 'When, on 3 May 1877, a 30-year old army officer was initiated into the Lodge, no-one dreamed that two years later he would be acclaimed as a national hero and be awarded the Victoria Cross for conspicuous bravery in battle. The young Mason was John Rouse Merriott Chard . . .'.

On 2 December 1878, Lieutenant Chard was with the 5th Field Company, which, along with the 2nd Field Company, moved out of

Chatham destined for South Africa and active service in the Zulu War. They landed at Cape Town on 28 December, and arrived in Durban on 4 January 1879. However, Lieutenant Chard and his men were greeted by a torrential downpour, in which the Engineers had to unload hundreds of tons of stores and equipment. To add to his dilemma the site of his vaccination had become inflamed and his right shoulder was very sore. He reported:

> An order came from Lord Chelmsford directing that an officer and a few good men of the RE, with mining equipment, etc, should join the 3rd Column as soon as possible. I was consequently sent on in advance of the Company with a light mule wagon containing the necessary tools, etc, and in which the men could also ride on level ground, with a corporal, three sappers, and one driver [Charles Robson], my batman, who rode one, and looked after my horses . . .

Chapter 4

The Zulu War

For most of the nineteenth century South Africa was disturbed by continuous friction between its mixed populations. After British troops had twice seized the Cape from the Dutch at the turn of the century, settlers began to arrive in 1820, and as they expanded the frontier there were many disputes over land boundaries between Cape colonists, Boer farmers and African Bantu tribes, which kept the British army on constant alert. These disagreements sometimes escalated and led to confrontations which came to be known as Cape or Frontier Wars.

However, the main threat to stability in the region came from the highly disciplined army of fearless Zulu warriors. General Garnet Wolseley stated: 'These Zulus are a great danger to our Colony.' The British government knew that they had to be subdued before there could be any progress towards a united nation under one flag, which would be easier for administration and the hard-pressed British army.

Cetshwayo became King of the Zulus on 1 September 1873. He was a cunning and prudent leader who hated the way his father Mpande had allowed the Zulu to lose their great military reputation during his rule from 1840 to 1872. Cetshwayo loved to hear the wonderful stories of the period when Shaka was chief of the Zulus from 1816 to 1828, when the Zulus became feared and respected. He modelled his style of leadership on that of Shaka, being more intelligent and at times equally ruthless. Under his leadership the Zulu army became feared again. He added new regiments, and by 1878 these numbered no less than thirty-three.

Born in 1787, Shaka was a tall, powerful figure, who ruled his people with an iron fist. His dreaded army slaughtered thousands of Bantu tribesmen during the Zulu rise to greatness. But he sealed his own fate when he began to exterminate his own people, and he was murdered in 1828.

Cetshwayo ka Mpande modelled his style of rule on that of his fearsome ancestor Shaka, the first Zulu king, being more intelligent and sometimes equally ruthless. He strengthened his army to retain independence for his people, but when his nation became a serious obstacle to confederation, the British invaded. When he came to Britain in 1882, he landed at Plymouth – the home city of the Chard family.

The Zulus used a tactical fighting formation in the shape of a bullock's horn, which was based on an old hunting technique. Cetshwayo's chiefs divided their armies into four groups, the bulk of the warriors forming a main central group – the chest – which faced and first engaged the enemy. Then two groups – the horns – moved swiftly round to attack the flanks and rear and encircle them. A reserve force – the loins – was kept in the rear ready to be used when needed, and was usually ordered to face away from the action to prevent them from becoming too motivated.

The warriors kept in shape with regular military exercises, which now included learning to use the firearms which Cetshwayo was able to acquire from white traders. But a Zulu warrior still prided himself on his ability to fight in close combat, and was always restless to gain military honour. They saw themselves as invincible, and among the local native tribes they were. Cetshwayo had as many as 40,000 of these efficient warriors at his disposal, and this threat naturally caused great unease among his European neighbours.

In order to deal with the Zulu threat the British issued a deliberately unworkable ultimatum to Cetshwayo, and British forces began to build up at strategic places along the border with Zululand even

As they were forming up for the attack, Zulu warriors made for a fearful sight. They used what became known as the horns of the buffalo tactic based on an old hunting technique. The centre, or loins, would attack the enemy face on, and then the horns came around on both sides to attack the flanks. It was a 'jolly deadly' manoeuvre.

before Cetshwayo had responded. The 3rd (Central) Column, under the Commander-in-Chief, Lord Chelmsford, marched towards a commandeered mission station known as Rorke's Drift. The main bulk of this section of the invasion force was made up of soldiers of Bromhead's 24th Regiment.

The Buffalo River at Rorke's Drift is wide, but there is an island about halfway across. It is dangerous and rocky in some places, and the recent heavy rains had swollen it, making the current strong and treacherous. An Irishman called James Rorke had established the trading post (KwaJim, or 'Jim's Place', in the local language), and he had cut away the banks to make it reasonably safe for transport. Engineers began to assemble two ponts for the purpose of ferrying the troops across. One was a raft on big barrels and the other was a pontoon supported on boats. These floating bridges were large enough to carry one Cape wagon and its team of oxen or about eighty men at a time.

Cetshwayo was aware that to accept some of the terms would mean the loss of Zulu independence and the eventual breakdown of Zulu

Following the usual practice on campaign, this warrior of the uDhloko regiment has discarded much of his ceremonial dress and retains only the otter-skin headband and cow-tail arm and leg decorations. Reflecting his married status, he wears the head-ring and also a charm necklace made up of small wooden blocks and pouches of animal skin. *(Illustration by Richard Scollins)*

society. No response to the ultimatum had been received from the Zulu king after twenty days, so a further ten days' grace was allowed. This expired at midnight on 10 January 1879, and the invasion of Zululand began on the morning of 11 January 1879.

Lieutenant Neville Coghill of the 1st Battalion recorded in his diary:

> On the morning of the 11th the rouse went at 3am and at a little after 5 the crossing commenced. It was a low misty morning . . . there was no sign of our enemy whom as we had been confidently assured by the best authorities in such matters would certainly oppose our crossing. Two ponts were kept constantly at work in the swollen river for the transport of European troops and supply waggons, the natives crossing at the drift.

The weather of late had been wet and the advance came to a halt when the condition of the track deteriorated as they moved further into enemy territory. They were forced to set up camp until the roads were repaired; a task which the Royal Engineers estimated could take as long as a week.

In the meantime, the British made an attack on the homestead of the Zulu chief named Sihayo situated among rocks overlooking the Batshe Valley, a few miles into Zululand. British casualties were minimal, including two corporals of the Natal Native Contingent, and the Zulus lost about sixty warriors.

The column eventually arrived at a distinctive sphinx-shaped rocky feature known as Isandlwana on 20 January 1879, and throughout the day a new advance camp began to take shape. Lieutenant Teignmouth Melvill of the 24th Regiment strongly advised that some kind of defensive preparation should be made, but other officers thought that it was only a temporary camp and his suggestions were not competently carried out.

Zulus had been sighted to the north of the camp and early on the morning of Wednesday, 22 January 1879, Lord Chelmsford had taken a mobile column amounting to about half of his force further into enemy territory to try to locate them and coax them into battle. There were now about 1,700 men left at Isandlwana, and the camp was under the command of Lieutenant Colonel Henry Pulleine of the 24th Regiment.

For various reasons the large Zulu army of about 25,000 warriors had decided to shelter in a valley and advance into battle the following day, but a detachment of colonial troops out scouting came upon them purely by accident, and having lost the element of surprise, they streamed out

A British army sergeant fighting at close quarters at Isandlwana. The foreign-service helmet has been dyed, and he wears the undress serge frock with grass-green facings. The regimental badge is a brass sphinx, and the number 24 on the shoulder strap is of white metal. His accoutrements are part of the valise pattern equipment first used in 1871. *(Illustration by Richard Scollins)*

of the valley and deployed across a wide area in their 'chest and horns' formation, and raced towards the British camp.

Pulleine was not aware of the full extent of the massive Zulu attack and sent his men out in thin ranks with large gaps between them in an effort to protect as much of the front of the camp as he could. When the horns of the Zulu attack appeared over the crest of the hills to the left

The British soldiers at Isandlwana had no choice but to stand and fight, knowing it was only a matter of time before they were overcome by the frantic warriors.

and right the British lines fell back about fifty paces to take advantage of rising ground closer to Isandlwana Hill, and even when the chest began to pour over the ridge line in full view of the defenders, the steady fire of the men of the 24th Regiment smashed into them and the attack showed signs of stalling.

However, the British line was too extended and the Zulus concentrated on running into the gaps to attack the soldiers in flank. The Brits fell back again towards the tents on the slopes of the mountain, which encouraged the warriors, who were shouting their battle cry '*Gwas Umhlongo! Gwas Inglubi!*', which means 'Stab the white men! Stab the pigs!' as they moved in for the kill. The last groups of men fought back-to-back on the nek of Isandlwana until they were overpowered and killed. Only about a hundred white men survived the carnage, in what was the most devastating single defeat inflicted on the British army in the Victorian era. The Zulus too had suffered fearful losses, in the region of 2,000 warriors killed and wounded. Lieutenants Melvill and Coghill would later be posthumously awarded the Victoria Cross for attempting to save one of the colours of their regiment from falling into enemy hands.

The following is the statement made by London-born James Page of the Royal Artillery, who returned to Isandlwana with Lord Chelmsford's

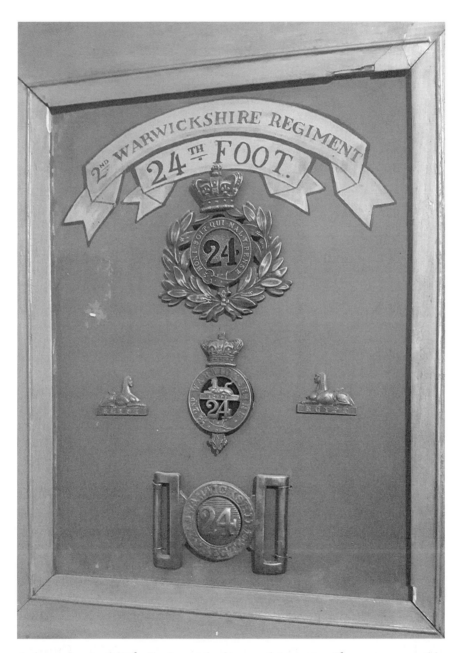

A framed set of 24th Regiment badges and insignia. They were possibly made for display on the wall of a regimental mess. The item at the top is a 24th Regiment helmet plate; the middle items are a pith helmet plate, with two sphinx badges either side. The bottom item is a belt buckle. *(Courtesy of Gary Richardson)*

force after the disaster. He referred to Cetshwayo as 'a big, fat, sulky ****'. He later fought with Major Chard at Ulundi, and against the Boers at Majuba Hill in the Transvaal War of 1881. He became a member of parliament in Australia.

> Then we went to Isandlwana . . . The Zulus began to get pretty thick on the hills, big bare mountains overlooking timbered kloofs, and when on the third day a very large force was reported about nine miles in front of the camp, Chelmsford left about 400 men in charge, and took the main body out to give battle. But the whole thing was only a ruse, and directly we had got out of the camp boundaries a huge impi appeared, and getting between us and the camp; came down on it and wiped it out. They got the whole equipment, including two field-guns, which the beggars didn't know how to fire – we got them back at Ulundi. The men in camp were all massacred – the Zulus took no prisoners, nor did we. Chelmsford immediately returned, but got there too late. Only about 20 men got away. Melville and Coghill were shot on the bank of the river, the [Zulus] waited for them; and three days later we found them with the colours wrapped round their bodies. We got back to camp at nightfall – the place was awful. The Zulus had stripped most of the bodies and ripped them up with their assegais, and they had hung the little drummer-boys up by the chins on the hooks of the shambles where we had done the butchering for the camp.*

Author's supposition: Because of their emphasis on close-quarter fighting, the Zulus were extremely vulnerable to concentrated firepower from a force protected by entrenched positions or behind barricades. Had the British kept every soldier available in the camp and entrenched the position or encircled the wagons, or both, therefore making a second line of defence to fall back on, the outcome of the battle might well have been much different. Indeed, Zulu losses may well have been so devastating that the war could have ended on that day. Consequently very few people would ever have heard of Rorke's Drift – or Lieutenants Bromhead and Chard.

---

* The statement concerning the treatment of the 'little drummer boys' is one of contention, even though it was repeated by others who were present in the theatre of war. Modern enthusiasts are of the opinion that it was too dark to have seen anything on the battlefield in detail. However, James Page stated that he was also with the troops who returned to Isandlwana to bury the dead a few months later.

The following account is by Colonel Alexander Tulloch, Welsh Regiment, from when he visited kraals near Eshowe in 1885, with George Mansell of the Natal Mounted Police:

One of these men was called 'Big Beard'. I asked the reason, as he had no beard, and Mansell said it was because at the battle of Isandhlwana he had killed an English soldier with a big beard. The Zulus who took part in that fight spoke enthusiastically about the grand way in which the two last small squares on the slope of the hill met death. With their ammunition all expended, and nothing but the bayonet left, the Zulus say the British made fun of them, chaffing and calling them to 'come on'. In the final melee the Zulus said our men fought so desperately that each English soldier killed at least ten Zulus. Of one man who had taken refuge in a deep crevice in the rock they spoke with unbounded admiration. This man, all alone, kept up the fight, firing steadily, killing with every shot, until his last cartridge was gone, when he coolly fixed his bayonet and dashed out amongst them, stabbing right and left till overpowered by assegai-thrusts.

Chapter 5

The Defence of Rorke's Drift

When the British crossed the Buffalo River on 11 January, Lieutenant Bromhead and B Company 2nd / 24th Regiment were left behind to guard the storehouse and field hospital at Rorke's Drift. Commissariat Officer Walter Dunne was supervising in the store, and Dr James Reynolds was in charge of the hospital. Overall command of the post was in the hands of Major Henry Spalding, who was one of Chelmsford's staff officers.

To the south of the two main buildings at Rorke's Drift the Oscarberg Hill overlooked the post, and from it the ground sloped quite substantially right down to the banks of the Buffalo River to the north-east.

Mr Dunne pictured the scene as the invasion had progressed. 'Heavily laden ox-wagons constantly came and went, accompanied by the usual yelling, whip cracking and bellowing; piles of corn bags, biscuit boxes, etc, rose up; detachments of troops were continually arriving and pitching their tents – all the bustle of a large camp and depot was apparent.'

Private Henry Hook remembered how things eventually died down and they went about their everyday duties. 'Everything was perfectly quiet at Rorke's Drift after the column had left, and every man was going about his business as usual.'

However, this was interrupted by an incident which was said to have 'cast a gloom over the whole camp'. Trooper Arthur Edward Dixon of the Newcastle Mounted Rifles had gone down to the Buffalo River early in the morning of 16 January 1879 to bathe. The weather was very hot and the river was in flood, and he had somehow got into difficulties and drowned. His body was not recovered until a few days later, when the Revd George Smith had the sad duty of performing the military burial service. Trooper Dixon's grave site is shown as note 6 on Trooper Lugg's sketch. This is close to where James Rorke had been buried on his death in 1875.

A warrior of the uThulwana regiment fighting at close quarters. He carries the full war shield and stabbing spear. A single chrome feather adorns his otter-skin headband, and at his neck he wears a horned snuffbox. *(Illustration by Richard Scollins)*

After the skirmish at Sihayo's Kraal, Trooper Harry Lugg of the Natal Mounted Police was ordered to ride to Pietermaritzburg with dispatches. He made a pony express-style ride, using ten horses in relays, and he was back at Rorke's Drift on 17 January. However, as he crossed the river his mount lost its footing and crushed his knee as it fell, resulting in him needing to go to hospital.

Because the rains had drenched the tracks the movement of wagons was slow, and it was not until 19 January that Lieutenant Chard and his party of weary Royal Engineers rattled by the mission station and down to the river, where the Sappers set to the task of fixing and securing the ropes that were used to pull the two large ponts across the water.

During the dark hours of the morning of 21 January Colonel Anthony Durnford of the Royal Engineers brought a strong force of Colonial units into Rorke's Drift, and after they crossed the river they took up camp which the main column had vacated. Among these units was Lieutenant Alfred Henderson with his Hlubi troop of horsemen.

That afternoon Chard received notification from Isandlwana, stating that his men were to move up to the base camp. He was confused about the orders because they did not seem to include him, so on the morning of 22 January he intended to accompany his men when they left.

There was drizzly rain during the night, and the morning of Wednesday, 22 January 1879 was cold and damp, with a hazy mist having settled on the hills all around. As the Rorke's Drift camp began to stir, a 19-year-old lieutenant named Horace Smith-Dorrien of the 95th Regiment, who was in charge of the transport, arrived back at the river border with a message from Lord Chelmsford asking Colonel Durnford to take his men forward to the base camp. After delivering the message, Smith-Dorrien requested for Chard to send one of the ponts across the river to collect him, and once across he rode up to the post to deal with some of his own transport duties, and to seek out Lieutenant Bromhead. The two officers had breakfast together, during which time he told all the news from Isandlwana, and informed Bromhead that 'A big fight was expected'. He borrowed eleven rounds of ammunition from Bromhead, after which he jumped on his horse and made haste back down to the river and beyond.

At the river, Chard and his men were squelching about in the heavy mud on the Natal bank, preparing to move up to the base camp, and they eventually set off soon after Smith-Dorrien, but the muddy tracks continued to slow the progress of the wagons and so Chard decided to ride on ahead. Being an engineer, on arriving at Isandlwana he would have been surprised to see that not much had been done to put the camp in a state of defence, but he went to the Headquarters tent to confer with the senior Royal Engineer, Lieutenant F.H. McDowell, to ascertain his orders, only to discover that McDowell had already left with Lord Chelmsford. He found that his duties were in the area around Rorke's Drift on the Natal side of the river, keeping the ponts in working order and maintaining the track back to Helpmekaar. He had his breakfast at the officers' tent of the 1/24th Regiment, and through a field glass he could see Zulus on the Nqutu plateau that overlooked the British camp, and as they seemed to be moving in the general direction of Rorke's Drift he set off back. He met Colonel Durnford on the way, so he told the Sappers to walk with Durnford's unit and told Driver Robson to turn the wagon around and accompany him back to Rorke's Drift; an order that was to save his life.*

Photograph of the terrain near the ferries on the Buffalo River close to Rorke's Drift, taken from the Zululand side in about June 1879. This was the area where Lieutenant Chard was camped when news of the massacre at Isandlwana reached the post. The ferries to the left of picture have been anchored together, and the Rorke's Drift post can be seen in the skyline to the north-west. The fort in the foreground just across the river was named after Lieutenant Melvill, one of the officers of the 24th Regiment who was killed in action as he and Lieutenant Coghill tried to save the queen's colour of the regiment from falling into enemy hands.

---

* The Engineers who carried on to Isandlwana were 7100 Corporal William Gamble, 9312 Sapper Henry Cuthbert, 13805 Sapper John McLaren and 12812 Sapper Marshall Wheatley. They all lost their lives in the battle.

Not far from the back of the storehouse there was a building described by Lieutenant Chard as a cookhouse, and there were two round stone ovens situated close by. These buildings are shown as note 3 on the Lugg sketch. Private Hitch had been busying himself in this area '. . . cooking the tea for the Company'. A sketch by Private Hook shows that there was a kitchen extension at the south-east end of the hospital, where he was busy '. . . making tea for the sick, as I was hospital cook at the time'.*

At about 2 o'clock in the afternoon, Major Spalding left for Helpmekaar to speed the relieving companies that had been ordered up to the mission station. Lieutenant Chard was given temporary command of the small Rorke's Drift garrison but took no action. He was probably convinced by Major Spalding who told him that 'nothing would happen'. Chard then went to his tent at the river to have lunch and to supervise the security of the ferries.

Mr Dunne remembered that the shock of the news of the disaster at Isandlwana had a strange effect on him:

Bromhead and I were resting after luncheon under an awning which we had formed by propping-up a tarpaulin with tent poles; everything was peaceful and quiet, when suddenly, we noticed at some distance across the river a large number of mounted natives approaching, preceded by a lot of women and children and oxen. We were going down to find out what they were, but had not gone many steps when we were called back by one of the men who said that a mounted orderly wished to see the officer in command. Turning back at once we met a mounted man in his shirt sleeves riding hurriedly towards us. His first words were, 'The camp is taken by the Zulus!' When I heard the words a strange feeling, which I cannot account for, came over me that I had heard this somewhere before. Though we could not realise it fully at first, we soon gathered the truth that a great disaster had befallen that portion of number 3 column which was left to defend the camp at Isandlwana, and that the Zulus, flushed with victory, were advancing to attack our post.

Perhaps the most viable warning from Isandlwana came in the hands of a Basuto, who brought a hastily written note from a staff officer named

---

* It was the author's original belief that Privates Hook and Hitch had worked together at the cookhouse and ovens. However, as Hook was looking after the patients in the hospital it is likely that he would have utilised the more convenient kitchen extension in that building.

Captain Alan Gardner of the 14th Hussars, stating that he wished the officer in command at Rorke's Drift to 'fortify and hold the house'.

Lieutenant Chard recorded:

At 3:15pm that day I was watching at the ponts when two men came towards us from Zululand at the gallop. They shouted out and were taken across the river; and I was then informed by one of them – Lieutenant [Gert] Adendorff of Commandant Lonsdale's regiment, who afterwards remained to assist in the defence – of the disaster befallen at the Isandlwana camp, and that the Zulus were advancing upon Rorke's Drift. The other, a Carbineer, rode on to take the news forward to Helpmekaar.

And then on to Pietermaritzburg; apparently 'spreading terror and dismay all along the way'.*

Chard continued:

Almost immediately afterwards I received a message from Lieutenant Bromhead – commander of the company of the 24th Regiment at the camp near the commissariat stores – asking me to come up at once. I gave instructions to strike tents, and to put all stores into the wagon, while I instantly made my way to the commissariat store, and there found that a note had been received from the Third Column, stating that the enemy was advancing in force against our post, which we were to strengthen and hold at all costs.

Lieutenant Bromhead was already most actively engaged loop-holing and barricading the store-building and hospital, and also in connecting the defences of the two buildings walls constructed of mealie-bags and wagons. I held a hurried consultation with him and Mr Dalton, of the commissariat – who was actively superintending the work of defence, and whom I cannot sufficiently

---

* The author has always believed that a man who can be considered to have been a defender of Rorke's Drift remains so until proved without doubt that he was not, and takes the view that it is not appropriate to dismiss any of them without such proof. This was the case in the author's 1988 book entitled *Rorke's Drift: The Zulu War, 1879*, which was the first publication to state without doubt that Lieutenant Adendorff was a defender when there had been doubts raised many times previously. By the same token it is the author's opinion that an account of the defence has to be considered to have been provided by a genuine eyewitness until proven without doubt that the teller of the story was an imposter or romancer.

thank for his most valuable services – and I entirely approved all his arrangements.

I then went round our position down to the ponts, and brought up along with their guard one sergeant and six men, the gear, wagon &c. I desire here to mention for approval the offer of these pont guards, Daniels and Sergeant Millne, of the 3rd Buffs, who, with their comrades, volunteered to moor the ponts out in the middle of the stream, and there to defend them from the decks, with a few men to assist. [*]

British soldiers began the task of emptying the storehouse of anything they could use to build a barricade. The men worked with a sense of urgency knowing that their lives might depend on whether they could complete a perimeter wall before the Zulus attacked. *(Illustration by Richard Scollins)*

---

* Lance Sergeant Thomas Williams was the senior NCO with the 24th Regiment fatigue party.

We arrived back at our post at 3:30pm, and, shortly after, an officer with some of Durnford's Horse came in and asked orders from me. [*]

I requested him to send a detachment to observe the ponts and drift, and to throw out vedettes in the direction of the enemy, in order to check their advance as much as possible, his men falling back on the post when forced to retire, and thereafter to assist in the defence. I next requested Lieutenant Bromhead to station his men, and, having seen every man thoroughly knew his post, the rest of the work went quickly on.

As Chard dismounted from his horse and handed the reins to his vorlooper boy, the lad jumped on its back, and 'wild with terror' he rode it all the way to Pietermaritzburg without stopping. At about the same time, his African wagon driver lost his nerve and on letting loose the mules in his care, he ran up the slopes of the Oscarberg and hid at the back of a cave throughout the battle. Some Zulus positioned themselves at the mouth of the cave to shoot down on the garrison, and a number of British bullets came into the cave and one of them killed a warrior. However, all the man could do was crouch in the darkness afraid for his life. Chard stated that when he came down in the morning he looked more dead than alive, and the mules he had abandoned were found grazing peacefully on the banks of the river.

Having played little part in the Battle of Isandlwana, men of the uNdi Corps of Zulu warriors crossed the Buffalo River into Natal on their way to attack the garrison at Rorke's Drift.

---

* This was Lieutenant Alfred Henderson and the Hlubi Troop.

Chard continued:

At 4:20pm, the sound of firing was heard behind the hill to our south. The officer of Durnford's Horse returned, reporting that the enemy was now close upon us. His men, he told me, would not obey orders, but were going off towards Helpmekaar, and I myself saw them in retreat, numbering apparently about one hundred, going in that direction. About the same time Captain Stevenson's detachment of the Natal Native Contingent left us – as did that officer himself.

I saw that our line of defence was too extended for the small number of men now left, and at once commenced an inner entrenchment of biscuit boxes, out of which we had soon completed a wall two boxes high.[*]

Trooper Lugg remembered how a man named Bob Hall, who had been out reconnoitring with Lieutenant Henderson, came back and announced the arrival of the enemy, 'Here they come, black as Hell and thick as grass!'

Four *amabutho*, or regiments, of Zulu warriors were advancing towards Rorke's Drift. They consisted of the uDhloko, about 2,000 warriors aged 41, and the younger iNdlondlo. The uThulwana, the unit that Cetshwayo had once belonged to, which totalled about 1,000 45-year-olds, and the inDlu-yengwe, another younger regiment, were known collectively as the uNdi Corps. Some carried white shields and others ruddy shields with white spots, and most wore the head-ring of the battle-experienced married regiments. They wore monkey-skin ear flaps, plumes from exotic birds such as the crane and the ostrich, otter skin headbands and ornaments of beadwork. Boxes filled with snuff, or other substances, dangled from their ears, and ivory spoons were fastened to their heads.

The British army adopted the Martini-Henry breach-loading rifle in 1871. It was a single-shot weapon, weighing just over 9lb, and the barrel was nearly 3ft in length. If not handled correctly the kick-back was severe enough to break a man's collar bone. It was nevertheless considered to be the best rifle of its day. The lever behind the trigger guard was depressed to uncover the breach chamber and eject the used

---

* Captain William Stevenson had been in charge of about 200 natives who were working on maintaining the road back to Helpmekaar, along with some European, or white NCOs.

A photograph of Rorke's Drift looking northward towards the post from the bottom of the Oscarberg, with the storehouse having been stripped of thatch and a more permanent stone wall having been built. The cemetery and monument can be seen to the left of the picture, and note the rocks in the foreground which is the area where Trooper Dixon and James Rorke were buried.

cartridge. A fresh round was then inserted into the chamber and raising the lever closed the breech for firing. It fired .45 bullets, and was most effective at about 400yd. The men wore a leather service belt, to which was attached an ammunition pouch which held four paper packets containing ten cartridges in each.

Chard and Bromhead were well aware that their weapons were far superior to those carried by the Zulus. Even if the Zulus had acquired firearms, they did not have the necessary skill to use them effectively. They could also gain comfort from the knowledge that the reputation of bravery attributed to Zulu warriors was matched by the tradition of coolness and gallantry of the British infantryman.

The feelings of isolation must have been dreadful, particularly in the face of an enemy with a reputation for ruthlessness. It was known that the Zulus took no prisoners. Hearts began to pound, and the only thing they could put their faith in was their tense and nervous comrades beside them and their own ability to defend themselves with rifle and bayonet. Thoughts of families and friends must have raced through their minds and brought sadness to their hearts to think that they may never see home again. As far as they were concerned nobody would ever know how they had fought and died in such a

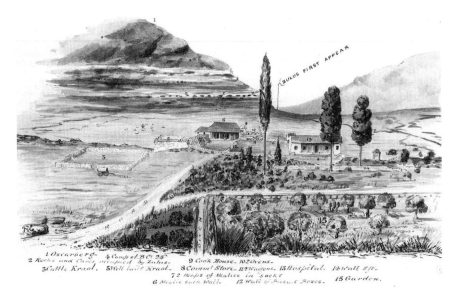

Lieutenant Chard prepared this detailed sketch of the Rorke's Drift post soon after the defence, with most of the significant positions clearly numbered and described. The tall, thin tree in the foreground was cut down when the stone wall was erected.

desolate place, and as the fight they were about to have would be no Waterloo or Balaclava they would have believed that even if the defence of Rorke's Drift was brought to the attention of the British public it would soon be forgotten.

Mr Dunne stated: 'The men knew what was before them – a struggle for life – but they one and all displayed the greatest coolness, though some of them were very young soldiers. On all faces there was a look of determination which showed that they meant to "do or die".'

Private John Williams stated:

What did I feel?' I don't know that I felt anything more than all the others felt. In his ordinary life a man often contemplates some possibility and feels that he would be unable to face it, but when it happens he does face it. He finds himself up against it and goes through with it. That's just what happened to all of us.

It is notable that early in the fight a controversial incident happened that was not recorded in either of Lieutenant Chard's accounts. Corporal Michael Anderson of the NNC had been ill with fever and the tension broke his nerve. The Revd Smith stated, '. . . one unfortunate Contingent corporal, whose heart must have failed him when he saw the enemy and heard the firing, got over the parapet and tried to make his escape on foot, but a bullet from the garden struck him [in the head] and he fell dead within a hundred and fifty yards of our front wall'.

Private Hitch eventually found himself in a most advantageous position on the roof of the storehouse to observe the Zulu advance. Armed Zulus took several shots at him, and he took a pot-shot at a Zulu on the top of the Oscarberg. He stated:

> I was cooking tea for the Company. I tried to get it done before the Zulus attacked the little post at Rorke's Drift, which I managed; taking the tea and my rifle and ammunition, and four kettles of tea.
>
> I just got into the fort when Bromhead asked me to try and get on top of the house. I at once mounted it. As soon as I got on the top I could see the Zulus had got as near as they could without us seeing them. I told Bromhead that they were at the other side of the rise and was extending for attack. Mr Bromhead asked me how

The sketch of the 'Mealie Fort' with certain relevant things numbered. It was prepared by Harry Lugg soon after the defence. It was passed to Alphonse de Neuville as background information for his painting. *(Courtesy of Bryn Lugg)*

many there were? I told him that I thought they numbered up to four to six thousand.

I stayed on the house watching the black mass extending into their fighting line. The same time a number of them creeping along under the rocks and took up cover in the caves, and keep trying to dismount me from the top of the house. Their direction was good but their elevation bad. A few minutes later one appeared on the top of the mountain; from the other side he could see us in the laager plain enough to count us.

I put myself in a lying position but the shot fell short of him. He then moved steadily to the right and signalled with his arm – the main body at once began to advance. I told Mr Bromhead that they would be all around us in a very short time. He at once told the Company to take up their post . . .

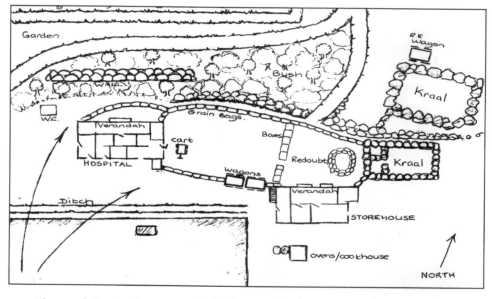

The north barricade consisted of a long wall of grain bags three units high, enclosing the front of the hospital and running along the ledge of the rocky terrace to the north-west corner of the kraal. Two wagons were incorporated into the south barricade facing the Oscarberg, which connected the north-west corner of the storehouse with the kitchen extension at the south-east corner of the hospital building. The arrows indicate the initial Zulu onslaught, and as the attack progressed the warriors moved around the barricades in a clockwise direction. The area where the biscuit boxes met the north rampart is where many of the defenders were shot. (*Courtesy of Tracey Bancroft*)

Private Hook recorded:

> After the enemy had fled the General's camp they came across the river here, and attacked our commissary stores, but fortunately we got an hour's warning, and made a fort. By-and-by down they came in thousands – one black mass – so many we did not know where to fire first, they being so many, and we were about a hundred all told.

Lieutenant Chard reported:

> Five hundred or six hundred of the enemy came suddenly in sight around the hill to our south. They advanced at a run against our south wall, but were met by a well-sustained fire; yet, not withstanding heavy loss, they continued to advance to within fifty yards of the wall, when their leading men encountered such a hot fire from our front; with a cross one from the store, that they were checked.

Drummer Patrick Hayes remembered:

> Suddenly the cry went up, 'Here they come,' and a black yelling mass of frenzied savages could be seen crossing the Buffalo River a short distance away and rushing towards us brandishing rifles and spears. It was a terrifying sight, but the enemy halted as we poured a deadly volley into their midst and followed it up with well-directed independent firing.

Private Caleb Wood recalled: 'Lieutenant Bromhead gave the order for three volleys, and at the first volley the Zulus went down as if they had been cut off at the knees. We had only a chance to fire one more volley when there came an order to fix bayonets.'

Sergeant Henry Gallagher later related 'the initial terror they all felt at the sight of so many Zulus in battle array'.

Lieutenant Chard reported: 'We opened fire on them, between five and six hundred yards, at first a little wild.' However, he was heartened by the way the marksmanship improved as trigger fingers steadied.

The Revd Smith recalled: 'One of the mounted chiefs was shot by Private [James] Dunbar, 2/24th, who also killed eight of the enemy with as many consecutive shots as they came round a ledge of the hill.' Private George Edwards Orchard claimed that it was his marksmanship, but the majority of witnesses stated that it was Dunbar.

Trooper Harry Lugg of the Natal Mounted Police recalled:

My carbine was broken, or rather the stock bent. I found a piece of rein, tied it up and fell in with the soldiers. I had the satisfaction of seeing the first I fired at roll over at 350, and then my nerves were as steady. I made sure almost before I pulled the trigger. There was some of the best shooting at 450 yards I have ever seen.

Corporal William Allan had taken out a party of skirmishers, and when he returned to the post he took up a position behind the south barricade, which included the two wagons.* Private John Lyons reported: 'I took up a position to check the fire from the enemy's right flank, as it was thought the crack shots would go up there [the Oscarberg]. Corporal Allen and several men were with me, and we consider we did good service.'

Chard recorded:

Taking advantage, however, of the cover afforded by the cook-house, and the ovens, they kept up thence heavy musketry volleys; the greater number, however, without stopping at all, moved on towards the left round the hospital, and thence made a rush toward our north-west wall and our breastwork of mealie bags. After a short but desperate struggle those assailants were driven back with very heavy loss into the bush around our works.

The main body of the enemy close behind had meantime lined the ledge of rocks, and filled some caves overlooking us at a distance of a hundred yards to the south, from whence they kept up a constant fire. Another body, advancing somewhat more to the left than those who first attacked us, occupied a garden in the hollows of the road and also the bush beyond it in great numbers, taking especial advantage of the bush, which we had no time to cut down. The enemy were thus able to advance close to our works, and in this part soon held one whole side of the wall, while we on the other kept back a series of desperate assaults which were made on a line extending from the hospital all along the wall as far as the bush. But each attack was most splendidly met and repulsed by our men, with the bayonet.

---

* Corporal Allan's surname is sometimes mistakenly spelt 'Allen'. However, his name appears as Allan on official documentation, and on his grave.

A scene at Rorke's Drift looking from the east, where the Engineers' wagon would have been situated. The rocks where the men are seated are the continuation of the ledge on which the defenders built the barricade to gain extra height. Much of the surrounding foliage and other terrain had been cut down and removed so it could not be used as camouflage if the garrison was attacked again.

Private Hook observed:

> The Zulus were swarming around us, and there was an extraordinary rattle as the bullets struck the biscuit boxes and queer thuds as they plumped into the bags of mealies. Then there was the whiz and rip of the assegais, the spears with which the Zulus did terrible work throughout the war, and of which I had had experience during the Kaffir campaign of 1877–78. We had plenty of ammunition, but we were told to save it, and so we took careful aim at every shot, and hardly a cartridge was wasted.

Private Hitch noted:

> There was a certain space of about nine yards where the barricade was uncompleted. It was, of course, the weakest link in the chain, and the Zulus were not long in discovering this fact. In this position eight of us, Bromhead, Nichols (Nicholas) Fagan, Cole, Dalton, Schiess, Williams and myself – made a stand, and it was here, I think, that the hardest work was done.

As more and more warriors moved around the barricades in a clockwise direction and came to the veranda at the front of the hospital, they began to clamber up the rocky ledge to get to the relatively open area described by Hitch. As they did so they began to push the defenders back, and tried to gain access to the hospital via the veranda. To counter this, Lieutenant Bromhead got together a detail of men, and placing himself at the forefront they charged forward with fixed bayonets, and repeated the action numerous times. The fighting became fierce as they were locked in the brutality of war. Bromhead and his men drove them out every time they got inside the compound. Weapons clashed as the Zulus kept one side of the barricade while the soldiers held their ground on the other. Each time the Zulus were driven back into the bushes they shouted their war-cry '*Usuthu!*' and the Brits replied with defiant shouts and curses.

A young warrior of the inDlu-yengwe regiment who first appeared on the neck of the Oscarberg Hill. The leopard-skin headband is the only item of ceremonial dress he has retained. He is carrying the small war shield bearing the colours of an unmarried regiment. (*Illustration by Richard Scollins*)

Fred Hitch remembered:

The Zulus pushed right up to the porch, and it was not until the bayonet was freely used that they flinched the least bit. Had the Zulus taken the bayonet as freely as they took the bullets we could not have stood more than fifteen minutes. They pushed right up to us and not only got to the laager but got in with us, but they seemed to have a great dread of the bayonet, which stood to us from beginning to end.

During that struggle there was a fine big Zulu see me shoot his mate down – he sprang forward, dropping his rifle and assegais, seizing hold of the muzzle of my rifle with his left hand and the right hand hold of the bayonet. Thinking to disarm me, he pulled and tried hard to get the rifle from me, but I had a firm hold of the small of the butt of my rifle with my left hand. My cartridges were on the top of the mealie bags, which enabled me to load my rifle, and I shot the poor wretch whilst holding on his grasp for some few moments.

We were so busy that one [a Zulu] had got inside and was in the act of assegaing Bromhead. Bromhead, not knowing he was there. I put my rifle on him, knowing at the same time that it was empty. Instead of him delivering the assegai, which no doubt would have been fatal, he dodged down and hopped out of the laager.

Dr Reynolds noted:

We found ourselves quickly surrounded by the enemy with their strong force holding the garden and shrubbery. From all sides but especially the latter places, they poured on us a continuous fire, to which our men replied as quickly as they could reload their rifles. Again and again the Zulus pressed forward and retreated, until at last they forced themselves so daringly, and in such numbers, as to climb over the mealie sacks in front of the hospital, and drove the defenders from there behind an entrenchment of biscuit boxes, hastily formed with much judgement and forethought by Lieutenant Chard.

All around them men were being hit by sniper fire and it must have occurred to Bromhead and Chard that they could not sustain the amount of casualties for long at the rate they were being inflicted. In his eyewitness account Private Hitch stated: 'It was then about when Mr Dalton was shot and Mr Dunne.' However, as there is no medical

Regular soldiers and men from Colonial units fought side by side in fierce close combat with ferocious Zulu warriors of the uNdi Corps. British dead and seriously wounded numbered less than 30, while Zulu casualties are believed to have totalled as many as 500. *(Illustration by Richard Scollins)*

report on Commissary Dunne being wounded and he does not mention it in his account, it seems that Hitch mistook Dunne for Commissary Louis Byrne.

Dr Reynolds stated: 'Early in the fight Mr Byrne was shot through the head, and later Dalton, when first standing at full height, received a bullet in the chest, but the wound fortunately did not prove fatal.'

Lieutenant Chard recorded: 'Mr Byrne, acting commissariat officer, and who had behaved with great coolness and gallantry, was killed instantaneously shortly before this by a bullet through the head, just after he had given a drink of water to a wounded man of the NNC.'

Chaplain Smith noted:

Presently Corporal C Scammell (Natal Native Contingent), who was near Mr Byrne, was shot through the shoulder and back. He crawled a short distance and handed the remainder of his cartridges to Lieutenant Chard, and then expressed his desire for a drink of water. Byrne at once fetched it, but whilst giving it to him, he was shot through the head and fell dead instantly.

The author originally believed that Corporals John Wilson, Carl Scammell and John Doughty, of the Natal Native Contingent, were patients in the hospital. However, there are no medical reports of injuries to any of the three men prior to the action at Rorke's Drift, and if the account by 'Old Soldier' is to be considered it seems that they were with Stevenson's party working on the road to Helpmekaar. He stated:

I was ordered to go and bring in Captain Stevenson and the 200 Kaffirs working on the road. When I told him what he was wanted for at the mission station he translated it to the Kaffirs, who immediately cleared off up the road towards Helpmekaar, and he went with them. I returned to the mission station accompanied by two European corporals (Doughty and Scammell), who had been with the party, and reported the matter to Lieutenant Chard.

Private Hook confirmed this in one of his accounts 'About this time Captain Stevens [Stevenson] and all his men, except one native and two Europeans, non-commissioned officers, deserted us and went off to Helpmekaar.'

Lieutenant Coghill stated in his diary that there were two NCOs of the NNC wounded at Sihayo's Kraal. They were Corporal Thomas Purvis, who did not take part in the battle, and Corporal Jessy Mayor.

Lieutenant Chard stated in his VC recommendation for Schiess that the corporal had been wounded in the foot at Sihayo's Kraal. However, it seems that Schiess was in the hospital with an injured foot caused by wearing ill-fitting boots.

Lieutenant Chard stated: 'The enemy stuck to this assault most tenaciously, and on their repulse and retiring into the bush, I called all the men inside our entrenchment – and the enemy immediately occupied the wall we had abandoned and used it as a breastwork to fire over.'

At the height of this hand-to-hand fighting a disaster almost occurred when the commanding officer came perilously close to being killed in action. Lieutenant Chard recalled:

While I was intently watching to get a fair shot at a Zulu who appeared to be firing rather well, Private [David] Jenkins, 24th, saying 'Look out, Sir', gave my head a duck down just as a bullet

Although they had been informed that Lord Chelmsford had divided his force, the defenders believed that the entire 3rd Column had been wiped out, and they stood on the defences and strained their eyes looking towards Helpmekaar for any sign of relief. *(Illustration by Geoff Dickson)*

whizzed over it. He had noticed a Zulu who was quite near in another direction taking deliberate aim at me. For all the man could have known, the shot might have been directed at himself. I mention these facts to show how well the men behaved and how loyally worked together.

Lieutenant Chard also reported:

All this time the enemy had been attempting to force the hospital, and shortly afterwards did set fire to the roof. The garrison of the hospital defended the place room by room, our men bringing out all the sick who could be moved before they retired. Privates John Williams, Henry Hook, Robert Jones and William Jones, of the 24th Regiment, were the last four men to leave, holding the doorway against the Zulus with bayonets, their ammunition being quite expended. From want of interior communication and the smoke of the burning house, it was found impossible to carry off all the sick, and, with most heartfelt sorrow and regret, we could not save a few poor fellows from a terrible fate.

The two commanding officers did not witness the action within the hospital, but the most descriptive accounts were provided by Private Hook. One of his reports recorded:

The Zulus kept drawing closer and closer, and I went on firing, killing several of them. At last they got close up and set fire to the hospital. There was only one patient in my room with a broken leg, and he was burnt, and I was driven out by the flames, and was unable to save him. At first I had a comrade [Private Cole] but he left after a time and was killed on his way to the inner entrenchment. When driven out of this room, I retired by a partition door into the next room, where there were several patients. For a few minutes I was the only fighting man there. A wounded man of the 24th came to me from another room with a bullet wound in the arm. I tied it up. Then John Williams came in from another room, and made a hole in the partition, through which he helped the sick and wounded men.

Whilst he was doing this, the Zulus beat in the door, and tried to enter. I stood at the side and shot and bayoneted several – I could not tell how many, but there were four or five lying dead at my feet. They threw assegais continually, but only one touched me, and

Lieutenant Bromhead posted six men of B Company inside the hospital to guard the sick and wounded. They fought with great gallantry, and of the six, two were killed in action and four were awarded the Victoria Cross. *(Illustration by Richard Scollins)*

that inflicted a scalp wound which I did not think worth reporting; in fact, I did not feel the wound at the time. One Zulu seized my rifle, and tried to drag it away. Whilst we were tussling I slipped in a cartridge and pulled the trigger – the muzzle was against his chest, and he fell dead. Every now and again a Zulu would make a rush to enter – the door would only let in one man at a time – but I bayoneted or shot every one.

When all the patients were out except one, who owing to a broken leg could not move, I also went through the hole, dragging the man after me, in doing which I broke his leg again. I then stopped at the hole to guard it whilst Williams was making a hole through the partition into the next room. When the patients had been got into the next room I followed, dragging the man with the broken leg after me. I stopped at the hole to guard it whilst Williams was helping the patients through a window into the other defences. I stuck to my particular charge and dragged him out and helped him into the inner line of defences.

Private Hitch stated:

The sun was just beginning to set at the time the Zulus came close up to the front; and after they had taken the hospital and was burning it, Lieutenant Bromhead and three privates, with Colour-Sergeant Bourne, kept the position in the right front, in order to keep the enemy from getting a line of fire at the men of the 24th, who were firing to the front from a line of biscuit boxes. I was here for about an hour, being all the time between three cross-fires.

We had to fall back to the second line of defence, and when the Zulus took possession of the hospital, Bromhead and myself and five others took up the position on the right of the second line which we were exposed to the cross-fire. Bromhead took the centre and was the only one that did not get wounded.

There was four killed and two wounded, myself was the last of the six shot. Bromhead and myself had it to ourselves about an hour and a half, Bromhead using his rifle and revolver with deadly aim. Bromhead kept telling the men not to waste one round. They seemed determined to move Bromhead and myself.

Lieutenant Chard reported: 'At about 6:00pm the enemy extended their attack further to their left, and I feared seriously would get over the wall behind the biscuit boxes. I ran back with two or three men to this part of the wall, and was immediately joined by Bromhead with two or three more.'

This meant that Lieutenant Bromhead and six of his men were now stationed at an extremely exposed position where the biscuit boxes met the northern breastwork. It was inevitable that some of them would be hit by enemy fire in such a dangerous area of the defences.

When studying the 'original' map prepared by Lieutenant Chard, it can be seen that Private Thomas Cole, known to his friends as 'Old King Cole', was able to get from the room he was defending with Private Hook to the hospital veranda by way of three escape doors without having to face the Zulus; and by the same token they were access doors for the enemy. It seemed he realised that if Bromhead and his small band of men failed to keep the warriors away from the veranda the occupants of the hospital would become sitting ducks, so he decided he would be better deployed outside.

Cole is believed to have been the first man to be killed here when he left the hospital to help out. A bullet went right through his head and killed him instantly, and the bullet then hit Private Bushe in the nose and caused him injury. Private Thomas Nicholas was noted as using his rifle well when he too was hit in the head by a Zulu slug. Private Hitch reported that 'his brains being scattered all about us!'. A Zulu bullet smashed into the left side of the chest of Lance Sergeant Thomas Williams, and he fell to the ground mortally wounded; and soon afterwards Private John Fagan was also hit in the chest. He fell against the biscuit boxes, but managed to keep hold of his rifle and remained at his post. Both men died later.

Private Hitch remembered:

Again, this was just before they tried to fire the other building, and they seemed to me as if they had made up their minds to take Rorke's Drift with this rush. They rushed up madly, not withstanding the heavy loss they had already suffered.

It was in this struggle that I was shot. They pressed us very hard, several of them mounting the barricade. I knew this one had got his rifle presented at me, but at the same time I had got my hands full at the front. I was at the present when he shot me through my right shoulder blade and passed through my shoulder which splintered the shoulder bone very much, as I have had in all 39 pieces of broken bone taken from my shoulder. I tried to keep my feet, but could not. He could have assegaied me had not Bromhead shot him with his revolver. Bromhead seemed sorry when he saw me down bleeding so freely, saying 'Mate, I am very sorry to see you down.'

I was not down more than a few minutes, stripping to my shirt sleeves, with my waist-belt on and valise strap; I put my wounded arm inside my waist-belt. I was able to make another stand, getting Bromhead's revolver, and with his assistance in loading it, I managed very well with it.

Mr Dunne stated: 'All this had not occurred without loss on both sides, numbers of the Zulus having fallen, and on our side Pte Cole (Old King Cole) and another man of the 24th had been shot dead [Nicholas], and three or four wounded. The doctor, Surgeon Reynolds, was busy attending the wounded as they fell.'*

Private Hitch recalled:

> We had to fall back to the second line of defence, and when the Zulus took possession of the hospital, Bromhead and myself and five others took up the position on the right of the second line of defence, in which we were exposed to the cross-fire. Bromhead took the centre and was the only one that did not get wounded. There was four killed and two wounded, myself was the last of the six shot.

However, it seems that initially two men were killed instantly (Cole and Nicholas), two were mortally wounded (Williams and Fagan) and two wounded (Bushe and Hitch).

Private Hitch stated: 'I saw one of my comrades – Private Nichols [Nicholas] – killed; he was shot through the head, his brains being scattered all about us! He had up to his death been doing good service with his rifle.'

Although he is not mentioned in any of the accounts as being involved, Private James Bushe must have been close to at least Private Cole when he was killed. Lieutenant Chard recalled after the battle: 'I was glad to seize the opportunity to wash my face in a muddy puddle in the company with Private Bush, 24th, whose face was covered with blood from a wound in the nose caused by the bullet which had passed through and killed Private Cole, 24th.'

In a newspaper interview dictated to a reporter Private Edward Savage recorded: 'In the night time, when under fire, Savage heard a fellow soldier of the name of Fagan cry out for water, and managed

---

* The men mentioned in various accounts concerning this part of the action are Lance Sergeant Thomas Williams and Privates Frederick Hitch, John Fagan, Edward Nicholas and Thomas Cole.

to crawl along to help his comrade in arms, who died before daylight next morning.'

Corporal Schiess showed particular gallantry at this point, and Lieutenant Chard reported:

Amongst many acts of his [Schiess] I may mention one I myself witnessed – after we had retired to our inner line of defence. The Zulus occupied the wall of mealie bags we had abandoned. Corporal Schiess without any order, crept out along this wall a few feet, to dislodge one in particular of the enemy who was shooting better than usual; on his raising himself to get a shot, the Zulu who was close to him on the other side of the wall, fired knocking off his hat. Cpl Schiess immediately jumped on the wall and bayoneted the Zulu, and in less time than I take to write it, shot a second and bayoneted a third, and then came back to the cover of the inner defence again.

The men defending the south barricade were also sustaining casualties. Private Lyons stated:

Lieutenant Bromhead was on the right face, firing over the mealie bags with a Martini-Henry. Mr Chard was also very busy. I only turned round once to see this, and in that brief interval I saw Private Cole shot and he fell dead. Seeing this I kept myself more over the bags, knowing that the shot that had hit him had come over our heads, and I was determined to check this flank fire as much as possible. I thus became more exposed, and so did Corporal Allen. We fired many shots, and I said to my comrade 'They [the Zulus] are falling fast over there', and he replied, 'Yes, we're giving it to them.' I saw many Zulus killed on the hill. About half past seven, as near as I can tell, after we had been fighting between two and three hours, I received a shot through the right side of the neck. The ball lodged in the back, striking the spine, and was not extracted until five weeks afterwards. My right arm was partially disabled.

I said, 'Give it to them Allen, I am done. I am dying', and he replied, 'All right, Jack', and while I was speaking to him I saw a hole in the right sleeve of his coat, and I said, 'Allen, are you shot?' And he replied, 'Yes, goodbye'. He walked away, with blood running from his arm, and helped to serve ammunition all night.

The awards of Victoria Cross to Corporal Allan and Private Hitch were announced together in the same citation, but in the author's view they did not actually fight together during any part of the battle, and their citations should have been recorded individually. Private Hitch spent some time on the roof of the store; then he was conspicuous in having taken part in Bromhead's bayonet charges, and in the defence of the biscuit box/north rampart danger area, where he was incapacitated by his wounds. Therefore, he had no time to help Corporal Allan. Allan was noted for providing cover fire for some of the hospital evacuees as they struggled across the compound, where he too was wounded. They were also noticeable for having given out ammunition to their comrades. The VC citation is scant on detail and probably they were cited together for convenience because they were both conspicuous in the compound area of the post.

Private Hitch recorded: 'I then knocked about as well as I could, serving the others with ammunition, until I became exhausted from loss of blood and fell down unconscious. I did not come to until the morning, just as peep of day, and I then found myself in a stable.'

Private Hook stated that 'Corporal Allen [Allan] and Private Hitch helped enormously in keeping up communication with the hospital. They were both badly wounded but when they could not fight any longer, they served out ammunition to their comrades throughout the night.' However, neither statement confirms that they worked together.

A trooper of the Natal Carbineers named J.P. Symons was told that the Revd George Smith:

> . . . carried ammunition round in his hat for the men. One man told me that a private was swearing because he could not get any ammunition and the Reverend George reproved him, saying he should not swear at such a time as this but to put his trust in God. Patting his rifle the soldier replied, 'I shall put my faith in this now and God afterwards.'

In later years Lieutenant Adendorff related to his friend, Captain Walter Stafford of the 1st Natal Native Contingent, who was a survivor of Isandlwana, 'A man was cussing all the time. Reverend Smith went to him and said, "Please, my good man, stop that cussing. We may shortly have to answer for our sins." The reply he got was, "All right, mister, you do the praying and I will send the black b's to hell as fast as I can."'

For the defenders thirst and fatigue had become as much an adversary as the Zulus; especially among the wounded. As 10 o'clock came and went many men were beginning to consider their situation as hopeless, and they could envisage no chance of escape. But they still intended to fight till the end. They had been firing their weapons continually for 5 hours, changing shoulders when they became bruised and sore from the recoil of their rifles, until they caused so much pain that the men had to hold their rifles at arm's length to fire. The rifle barrels became so hot that their fingers and the palms of their hands became scorched and they had to use rags to enable them to hold the weapon. Others picked up the rifles of their dead and wounded comrades and used them alternately. They had to clear the barrels frantically with a ramrod when they clogged up and jammed, and their hands became cut and splintered as they fumbled for cartridges in the ammunition boxes.

Private Edward Savage recorded: 'Lieutenant Bromhead assisted to open a cartridge box. In doing so in the dark, Savage cut his hand. He, however, kept "pegging" away and did some execution.'

The bayonets were effective, but they were not strong, and most of those that had not been snapped from the rifles had bent during the struggle. Their uniforms were ripped and begrimed, and their faces were dirty and slashed with blood. Some men could no longer speak from exhaustion and the smoke that parched their dry, burning throats.

As the battle went on the Zulu chiefs were also becoming more anxious. They were used to fighting out in the open and not against rapid-firing rifles from behind frustrating fortifications. They had not eaten properly for days, and had run over 16 miles to get to Rorke's Drift. They had disobeyed Cetshwayo's orders not to attack fortified positions, and they could only justify their defiance

`For how can man die better,
Than facing fearful odds.
For the ashes of his fathers,
And the temples of his gods.'
Thomas Macaulay

by taking back to Ulundi a report of unqualified victory. However, they had already launched their best attacks and the soldiers were still secure in the enclosure. Even if they did finally succeed their losses were already heavy and rising. They were finding it increasingly difficult to stir up morale and fighting spirit and they could see signs that their warriors were losing heart.

Chard recorded: '. . . we now converted two mealie-bag heaps into a sort of redoubt, which gave a second line of fire all along, Assistant Commissary Walter Dunne working hard at this though much exposed; thus rendering most valuable assistance'.

Mr Dunne remembered:

However, the position was a desperate one and our chance of escape seemed slight indeed, so Chard decided to form a sort of redoubt of mealie bags, where a last stand could be made. We laboured at this till we dropped with exhaustion, but succeeded in building it up to about eight feet high on the outside, and here the wounded were brought for protection. It was hard work, for the bags of mealies weighed 200 pounds each.

Surgeon Reynolds stated: 'Lieutenant Chard here again shined in resource. Anticipating the Zulus making one more united dash for the fort, and possibly gaining entrance, he converted an immense stack of mealies standing in the middle of our enclosure, and originally cone fashioned, into a comparatively safe place for a last retreat.'

After their failure to overcome the defenders at the north barricade, the Zulus turned their attention to the south-east of the defences at the back of the store, where the glow from the burning roof of the hospital was less effective. However, even here they had little success, as the men defending the back of the building fired through windows and loopholes and brought them crashing down as they ran in with flaming torches in an effort to set light to the thatch on the roof.

One of these men was Corporal Francis Attwood of the Army Service Corps, who was stationed at the top floor. In a letter to his aunt and uncle he stated:

I must tell you that I made an awful mess of one fellow. He was running towards the house in a slightly stooping position, when I let fly at him and struck him in the crown of the head, the effect of which was to blow the entire side of his face away. I must tell you that I was at an upper window, the only one in the barn, I call it.

Corporal Attwood was awarded the Distinguished Conduct Medal for his part in the defence.

However, he was not the only one defending the store building. Lieutenant Adendorff was firing through a loophole in the back wall, and Chard reported, 'Seeing the Hospital burning, and the desperate attempts being made by the enemy to fire the roof of our Store (one man was shot, I believe by Lieutenant Adendorff, who had a light almost touching the thatch) . . .'.

Trooper Lugg had decided that he wanted to play his part in the action and at some time during the morning he '. . .fell in with the soldiers'. He continued: 'I thought, if I can get somewhere I can sit down and pop away I shall be alright, because my knee was much swollen. I was told off in my turn to take a loophole and defend the roof from fire.' His sketch note number 9 shows: 'The loophole near the roof was my position to defend roof from fire.' He also explains with note 3 that the 'washhouse' was where the Zulus '. . . made themselves at home by smoking, boiling coffee, and otherwise enjoying themselves'. This audacious behaviour must have really annoyed the defenders, as it was their coffee the Zulus were drinking.

Lugg's son later recorded: 'One of the stories Henry used to recall was of a Zulu, who, during the height of the fight, availed himself in the semi-darkness, to creep into the kitchen to light his smoking horn or *gudu* from the glowing embers, and was promptly shot by Henry.'*

Lieutenant Chard remembered: 'We were sustaining throughout all this a desultory fire, kept up all night, and several assaults were attempted, but always repulsed with vigour, the attacks continuing until after midnight, our men firing with the greatest coolness, not wasting a single shot. The light afforded by the burning hospital proved a great advantage.'

As daylight came Mr Dunne recalled: 'Overhead, the small birds, disturbed from their nests by the turmoil and smoke, flew hither and thither confusedly.' Trooper Lugg added that there were some less welcome creatures too – 'Vultures'.

---

* Many years later Henry Lugg was informed that the Zulu he had killed was named Mngumle. The use of the words 'glowing embers' suggests that Mngumle crept into the kitchen extension of the burning hospital to light his pipe; a distance of at least forty paces from where Henry was stationed. Henry was in a good elevated position to take such a shot, and the fact that he hit his target with a damaged weapon must have gained the admiration of his comrades.

Lieutenant Chard reported:

At four o'clock on the morning of 23 January firing ceased; and at daybreak the enemy were passing out of sight over the hill to our south-west. We then patrolled the ground, collecting arms from dead bodies of the Zulus, and strengthening the position as much as possible. We were still removing thatch from the roof of the store, when about seven o'clock, a large body of the enemy once more appeared upon the hills to the south-west. I now sent a friendly kaffir, who had come in shortly before, with a note to the officer commanding at Helpmekaar, asking help. About eight o'clock, however, the British Third Column appeared, and at sight of this the enemy, who had been gradually advancing towards us, commenced falling back as our troops approached.

Lieutenant John Maxwell, 3rd NNC, was with the British column as it approached. 'Those that had glasses eagerly scanned the place; but I was

At about 8 o'clock in the morning on 23 January 1879, the defenders were suspicious when they saw a long column of figures marching towards them from the direction of Isandlwana, thinking they were Zulus dressed in the tunics of their dead comrades. However, they were relieved when a unit of British cavalry rode into the camp and their dreadful ordeal was over.

IN LOVING MEMORY OF
WILLIAM NEVILLE,
WHO DIED ON THE 28TH DAY OF AUGUST, 1895,

AGED 37 YEARS,

And was Interred at Ince Cemetery August 31st.

Farewell, dear wife, my life is past,
Faithfully I loved you to the last ;
And on my children pray pity take
And love them for their father's sake.

My sufferings so long time I bore,
Physicians were in vain ;
Till death did seize and God did please
To ease me of my pain.

A loving husband, a father dear,
A faithful friend when he was here ;
He lived in hope, his end was peace,
We hope his joys will never cease.

＋ IN LOVING MEMORY OF ＋
Alice Neville,
WHO DIED MAY 14, 1897,

AGED 1 YEAR AND 10 MONTHS,

AND WAS INTERRED AT INCE CEMETERY MAY 17th.

We had a little darling girl,
She was our grateful pride ;
We loved her, ah, perhaps too well,
For soon she slept and died.

We often talk about her yet,
Her little ways we can't forget,
Yet we submit while here below,
That we may meet where death's not known.

The memorial card for a Rorke's Drift man. The men under Lieutenant Bromhead's command were mainly rough and ready lads from the industrial and rural areas of Britain. After military service they returned to a life that was extremely difficult for the working classes of the time. William Neville struggled to look after his family, and he got into several scrapes with the law. He died of heart failure at the relatively young age of 37.

76

looking at the river, which seemed to be a perfect torrent. The ponts appeared all right, so the regulars would have no difficulty in crossing.'

After his unit made a difficult crossing of the river, Lieutenant Maxwell continued:

> We formed up, and marched on the temporary fort, and as we approached we could distinguish several soldiers waving their helmets and apparently very glad at our arrival. There were several dead bodies of the enemy scattered about which at once told us the place had been attacked. It was about 8 o'clock when we arrived at the front of the place, and I should say there were from 150 to 200 bodies about here.

Lieutenant Chard continued:

> There were a great many of our Native Levies with the Column, and the number of red coats seemed so few that at first we had grave doubts that the force approaching was the enemy. We improvised a flag, and our signals were soon replied to from the column. The mounted men crossed the drift and galloped up to us headed by Major Cecil Russell and Lieutenant Walsh, and were received by us with a heavy cheer.

Chard must have found great comfort on hearing the familiar Taunton accent of Major Henry Walsh of the 13th (Somerset) Light Infantry.

Lieutenant Bromhead ran out to greet some fellow officers of the 2nd Battalion, a highly memorable moment. Lieutenant Henry Mainwaring stated, 'I shall never forget seeing Gonny Bromhead come out to meet us as we formed in quarter column outside the gate. He told me afterwards he felt as if he was walking on air as he never expected to see daylight again.' Lieutenant George Bannister 'found old Gunny as cheery as ever and not a scratch about him'.

For most of the battle Driver Robson had been concentrating his fire on the warriors who were ransacking the Engineers' wagon with all the equipment in it. Lieutenant Chard reported: 'In wrecking the stores in my wagon the Zulus had brought to light a forgotten bottle of beer, and Bromhead and I drank it with mutual congratulations on having come safely out of so much danger.'

Edward Savage said to a reporter: 'He never spent such a miserable night in all his life. There was the momentary danger of being shot, and the likelihood of perishing from the cold and hunger. He has no recollection of ever having gone through such hardship as while invalided at Rorke's Drift.'

Dr Reynolds stated proudly, 'I do not think it possible that men could have behaved better than did the 2/24th and the Army Hospital Corps (three), who were particularly forward during the whole attack.'

Perhaps the last statement concerning the defence of Rorke's Drift should be made by the only man of God who was present, the Revd George Smith:

> At last daylight dawned, and the enemy retired round the shoulder of the hill by which they had approached. Whilst some remained at their posts, others of our men were sent out to patrol and returned with about one hundred rifles and guns and some four hundred assegais left by the enemy upon the field; and round our walls, and especially in front of the hospital, the dead Zulus lay piled up in heaps. About three hundred and fifty were subsequently buried by us. They must have carried off nearly all their wounded with them . . . It was certainly of the upmost strategic importance that this place should not be taken. Perhaps the safety of the remainder of the column, and on this part of the Colony, depended on it.'

The cemetery at Rorke's Drift. Private Hook remembered: 'Soon afterwards the little cemetery was walled in and a monument was put up in the middle. The lettering was cut on it by a very clever bandsman named James Mellsop, who used bits of broken bayonet as chisels.'

Speaking in Adelaide, Australia in May 1913, he stated:

'Do I remember Rorke's Drift?' he repeated. 'I do, indeed: vividly and clearly. Every occurrence of that day was not of the kind that could be easily dropped from the mind. The attack took place in the afternoon. They came upon us suddenly. We were kept going till the relief came. We knew the relief was coming from the natives themselves. When the first soldiers appeared they [the Zulus] drew off for a little while, but came on to the attack again, as they thought the soldiers they saw were only the ghosts of the men killed at Isandlwana. When they found that the ghosts were firing on them they soon left, and when Lord Chelmsford's force came up to us we were pretty well worn out.

The monument erected as a memorial to the Zulu warriors who fought at Rorke's Drift. (*Courtesy of Lenny Hodges*)

Chapter 6

Reluctant Heroes

Lieutenants Bromhead and Chard remained stationed at Rorke's Drift for a while after the battle in dreadful conditions. Chard was tasked with supervising the burial of hundreds of dead Zulus in mass graves, and to work on a more permanent stone perimeter.

Lieutenant Bromhead oversaw the awful work of burying the British dead, and the construction of a cemetery. Private Hook recalled:

> As for our own comrades, we, who had fought side by side with them, buried them. This was done the day after the fight, not far from the place where they fell, and at the foot of the hill. Soon afterwards the little cemetery was walled in and a monument was put up in the middle. The lettering was cut on it by a very clever bandsman named James Mellsop, C Company, 2nd/24th Regiment, who was a former stonemason, used bits of broken bayonet as chisels. He drew a capital picture of the fight. Those who had been killed in action were buried on one side of the cemetery and those who died of disease on the other side. A curious thing was that a civilian named Byrne, who had taken part in the defence and was killed, was buried outside the cemetery wall. I don't know why, except that he was not a regular soldier.

Colonel Henry Harford described the situation after the battle in his *Zulu War Journal*:

> With the disbandment of our men, the officers and NCOs of the Contingent were brought into the Fort and given the north-east corner of it to hold, and a very tight fit it was for everyone as the place was overcrowded with the number of men in occupation.

To make matters worse we had a lot of rain, and the interior of the Fort became a simple quagmire from the tramping of so many feet. Fatigue parties were employed for the best part of the day in carrying liquid mud away and emptying the slush outside. In this state of filth we lived and ate and slept for more than two months, no-one being in possession of anything more than a blanket and the clothes that he stood up in.

An exception was made, however, with B Company, 2nd Battalion, 24th Regiment, who had made such a gallant defence, and they were housed in the attic of Rorke's House with a tarpaulin thrown over the rafters (from which the thatch had been removed) to shelter them from the wet, a well-deserved honour.

However, even they had their troubles in trying to keep dry, as the tarpaulin often bagged in between the rafters with a collection of water which had to be ejected, and I shall not easily forget one particular night when Dr [Surgeon Major James] Reynolds, who got the VC, and I met in the dark having been literally washed out of our sleeping place, and mooched about, endeavouring to find a more sheltered spot.

Suddenly we hit upon the idea of lying down under the eaves of B Company's roof, so coiled ourselves up in our soaking wet blankets thanking our stars that at all events there would be no river running under us, when presently swish came about half a ton of water clean on top of us – B Company were emptying their tarpaulin! It was useless moving as we couldn't better ourselves, and wet as we were, thanks to the temperature of the atmosphere and the heat from our bodies, was comfortably warm as long as we lay still.

This terrible state of things, living in such slush, caused a lot of sickness from fever and dysentery which carried off a large number of men and one or two of the officers.

Chard was struck down with fever, and on 17 February he said goodbye to Bromhead and most of the other defenders as he was taken by ambulance wagon to Ladysmith. There he was looked after by a fellow West Country man named Dr Hyde Allen Park and his wife. After showing signs of improvement, he suffered a relapse, and just after the announcement of his Victoria Cross award it was reported in local newspapers that he had died. However, he was nursed back to health, and was able to report back to duty in time for the re-invasion of Zululand.

Before the awards of Victoria Cross were announced on 2 May, the people of Harrismith in the Orange Free State sent a calligraphic manuscript address to Chard and Bromhead and other officers and men who defended Rorke's Drift. 'We believe that your gallant conduct has been the means of averting much bloodshed throughout South Africa, and that Her Majesty and Her Government will be pleased to give such recognition of your services as we believe you are entitled to receive.'

Chard wrote back from the British camp at Conference Hill in the Transvaal on 22 May 1879, to John Emmett, C.A. Barrett and Thomas F. De La Mare, and the people of the town, thanking them 'on behalf of the defenders of Rorke's Drift for your complimentary address . . . we deeply appreciate the great honour done to us by this kindly expression'.

Chard joined Colonel Wood's column at Landman's Drift to inspect the fortifications, and he was involved in all the engineering activities during the Flying Column's advance on the Zulu capital at Ulundi. His unit followed up Colonel Buller's scouting activities, building bridges and repairing roads. While the Second Division was halted at Fort Newdigate to await supplies on 6 June 1879, Chard was out on picket duty when he was caught up in a false alarm which caused the British

About 12,000 Zulus attacked the British square early on the morning of 4 July 1879. The leading warriors got to within about sixty paces of the square before ferocious British firepower stalled their attack. Shells and bullets rained down on the warriors until they broke and ran. Then a section of the square opened to allow the 17th Lancers to charge out and run them down.

to open fire. Several of his men were wounded and some horses were killed, and he and his men spent an uncomfortable time sheltering in a muddy trench with British bullets whizzing about above them.

Chard was in the classic British square formation, as his local regiment's band, the 13th Somerset Light Infantry, led them into the final battle of the war at Ulundi on 4 July 1879. Devastating British firepower delivered the final crushing defeat of the Zulu army.

Lieutenant R. de C. Porter of Chard's company, whose father wrote a history of the Royal Engineers, kept a diary of the advance on Ulundi, extracts from which follow:

2 July: Commenced building a small pentagonal stone fort. The ideas for the future are these. Tomorrow or next day the army is to cross the Umvalosi, without wagons, except such as are necessary for ammunition and tools. The men are to carry two days' provisions. The wagons are to be left behind in laager; one battalion guarding them. All day long we could see large numbers of Zulus in the big kraals across the river. Some of them have been dancing war dances.

4 July: Started in the dark to cross the river. The river was about 50 yards wide, nowhere more than eighteen inches deep; the bottom sandy. After crossing we commenced at once to ascend through a somewhat broken country towards the open plains where the kraals lay. About two miles from the river we got into open grassland, and here we formed a large square two deep. The Engineers (only the 5th Company, as the 2nd company had been left on the other side of the river with the force guarding the laager) were in reserve on the front face, behind the Gatlings.

About 8 o'clock, large bodies of the enemy began to appear, both to the right and left of us, and soon after on our front also. We did not see any in our rear, but we heard afterwards from the garrison left behind in the laager, that a large force, estimated at about 10,000 men, had passed down the valley of the river shortly after we had crossed. It appears from the accounts of prisoners taken during the battle that the Zulus intended to attack the camp that morning. For this purpose a large body was sent down the river; this afterwards came up on our rear. The two other bodies began working through the hills on each flank, and had we not advanced ourselves a concentric attack would have been made. As it was we came out into the open, to the vast astonishment of the Zulus, who thought we were moonstruck and delivered into their hands. They accordingly made arrangements to surround us on the line of march. The people on the two flanks turned about and came abreast of us at a distance of a mile and a half, while the body originally intended to act as reserve attacked our front face. Altogether there were about 20,000 of the enemy present, but only about half of that number ever got close to us.

At 8:50 am our cavalry on the front and flanks became engaged, and about ten minutes after they had to retire on the main body and get inside the square. About this time the first bullets began to whistle about our heads. By 9:05 am all four faces were attacked, and a heavy fire opened by both sides. About 9:25 am the pressure on the left of the left face began to be rather great, and our company was moved there in support. At 9:35 am the Zulus retired, and a few minutes afterwards the cavalry was sent out to follow them up.

Notwithstanding the somewhat heavy fire to which my company was exposed, we had only a sergeant [Wood] wounded, and this seemed the more surprising as a good many bullets struck the ground among us. About 11 o'clock the cavalry set fire to Ulundi, and the army was marched towards the kraal to see the burning.

Archibald Forbes, the well-known *Daily News* correspondent, was eager to be first to report the news of the victory. After a ride of 110 miles in 20 hours from Ulundi to Landman's Drift, he went straight to the telegraph office and reported:

Archibald Forbes to Sir Garnet Wolseley, 5 July 1879 – Brilliant success yesterday. While both columns were marching on Ulundi in a hollow square, and we were attacked at 9am on all four sides by 12,000 Zulus. Affair lasted half-hour. All troops behaved admirably. The Zulus came within 60 yards of the square, when they began to break. The cavalry slipped at them. Lancers cut fugitives into mincemeat. Shell fire rained on Zulus till last man disappeared. Our loss 10 killed and 60 wounded. I calculate dead Zulus about 800. After short rest columns moved on Ulundi. Cavalry preceding fired it, and all other military kraals surrounding it. Forces returned to laager before night.

The Distinguished Conduct Medal was instituted on 4 December 1854, for gallantry in the field performed by 'other ranks' of the British army, and the Conspicuous Gallantry Medal was established on

A contemporary sketch of the interior of the British square at Ulundi. The battle was said to have lasted about half-an-hour. The well-know newspaper correspondent Archibald Forbes stated that 'All troops behaved admirably', and he described the battle as a 'Brilliant Success.' Major Chard and the Royal Engineers were station behind two Gatling guns to the left of the sketch.

13 August 1855, as the naval equivalent of the DCM, but there was no universal medal that could be awarded for all ranks of the British armed forces. However, stories of the gallantry being performed by her soldiers in the Crimea, set against reports from the first war correspondents of their neglect and suffering which was causing discontent among the British public, prompted Queen Victoria to try to do something within her power to give them recognition. Consequently, the Victoria Cross was instituted by her royal warrant on 29 January 1856, and 111 men who fought in the Crimean campaign became the first recipients for 'Conspicuous bravery and devotion to country in the presence of the enemy.' Rank, long service or wound was to have no special influence on who qualified for the award.

Queen Victoria took a great interest in the establishment of the award and in the design of the medal. Prince Albert suggested that it should be named after her, and the original motto was to have been 'For the Brave', but Victoria was of the opinion that this would lead to the inference that only those who have got the cross are considered to be brave, and decided that 'For Valour' would be more suitable. The design was not to be particularly ornate and not of high metallic value. All the medals have been cast from the bronze cascabels believed to be from two guns, said to be of Chinese origin, which the British had captured from the Russians at Sebastopol. The original ribbons for the medal were blue for the navy and crimson for the army. Queen Victoria thought that 'the person decorated with the Victoria Cross might properly be allowed to bear a distinctive mark after their name'. She pointed out that at that time 'VC' meant Vice-Chancellor, and she suggested 'DVC' ('Decorated with the Victoria Cross') or 'BVC' ('Bearer of the Victoria Cross'). However, just 'VC' was finally agreed on. On its institution it carried an annuity of £10. Many rank-and-file soldiers who gained the Victoria Cross are known to have felt great satisfaction from the fact that military regulations state that all officers must salute a man of any rank who passes by them wearing the Victoria Cross on his breast.

The first investiture took place at Hyde Park in London on 26 June 1857, when sixty-two Crimean veterans received the medal from the queen herself, in a ceremony which is said to have taken only about 10 minutes. She performed the deed in the rather awkward position of side-saddle on a horse, presumably because most of the men were tall and it would be easier for her to reach them, and she actually pinned the medal to the skin of Commander Raby, who was first in the queue and therefore became the first man ever to wear the Victoria Cross – literally! It seems she didn't get much better with practice, as she did it again to Lieutenant Graham who was twenty-fourth in line. The queen recorded in her diary: 'It was indeed a most proud, gratifying day.' However, even after seeing men in the line with limbs and eyes missing, and other disfigurements, it is unlikely that she or any British civilians really understood what horrors they had witnessed and experienced to gain the award. Prior to the beginning of the Anglo-Zulu War in January 1879 the Victoria Cross had been awarded 345 times.

For their gallant conduct at the defence of Rorke's Drift, Lieutenants Gonville Bromhead and John Chard were Mentioned in Dispatches and awarded the Victoria Cross, which was announced in the *London Gazette* on 2 May 1879. The official citation for the Victoria Cross stated:

The Lieutenant-General commanding the troops reports that, had it not been for the fine example and excellent behaviour of these two Officers (Lieutenants Chard and Bromhead) under the most trying circumstances, the defence of Rorke's Drift post would not have been conducted with that intelligence and tenacity which so essentially characterised it. The Lieutenant-General adds that its success must, in a great degree, be attributable to the two young Officers who exercised the Chief Command on the occasion in question.

Eleven men in all were awarded the Victoria Cross for the gallant defence of Rorke's Drift, a total which has never been equalled since, and five men were awarded the Distinguished Conduct Medal, although one was later cancelled. In addition to Bromhead, the record seven VCs to soldiers of the 24th Regiment included Corporal William Allan and Privates Fred Hitch, Alfred Henry Hook, Robert and William Jones, and John Williams. Surgeon James Henry Reynolds received the Victoria Cross and a promotion, as did Commissary James Langley Dalton and Corporal Friederick Schiess. The awards appeared in the *London Gazette* for 2 May, 17 June, 18 November and 2 December 1879.

Major Chard was decorated by General Sir Garnet Wolseley during a parade of the troops at St Paul's Camp, Zululand, on 16 July 1879. For his service he also received the South Africa Medal with *1879* clasp.

According to the Record of Service Ledger for the 2nd/24th Regiment, Major Bromhead and Private Robert Jones received their Victoria Crosses from General Wolseley while they were still on active service at Utrecht, on 11 September 1879; although several sources state that it was earlier. For his service at the Cape he also received the South Africa Medal with *1877–8–9* clasp.

Numerous sources have stated that the most Victoria Crosses awarded for a single action were gained for the defence of Rorke's Drift on 22/23 January 1879, during the Anglo-Zulu War. However, while the eleven Victoria Crosses for that battle has never been equalled since, and it did produce the record of seven Victoria Crosses awarded to one regiment for a single action, the author's original research from 1992 to 1994 when compiling *The Chronological Roll of the Victoria Cross* first brought to light that there were three prior superlatives.

At that time, the author carried out a comprehensive study of all the citations for the Victoria Cross which were announced in the *London Gazette* from 24 February 1857 to date, and the findings were published in his 1994 book *Deeds of Valour*, announcing that the superlative award of the Victoria Cross for a single action is the twenty for the first attack on the Great Redan at Sebastopol on 18 June 1855, during the Crimean War. This is followed by the seventeen awarded for the assault on the

Sikandar Bagh at Lucknow, during the India Mutiny, on 16 November 1857, and the twelve (probably thirteen) for the second attack on the Great Redan on 8 September 1855.

Some military enthusiasts consulted still want to believe that the eleven Victoria Crosses awarded to the defenders of Rorke's Drift should be recognised as the highest, based on the fact that it was an individual fight, while the assault on the Sikandar Bagh was part of a continuing battle (the twenty-four Victoria Crosses gained at Lucknow on 16/17 November 1857 was the most for a single 24-hour period), and the men who were awarded the Victoria Cross for both attacks on the Redan performed other acts of gallantry which were recorded. However, if an action is mentioned in a Victoria Cross citation then it should be included in the total number for that particular man, and should not be devalued because other deeds are quoted in the same citation.

However, John Chard may have been too modest for his own good, and seems to have been a man with no particular ambitions. This attitude caused animosity towards the already reluctant hero, and he began to find himself on the rough end of some jealousy fuelled criticism. Some senior officers, including General Wolseley, who was not a supporter of the awarding of gallantry medals, and General Buller, a fellow West Countryman, who was himself awarded the Victoria Cross on 17 June 1879, made less than complimentary remarks about his ability in the field, and some unnecessary personal insults. On recording the presentation of the award of the Victoria Cross to Major Chard, Wolseley wrote:

> A more uninteresting or more stupid-looking fellow I never saw. Wood tells me he is a most useless officer, fit for nothing. I hear in their camp also that, the man who worked hardest in defence of Rorke's Drift Post was a commissariat officer, who has not been rewarded at all. The only one who behaved badly was the doctor and reports say he was a coward. Bromhead, of the 24th Regiment, who was the second-in-command of the Post, is a very stupid fellow also.

The commissariat officer was of course Mr Dalton, who, thanks in part to Major Chard, was later awarded for his gallantry.

For some unknown reason Colonel Wood had taken a dislike to Major Chard, and made no secret of the fact that he disapproved of his gallantry award. As Wolseley stated, Wood considered Chard to be 'a most useless officer' and did his best to damage Chard's reputation whenever he could – which unfortunately to some extent he succeeded in doing.

Major Chard was decorated by General Sir Garnet Wolseley during a parade of
the troops at St Paul's Camp in Zululand on 16 July 1879. General Wolseley also
decorated Major Bromhead at Pine Tree Camp in Utrecht on 22 August 1879.

Captain Walter Jones of the Royal Engineers, who was a friend, said of Chard:

> He is a most amiable fellow, but as a Company Officer he is so hopelessly slow and slack . . . With such a start as he got, he stuck to the company doing nothing. In his place I should have gone up to Lord Chelmsford and asked for an appointment. He must have got it, and if not he could have gone home soon after Rorke's Drift, at the height of his popularity and done splendidly at home. I advised him, but he placidly smokes his pipe and does nothing.

In mid-April Major Bromhead and the men of B Company moved to Pine Tree Camp in Utrecht, where his 'quiet and unassuming demeanour' had not faded with the fame he was beginning to have thrust upon him, and which he found difficult to accept. A contribution to this would almost certainly have been because he, like Major Chard, had already begun to suffer the effects of the jealousy their unwanted hero status would also create.

Major Francis Clery, of the 32nd (Cornwall) Light Infantry, observed:

> . . . the height of his enjoyment seemed to be to sit all day on a stone on the ground smoking a most uninviting-looking pipe. The only thing that seemed equal to moving him in any way was an allusion to the defence of Rorke's Drift. This used to have a sort of electrical effect upon him, for he would jump up and off he would go, not a word could be got out of him. When I told him he should send me an official report on the affair it seemed to have a most distressing effect on him.

Although Charles Bromhead had become a favourite of Sir Garnet Wolseley, it did not stop the general from remarking in his journal of 11 September 1879: 'I have now given away these decorations [the Victoria Cross] to both the officers who took part in the defence of Rorke's Drift, and two duller, more stupid, more uninteresting men or less like gentlemen it has not been my luck to meet for a long time.'

However, at the time of Bromhead's death in 1891 the *World* newspaper had printed an obituary which reflected these jealous sentiments, and Colonel Glennie responded:

> It is with feelings of pain and regret that the officers of the 24th Regiment (the South Wales Borderers) have read a paragraph . . .

relative to the late Major Gonville Bromhead VC. The whole paragraph as applied to him is a shameful slur on the memory of a gallant officer, and is inaccurate in his name and all its facts. Gonville Bromhead was unfortunately deaf, but by no means dull-witted, and I never heard that he ever failed in any examination; indeed, when promoted Major, although a letter was sent to him stating he was not required to pass he refused to take advantage of this privilege. The *World* calls him 'a big, clumsy, dull-witted Subaltern' and 'clownish hero,' but he was the reverse of all this. To those who knew him he was a thorough good-hearted fellow, *bon camarade*, and English gentleman. The name of Gonville Bromhead and the gallant deeds of B Company, 2nd Battalion, 24th Regiment on the night of January 22, 1879, will ever be remembered in his regiment, and will be handed down to future generations, notwithstanding the unfeeling remarks of the *World* newspaper.

Bromhead also received the South Africa Medal with *1877–8–9* clasp. He and Chard were promoted captain and brevet major, dated back to 23 January 1879, and he was twice Mentioned in Dispatches, on 1 March and 15 March 1879. He and Major Chard had the rare distinction of being thanked by both Houses of the British Parliament. As a major Bromhead's pay rose to 16*d*. a day.

General Wolseley had selected Bromhead's unit to take part in the expedition against Sekhukhune, but at about the time when Wolseley presented the VCs he also told them that they were to be posted to Gibraltar. When the garrison finally marched out of the war, they were cheered through the streets of colonial towns along the way.

In 1879 the *Sheffield Telegraph* published several letters which had come from soldiers serving in the Anglo-Zulu War. This stirring of public awareness of the war, combined with the fact that the game of football was becoming highly popular in the area, prompted a local businessman to put together a team of players to try to raise funds for the widows and families of men who had lost their lives in the Anglo-Zulu War.

The real Zulus had gained some degree of notoriety in Britain after the initial phases of the war, particularly the massacre at Isandlwana. Contemporary news reports from Nottingham, Dublin and Glasgow refer to black men being heckled, abused or even assaulted after being accused of being Zulus. However, it also meant that the word 'Zulu' invoked curiosity, which was exploited by the football team.

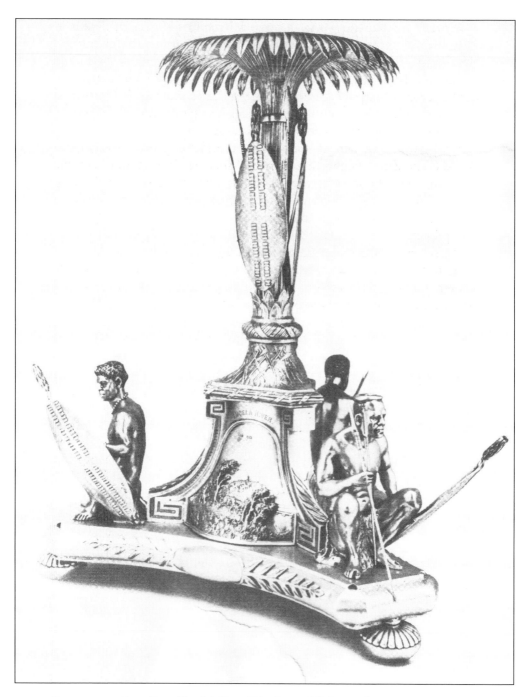

Commemorative silver, like this Royal Engineers' dish stand, was commissioned by many of the regiments that had fought in the Zulu War.

In order to make the project as authentic as possible, the men donned Zulu attire and acquired Zulu weaponry which was picked up from ships returning from the conflict in South Africa. They took on Zulu names and even blacked their faces with cork, which would of course not be acceptable in modern times. They usually did a tour of the towns in which they were playing to promote the game; and 'Cetshwayo' gave out the programmes before the kick-off. The Zulus also performed a tribal dance to entertain the crowd, brandishing their assegai and shields. The Zulus began their series of matches in England, winning them all, before taking on teams from Scotland, and lost them all.

However, it was a time when football was considered to be a recreational game, and it was frowned upon for players to be paid. The project eventually ran into controversy when FA officials started to receive reports that the Zulus were being paid for their appearances. William Pierce-Dix, honorary secretary of the Sheffield FA and a well-known referee, was fiercely opposed to professionals. The Football Association got involved and the Sheffield Zulus were no more.

Chapter 7

Homecoming

On arriving at the station in Durban to begin his journey back to England aboard the *Eagle* troopship, Major Chard asked a porter to get him some kaffirs to carry his bags to the hotel. The first lad who came running up got the shock of his life when he saw the officer. It was the vorlooper boy who had ridden away from Rorke's Drift on one of Chard's horses. He stopped in his tracks and looked shocked, and Chard had to grab hold of him to stop him from running off. The boy was convinced that they had all been killed by the Zulus and that the man standing in front of him was a ghost. When Chard asked the boy how he thought he had got away, he answered, 'I know, you rode away on the other horse.' The horse had been taken off him by the authorities.

Chard arrived at Spithead on 2 October 1879, along with Dr Reynolds and Charles Robson. The Duke of Cambridge welcomed him and delivered a message from Queen Victoria inviting him to an audience with her at Balmoral Castle.

A reception awaited him on his return to Somerset. It was mainly organised by his oldest sister Charlotte, and her husband Major Barrett, and was also attended by his sister Florence and her husband, the Revd Lathom-Browne, and by his two brothers. Charles Robson was with him.

The *Royal Engineers Journal* for 1 November 1879 recorded: 'Major Chard was accompanied by his military servant in full regimentals and the appearance of this soldierly young fellow bearing an armful of Zulu assegais and other trophies of the campaign excited much interest.'

Chard was surprised to be greeted by the same Major Walsh who had greeted him after the defence of Rorke's Drift. It was a grand affair, and was reported in the *Tiverton Gazette and East Devon Herald* for 7 October 1879 under the title 'Reception of Major Chard at North Curry':

The rural village of North Curry was *en fete* on Friday last on the occasion of the visit of Major Chard, VC, of Rorke's Drift renown, to his brother-in-law, Major Barrett, at Moredon. The gallant major landed at Portsmouth on Thursday, and on Friday he proceeded direct to Taunton, via Yeovil, reaching his destination at about one o'clock. At Durston Junction he was greeted with the first instalment of the reception which awaited him, for as the train came in it was received with a kind of *feu de joie* from ten or twelve detonators placed on the line. About a dozen gentlemen collected on the platform, raised a hearty cheer for Major Chard, and afterwards shook hands with him before the train left. At Taunton he was met by the major and Corporation, and the former addressed the hero in appropriate terms, reverting to incidents in his early life, and to the events connected with the defence of Rorke's Drift, which gained him his promotion from the rank of lieutenant to that of major, and also his Victoria

Two members of 'a very energetic committee' stand proudly before the principal triumphal arch in North Curry to welcome John Chard home. The archway was emblazoned with the names Chard and Bromhead, and was composed of mock-up biscuit tins and mealie bags and featured the motto 'Joy to the Defenders of Rorke's Drift'. All the streets were decorated with flags and streamers.

Cross. Major Chard briefly responded, and afterwards drove off for North Curry, accompanied by Major and Mrs Barrett, Captain Chard, and another brother.

At North Curry extensive preparations had been carried out, under the management and at the expense of a very energetic Committee, and all the streets were decorated with flags, streamers, evergreens, mottoes, etc. Innumerable triumphal arches crossed the road at various points. Opposite the post office was one bearing the motto 'The Natal Preservers', and near Mr Temblett's house was another with 'Welcome'. In the square in the centre of the village was the principal arch, composed of biscuit tins and bags containing the word 'Mealies' – (biscuit tins and mealie bags it will be remembered were the materials with which Chard and Bromhead constructed their barricade), and upon it was the motto 'Joy to the defenders of Rorke's Drift.' Along the road from here to Moredon were the mottoes 'Welcome to the valiant hero of Rorke's Drift' (on Mr R R Batten's house), 'Health and Happiness' (on an arch), and 'Peace and Prosperty' (another arch). At the first gate at Moredon was an arch bearing the two words 'Ulundi – Home,' and on the second was 'Welcome to Moredon' surmounting a Victoria Cross. The decorations were continued along the road towards Taunton, as far as the four cross roads and some of the mottoes were 'Chard and Bromhead' (at the *Bird in Hand*), 'Health and Happiness Welcome to the gallant Major Chard, the hero of Rorke's Drift' (at Mr Lockyer's house), a portrait of Major Chard (on the front of Mr Foster's house), 'God bless the Queen' and 'God bless the Prince of Wales' (together with other decorations, on the front of the house occupied by Dr Olivey, who was a prime mover in getting up the demonstration), 'J R M C, VC.' surmounting a laurel wreath (on an arch at the beginning of the Windmill Road), 'Long life to Major Chard' (opposite the Wesleyan chapel, at the beginning of the Greenery), 'Honour to the brave', an arch supporting the Chard crest (a shield, bearing an eagle, and the motto 'Nil Desperandum'), and a very large triumphal arch by the cross roads. Here the carriage containing Major Chard arrived at about half-past two, and was met by a procession from the village. The band greeted the arrival with *See the Conquering Hero Comes* and during a halt the following address was read and presented by the Reverend R C L Browne (vicar).

'To Major John Rouse Merriott Chard, RE, VC.

'We, the inhabitants of North Curry, Othery, and neighbourhood, with whom you and your family have been and are connected, whilst thankfully acknowledging the goodness of Providence in specially preserving and shielding you from the dangers to which you have been exposed, cordially and affectionately welcome you on your safe return to your family and country, and take this opportunity of respectfully expressing our heartfelt admiration of your self-devotion, talent, and gallantry during the Zulu War, particularly during the trying night at Rorke's Drift, when, with only a handful of brave soldiers, and with merely extemporized defences, you kept at bay an almost overpowering force of the enemy, and thus probably, under Divine providence, saved the colony of Natal from destruction, and defended the honour of your country.

'It is an additional cause of gratitude to us that Her Most Gracious Majesty has recognised your services as well by the promotion which you have so well earned, as by investing you with the Victoria Cross, the highest distinction for personal bravery which can be conferred upon the British soldier or sailor, whatever rank he may hold in the service of his sovereign. And in conclusion we wish you health and happiness, and pray that your valuable life may long be spared to enjoy the honours you have gained, and to be of further benefit to your family and country.'

The address, which was beautifully illuminated by a firm in London, bore the Chard crest, and corner ornaments composed of Zulu shields crossed with bundles of assegais, was signed by the Committee, comprising the following gentlemen:- Reverend R C L Browne (chairman), Messrs C R Mottis, J Ellard, W W Lock, Reverend E Godson, Messrs H Lockyer, G Goodson, J Badcock, J H Dinning, C E Vile, G J A Rouse, P Foster, J Southwood, J Temblett, H Barrington, T Hemborough, Reverend Coddrington, Reverend E Gillam, Doctor H P Olivey, Messrs C Lockyer, F J Coombes, J Meaker, H M Hunt, W House, R Turner, J F Collier, C Glyde, and W Pyne (secretary).

Major Chard (who looks remarkably well after his experiences) then rose to reply, and was received with enthusiastic cheers. He said he saw so many people around whom he knew, and so many whom he did not know but whose faces he recognised, that his heart was too full for him to say how deeply he felt the great honour that was now done him. He mentioned that on arriving at Taunton station, Mr Walsh, of the 13th Regiment, was one of the first to shake him by the hand, as he was the first to shake hands with him after the defence of Rorke's Drift. He was very glad to see around him some of the men of the 13th Regiment, who served in the same column with him under General Wood in Zululand. In the address, allusion had been made to the great mercy shown in his coming home safe and sound. He could assure them he felt very deeply at having been brought safely through all the dangers of the enemy and disease. They would feel thankful as he did, that he was taken to the house of Dr Hyde, a Somerset man, but for whose kindness and that of his wife, he much feared he should not have been standing here at this moment. He much regretted that Major Bromhead, who was still serving his country in Zululand, and Dr Reynolds, whom he left at Portsmouth on the previous day, and the others who were with him at Rorke's Drift, were not here to see this reception. There was one man present who was with him at Rorke's Drift, and that was the Engineer now sitting on the box of the carriage. He thanked all most sincerely for the reception.

Three hearty cheers were given for the Major Sir Percy Douglas then, as an old general officer, called for three cheers for the sapper on the box, which was immediately given.

The man in question was Driver Charles Robson, the only Engineer present at the defence of Rorke's Drift besides Major Chard.

The horses were taken out of the carriage, which was drawn through the village by tenants. The procession was re-formed, headed by a pensioner from the Life Guards bearing a large Union Jack; and comprising the band of the 3rd S.R.V. Corps; members of the Forester's, Old Fellows, and North Curry Friendly Societies; townsmen four abreast; the reception committee on horseback; Major Chard's carriage, with an escort of four men of the 13th Regiment; private carriages; and the Othery and North Curry tenantry on horseback. The Committee had applied for an escort of the Ilminster Troop of Yeomanry, but while the members were willing enough, this had to be refused as the War Office regulations will not permit them to furnish an escort for any less than members of the Royal Family. The tunes played by the band were *See the Conquering Hero Comes – Home Sweet Home* and *The Gallant 24th.*

Arrived at Moredon, in front of the house, cheers were given for Major Chard, Major Barrett, Mrs Barrett, Captain Chard, Sir Percy Douglas, Captain Acock, and the Sapper.

Major Barrett, in response, expressed his gratification at the reception, which he said had come spontaneously from the hearts of the people, and he knew nothing about it. He invited all present to enjoy themselves. – Captain Chard also responded.

Sir Percy Douglas, as an old officer in the army, and the predecessor of Lord Chelmsford in the command in South Africa, which he held ten years ago, paid a high tribute to the gallantry of the British soldiers in Zululand, and said they were but giving utterance to the truth in thus paying honour to Major Chard.

A move was then made into Mr Jeanes' field, where tents had been erected, and refreshments were provided for all. Mr Denman, of Bridgwater, was the caterer, and acquitted himself to the satisfaction of all.

In another part of the field Major and Mrs Barrett and their friends had assembled to do honour to another brave action. It appears that some little time back two lads were bathing in the Tone near here, and getting out of their depth, were in danger of both being drowned. A lad named Fred Brewer, without waiting to strip jumped in, rescued one, and went in after the other, but failed, and was so exhausted by his efforts, that had it not been for two other lads, Charles and Henry Hayes, he would also have been drowned. Dr Olivey took an interest in the matter, and after laying the matter before the Royal Humane Society, succeeded in getting their medal for Brewer, and certificates for the other two lads. The medal and certificates were presented by Mrs Barrett, the circumstances being detailed by Major Barrett, who said he and his wife were eye-witnesses of the affair.

Speeches were made by the Reverend E Godson, vicar of Burrow Bridge, who said that the lads were carrying out the same principles as those which actuated Major Chard, and urged other lads to take the good old advice in respect to any deed of duty, 'Go thou and do likewise'; and also by the Reverend E Gillam, of Othery, who mentioned that the Chards were connected with his parish. In the church was a memorial window to the Major's father, and he found that one of the Major's progenitors was formerly a vicar of his parish.

Various sports were engaged in and the proceedings were kept up till dark, when they were brought to a most successful termination with a grand display of fireworks.

Major Chard and Robson travelled up to Balmoral for the arranged audience with Queen Victoria, which took place on 10 October 1879. Queen Victoria was appreciative of his unassuming manner and the modest way in which he told of the events at Rorke's Drift, and it was said at the time when he submitted his official report, which was modest and to the point, that 'He has spoken of everybody but himself.' He gave a verbal account of the battle to Queen Victoria, after which she presented him with a gold ring. He did the same to the queen's private secretary, who was not influenced by regimental jealousy, and noted:

> Chard has been here this morning. He explained the defence of Rorke's Drift to the Queen, Prince Leopold, the Grand Duke of Hesse, and Princess Beatrice, in the Queen's private room, and did it all very clearly and modestly. After dinner he did likewise to us in the billiard room on the table, where store and hospital were books and boxes, and mealie bags and biscuit tins were billiard balls. I gather from all I hear that Dalton was quite as much (if not more) of the presiding genius here, as himself. He conceived the idea of joining the two buildings with mealie bags, etc, before Chard's arrival on the scene; though perhaps Chard would have done so, had he not found it in operation. The inner line, which was their great safeguard, was Chard's own idea, I fancy, and when they were deserted by so many of the defenders (natives, etc) it was soon found that the first line of defence was too extended. Bromhead (commanding B Company, 2/24th Regiment) had of course great influence over his men, and kept them in their places or moved them about, controlled their fire with great judgement. Only one and a half boxes of ammunition were left when morning came, beside what they had in their pouches. Chard made no complaint, but it seemed odd to me that he was not consulted as to the distribution of the Victoria Cross. He is not a genius and not quick, but a quiet, plodding, dogged sort of fellow who would hold his own in most of the situations in which, as an Engineer officer, his lot may be cast . . .

On 13 October 1879 he received a signed presentation copy of Queen Victoria's book, *Leaves from the Journal of Our Life in the Highlands from 1848 to 1861*, which she had published in 1868.

Of all the conflicts fought by soldiers of the British Empire, Queen Victoria seems to have taken a particular interest in the Zulu War. Newspapers in April 1880 reported:

The Queen and the Zulu War

Her Majesty's interest in the Zulu War has been shown in a very sympathetic and touching manner. A few days ago several noblemen and their ladies were favoured with the view at Buckingham Palace of a splendid silver-gilt casket, ordered by the Queen, In this were placed lockets of pure gold; containing locks of hair of thirteen officers who fell at Rorke's Drift [probably Isandlwana], each locket being engraved with an 'In Memoriam' and the name of the officer, together with the date of his melancholy death. The casket is in the shape of a Greek cross, and the lockets are arranged in that form. The jewellers who have executed the work have been authorised by Her Majesty to receive and treat in a similar manner all-like relic or souvenir of officers or men who fell in the South African campaign.

Chard and Doctor Reynolds were invited to a special dinner held at the Wanderers Club in Pall Mall. In his *Dictionary of London* for 1879, Charles Dickens junior described the club:

For members of town and country society and for gentlemen who have associated in various parts of the world. It cost ten guineas to join. Among the members present was Crimean War veteran, Colonel William Hope, who, as a lieutenant with the 7th Royal Fusiliers, had gained the Victoria Cross for gallantry during the disastrous first attack on the Great Redan at Sebastopol in 1855; and Sir Charles Hastings Doyle, another Crimean War veteran, whose mother was a relative of Lieutenant Coghill.

The Times reported on 18 October 1879:

Last evening Major Chard VC, and Surgeon-Major Reynolds VC were entertained at dinner by The Wanderers Club at Pall Mall, in recognition of their splendid defence of Rorke's Drift. There was nothing formal about the proceedings which were altogether of a friendly and social character.

Lord Headley was in the chair, and had the guests of the evening on his right and left. Among the company which numbered about one hundred, were Major-General, Sir Hastings Doyle, Colonel Hope VC, Colonel Bousfield MP, Major-General Raines CB, Sir F Perkins MP, Colonel J Ward, Colonel E Galt, Doctor Swettenham, Captain W Oughton Giles, Mr W Jameson,

Mr P Penn-Gaskell, Captain Jameson, Mr C Armstrong and Mr C W E Pineo (secretary).

After the usual loyal toasts the chairman proposed 'The Army, Navy and Auxiliary Forces.' Sir Hastings Doyle, in returning thanks for the army, remarked that he had spent 21 years serving with the gallant 24th Regiment (cheers). Mr C Armstrong responded for the Navy, and Captain W Oughton Giles and Colonel Bousfield for the Auxiliary Forces.

An illuminated address was presented to him by the borough of Langport in Eastover (Somerset), on 1 November 1879, and the St George's Lodge of Freemasons prepared an Illuminated Address which was presented to him in Exeter on 14 November 1879 by the Master Wardens and Brethren of the Lodge, for his 'courage and gallantry at Rorke's Drift'. Within the decorative border was incorporated images of Zulu shields, spears and clubs, the Royal arms, the Lodge arms, all surrounded by acanthus leaves and flourishes.

On his arrival in Plymouth on 18 November 1879, Major Chard was greeted at the Guildhall by the largest gathering in the town 'since the Prince of Wales opened the municipal buildings. Thousands of people of all grades were present, and a more striking scene would be hard to produce in Plymouth.' The people of the town had raised three hundred pounds for the purchase of a sword of honour and a gold chronometer. The sword had been specially manufactured by Messrs Hunt and Roskell, goldsmiths to Queen Victoria, and the silver scabbard was richly ornamented.

Plymouth newspapers recorded:

His home town of Plymouth did not forget Chard. Mr W Derry was mayor, and in the present Guildhall there was a brilliant and never-to-be-forgotten scene. Major Chard advanced up the hall with Mr Derry to the orchestra where he was welcomed by the present Earl of Mount Edgcumbe and a former Earl of St Germans. A sword of honour and a gold chronometer watch were the tokens of a West Country regard for the blushing brevet-major.

In his dedicatory address Mr Derry told Chard that his actions at Rorke's Drift had instilled in the men of Devonshire . . . something of the old pride which filled the hearts of their forefathers in the days of Drake and Raleigh.

In his acceptance speech Chard thanked the crowd for their welcome back to his birthplace: 'to which I am attached by the associations of my whole life. The smiles of my own Plymouth friends, and particularly the ladies, have made me very nervous. I almost fancy I would rather meet the Zulus again.' And then followed a magnificent tribute to all the officers and men of the heroic garrison he was called upon to command at Rorke's Drift. He added: 'The Zulus were an enemy it was a credit to us to defeat. They showed such discipline and courage as were a lesson to any civilised nation. Cruel and savage as they were, they showed courage that could not be excelled by anybody, and their military organisation and their discipline might have given a lesson to more civilised nations.' The report went on to state that he repudiated the assertion that the British soldiery had treated them with barbarity.

The sword was described in the *Illustrated London News* for 22 November 1879:

The panels represented - 1 The mission house at Rorke's Drift; 2 shields bearing the arms of Plymouth and England; 3 'Vulcan forging the arms of Achilles', in allusion to the generally defensive character of the Royal Engineers; 4 A trophy of broken Zulu weapons; 5 an allegorical device of lion and elephant, symbolising the pursuit and defeat of the enemy, and the triumph of British arms in South Africa. The opposite side has corresponding panels showing – 1 The Victoria Cross 2 Shields with the arms of Major Chard and the Royal Engineers; 3 Britannia; 4 Trophy of Engineers' tools crowned with laurel by Fame; 5 St George of England vanquishing the dragon. The guard is of silver, pierced and richly carved with the rose, shamrock and thistle, surrounded by oak leaves. The blade, of the finest tempered steel, bears on one side the motto 'Strong to defend the right – swift to avenge the wrong'. On the other a record of the presentation of the sword 'in recognition of his gallant defence of Rorke's Drift.'

A sketch of the commemorative sword presented to John Chard by the people of Plymouth at the Guildhall on 18 November 1879. The sword was among several items that were auctioned in 2020 and achieved a price far in excess of that which was expected.

Driver Robson was due to leave the army and was looking for employment, so Major Chard tried to use his new-found influence to help him, and he wrote a testimonial for him from his sister's home in Moredon, dated 17 November 1879:

> Driver Charles Robson, Royal Engineers, served with me in the 5th Company, RE as my batman, for some months before and during the whole of the Zulu campaign. His conduct has been very good and he has given me great satisfaction – He was the only Royal Engineer with me at Rorke's Drift on the 22 January, where he did good service. He was also present at the action of Ulundi. I sincerely hope he may get on and do well.

Queen Victoria requested Chard to prepare a detailed account of the defence, which was presented to the sovereign on Chard's behalf at Windsor Castle on 21 February 1880, by Captain Fleetwood Isham Edwards, the queen's groom-in-waiting. Captain Edwards described the account as: 'a simple soldier-like account of very gallant deeds, and a thrilling record of a terrible night's work. Major Chard much regrets the unavoidable delay which has occurred in its preparation, but, as perhaps your Majesty may remember, he lost most of his notes.'*

Chard's niece, Dorothy, remembered him from when she was a child. Her story of his arrival back in Somerset sums up the type of man he was. Told by his sister to take off his hat and wave back to them, he reluctantly did so, muttering sheepishly, 'All I did was my duty.' Whatever people thought of him, civilian or military, Queen Victoria grew very fond of him, and he was held in the highest regard in the West Country for the rest of his life.

* * *

It is sometimes stated that Major Bromhead missed attending an audience with Queen Victoria because he had gone fishing. However, while home on leave on 17 May 1880, he was invited to Windsor Castle for an audience with his sovereign, who gave him a signed photograph of herself. The audience was confirmed by the Mayor of Lincoln. He was guest of honour at several functions, and on 25 June he was

---

* Interestingly, a draft of this account – with extensive annotations, additions and corrections – was sold at auction in 2020.

Brevet Major Gonville Bromhead wearing his Victoria Cross. It is likely that this photograph was taken during his audience with Queen Victoria at Windsor Castle on 17 May 1880.

invited to Lincoln Masonic Hall, where the mayor presented him with a jewelled sword and an illuminated address.

Local newspapers reported on the public meeting at the Masonic Hall, under the headline 'Public Reception to Major Bromhead at Lincoln':

On Friday, Major Bromhead VC, of Rorke's Drift celebrity, was publicly received at Lincoln, on the occasion of his visiting the city. A public meeting was held at the Masonic Hall in the afternoon, where an illuminated address and a magnificent dress sword were presented to Mr Bromhead; and in the evening a banquet was given in the Assembly Room. There was a large and influential gathering at the afternoon meeting, where the mayor, F J Clarke, presided.

In opening the proceedings the mayor called upon Mr Dashper to read the address, which was as follows:

The Major Bromhead VC of Her Majesty's 24th Regiment of Foot
'We, the citizens of Lincoln, and residents in the county of Lincoln, have the utmost pleasure in tendering you our hearty congratulations on your safe return to England and to Lincoln after your hazardous and perilous campaign in Africa. As one of the chiefs in the ever-memorable defence of Rorke's Drift, where a small band of England's troops nobly sustained their renown for bravery and endurance against the overwhelming host of the Zulu forces, we welcome you to your home.

We esteem you for your devotion to the noble profession which you have chosen – a profession requiring coolness and courage in the hour of danger. That coolness and courage have been displayed in a marked degree not only by your ancestors and near relations, who were soldiers before you, but also by you in the heroic defence to which we have already referred, and which will ever be recorded in the annals of our country.

The spirit of the brave which you possess is the beacon that will light you on to fame and as a suitable emblem of your profession, and as a token of our admiration, we are pleased to present you with the sword which accompanies this address. Should you ever be called upon to wield the gift, we pray that, as in times past, so in the future, the weapon will be used in the interest of our beloved Sovereign and country, and for the promotion of the peace of the world.'

Date this 25th day of June, 1880
J T Tweed, Town Clerk
F J Clarke, Mayor

The Mayor, addressing Major Bromhead, said he was proud and happy to have the privilege on behalf of the citizens of Lincoln and the inhabitants of the county, to present him with the sword and address as a small token of their appreciation and admiration of his gallant conduct in Zululand. When the electric wires first flashed this intelligence to England of the gallant defence made at Rorke's Drift after the disastrous defeat at Isandula, it sent a thrill of joy and gladness throughout the kingdom, and they, as Lincolnshire men, felt doubly proud, because one who took a conspicuous part in the defence was so closely connected with this county. He was received the other day by our noble Queen, and received the decoration of the Victoria Cross, a decoration only given to the bravest of the brave. He (the Mayor) trusted that he would live many years to enjoy the honour conferred upon him, and he was quite sure that if ever he was called upon again to draw his sword in defence of the glorious old country, which we all love so well, he would gain and add fresh laurels to a name which for a century and a half had been conspicuously known in history. He found by some records which he had been looking over that twelve of his ancestors, during the past century and a half, had made a name on the battlefields in all parts of the globe. He had great pleasure in presenting him with the sword before him.

Major Bromhead was loudly cheered on rising. He said:

'Mr Mayor and citizens of this ancient city of Lincoln, I beg to thank you very much for the very kind and flattering address with which you have presented me this day, and also for this magnificent sword, which I assure you will always remain in my family as an heirloom forever. I feel great difficulty in adequately expressing to you my deep sense of the sympathy and kindness with which I have been received since my return to England, but I assure you nothing had given me greater gratification than the splendid reception I have met with this day, especially, as since my boyhood, when I left Thurlby, I have been personally almost a stranger in these parts. I am not vain enough to take this great reception all to myself, and I beg to thank you on behalf of Major Chard, Surgeon-Major Reynolds, Mr Dalton, Mr Dunne and the Reverend Mr Smith, all brave and stalwart men, who were with us on 22 January 1879, and the greater part of whom I am proud to say I still retain in the company which I have the honour to command. I beg to thank you again for the very kind reception which you have given me.'

Mr Melville, in proposing a vote of thanks to the Mayor far calling the meeting together, said the name of Bromhead, as the Mayor had remarked, had been handed down through several generations, but he did not think it stood so high in their love and esteem as at the present day. Not only was the name connected with the defence of the country, but also with the alleviation of the suffering and the sick, and all through England the name of Bromhead had become a household word. He was sure that in future times the defence of Rorke's Drift would be handed down to our children and grandchildren as one of the noblest feats of arms that was ever accomplished by Englishmen.

Colonel Ancotts [probably Amcotts, a well-known family in Lincoln at the time], who was received with loud applause, said that the Mayor had alluded in his address to the Bromheads as a family of warriors, and he would relate to them an anecdote of the late Colonel Bromhead. In the Peninsula War there was fought a very gallant action at El Bodon, in which his Majesty's 11th [North Devonshire] Regiment of Foot together with his (the Speaker's) father's own regiment, the 11th Light Dragoons, succeeded in beating off a force of no fewer than 10,000 Frenchmen. Colonel Bromhead, who commanded before the battle, addressed his regiment in the following short and economic words – 'Men of the 77th. You see the enemy; if you don't kill them they will kill you, and now let's go at them!' They did go at them, and the result was the victory of El Boden. And he (the Speaker) had never yet made out why the gallant 77th did not put the action on its regimental colours.

The spirit of his ancestors, perhaps unknown to himself, was in Major Bromhead that dreadful night at Rorke's Drift. It is true that Rorke's Drift could not be compared with battles which had either placed the nation at the head of civilisation or reduced it, for instance Waterloo or Marahbohn [probably Marathon], where, at the former place, the greatest conqueror of modern times was defeated by the great Duke of Wellington, and like many other actions in which the British troops had distinguished themselves. They had all seen in the papers a description of the action at Rorke's Drift, where a few men, only three commissioned officers, including the gallant surgeon – who bound up the wounds of the soldiers with one hand, whilst he fought with the other – and a few rank-and-file with a few non-commissioned officers, who maintained their position against overwhelming numbers. He hoped that Majors Bromhead and Chard might never have to stand and fight out such a night again; and that it would never fall to the lot of any of those present, but he would say that if such a thing should happen he hoped that they would take Majors Bromhead and Chard, and those gallant soldiers as an example. He had great pleasure in seconding the vote of thanks to the Chairman.

The Mayor briefly returned the thanks, and the meeting was brought to an end.

The tenants of Thurlby Hall presented Major Bromhead with a commemorative revolver, and the address which accompanied it stated:

We the undersigned living in Thurlby, justly proud of the part which you took in the heroic defence of Rorke's Drift, beg your acceptance of the accompanying revolver as a token of our esteem and admiration of your gallant conduct which has brought honour to the name of England and especially to Thurlby, your native place. We would, at the same time, take this opportunity of offering to you our congratulations on your obtaining the rank of Captain and Brevet Major; and of your receiving the Victoria Cross.

We trust that you may be spared to a long life of usefulness in the service of our country and that we may see you amongst us again in Thurlby.

We hope that you may never find yourself face to face with such numbers as you successfully met at Rorke's Drift, but should this occur, we trust that our revolver may not fail you in the hour of need and we are certain that it could not be held by a worthier hand.

In autumn 1879, the artist Lady Elizabeth Butler was passionately involved in the production of her painting entitled *Scotland the Brave* when Sir Henry Ponsonby, the keeper of the queen's privy purse, called at her studio to convey the queen's wish to have a picture painted of a war from her own reign, and she had also expressed her desire that the British troops should be shown engaged with the enemy. She did not like having to put aside the work that was the focus of her attention, but the sovereign has desired that she wanted it ready in time to be shown at the next Academy. The artist's friends tried to influence her to choose the defence of Rorke's Drift as the subject, while it was still in the forefront of the public's mind.

However, it was a rule of Lady Butler never to portray actual conflict, and she was aware that her husband William had shown his disapproval of the conduct and inefficiency of the Zulu War. In his capacity as quartermaster-general at Durban he had visited Cetshwayo in prison at Cape Town, and as a humanitarian gesture he had taken with him some bundles of rushes to allow him to make a mat and sleep more comfortably. The gesture is said to have moved the Zulu king to tears.

Lady Butler initially chose to depict the finding of the body of Louis Napoleon of France, who had been killed in a Zulu ambush. Victoria agreed with the subject at first, but decided firmly that she wanted a picture of the defence of Rorke's Drift, and that she wanted the portraits of some of the men who had participated in the defence to be included in it.

It is believed that when the men returned to England, Bromhead and Chard were summoned to Lady Butler's studio, along with some of the others who had gained the Victoria Cross, and the artist also made the trip to Portsmouth, where the 24th was quartered, to make studies of the 'principal heroes' who were ordered to present themselves in their uniforms. For accuracy she constructed a model of Rorke's Drift post in her garden, and related that she had managed to include portraits of all the Victoria Cross winners, with Lieutenants Chard and Bromhead in the centre of the scene: 'Of course, the result was I reproduced the event as nearly to the life as possible . . .'.

This was followed-up by the military artist Alphonse de Neuville. His painting was based on eyewitness accounts and depicts several known Victoria Cross actions happening at the same time. It was first shown in 1880 and was bought by the Art Gallery of New South Wales in Sydney, where it has remained ever since.

Newspapers reported:

Mr de Neuville's celebrated picture of the 'Defence of Rorke's Drift' which has been purchased for the Sydney Museum has been withdrawn from public exhibition in this country and is now being prepared for shipment. The last place in which it was exhibited was Plymouth, where it excited more than ordinary notice, from the personal interest the inhabitants have in the chief actor in the defence, Major Chard VC, RE, who commanded on the occasion, being a native of the place, and his family residing there; the gallant officer himself is stationed in the garrison, and he has paid several visits to the gallery in which the picture has been exhibited. In painting it Mr de Neuville had his personal assistance and advice, as well as others who took part in the fight. Of course the major occupied a prominent position in the picture, and he is shown as handling a rifle at the barricade, and taking a cartridge, which is handed to him by a non-commissioned officer. One slight defect is the representation of Major Chard, who is decidedly short, as a taller man than he actually is, but this, perhaps, is artistic licence.

On one day during the time it was in Plymouth the picture was taken to the residence of Mrs Chard, the mother of the major, who was too ill to go to the gallery. Another incidence was the visit of Mrs Butler *nee* Thompson, the well-known painter of 'Quatre Bras', the 'Roll Call', and other battle pieces, and who has painted a picture of Rorke's Drift for the Queen. Colonel Butler, Mrs Butler's husband is like Major Chard, stationed in the garrison, and holds the appointment of Assistant-Adjutant and Quartermaster-General.

It was probably at about this time that Alphonse painted a head and shoulders portrait of Chard in Royal Engineers uniform which remained unknown outside the family until it was purchased by the Royal Engineers Museum in 2020.

It is interesting to note that when Cetshwayo came to Britain in 1882, he actually docked at Plymouth on his way to be feted in London. A large crowd greeted him, and one wonders if any members of the Chard family were among the people who went to see the chief whose warriors came close to killing a member of their family. A heritage blue plaque has been placed at the house where he stayed in Kensington.

Chapter 8

Devotion to Duty

On leaving Durban Major Bromhead's unit was stationed at Casement Barracks in Gibraltar until August 1880. On 1 March 1880, Private John Williams received his Victoria Cross from Major General Anderson on the Almeda Parade Ground. They were then posted to Secunderabad in India, although Major Bromhead remained in England. On 1 July 1881 the 24th Regiment was re-designated the South Wales Borderers.

On the eve of the Crimean War in 1853, the British army established the School of Musketry at Hythe in Kent. From 1 October to 5 December 1882, Major Bromhead attended two courses at the school, where he gained a 1st Class Extra certificate.

The great Rock of Gibraltar rises commandingly over the Casement Barracks, where Bromhead and his unit were stationed after their service in the Zulu War.

On 2 January 1883 he sailed from Portsmouth on the *Serapis,* to join the 2nd Battalion, South Wales Borderers at Secunderabad, where he was promoted full major on 4 April 1883. On 8 May 1886 the battalion received orders for active service in Burma, in what became known as the 3rd Anglo-Burmese War. The region was extremely inhospitable, which cost the South Wales Borderers more casualties from disease and sickness than from the extremely hostile enemy, and they were relieved to get back to India.

Thibaw, the king of the Burmese, had been expressing much anti-British sentiment for many years. In 1885 a British force had advanced up the Irrawaddy River and occupied Mandalay in a swift, almost bloodless campaign. Upper Burma was annexed to the British Crown, to be administered as a province of India. However, the Burmese army refused to surrender and took refuge in the vast, thick jungle, from where they launched a campaign of guerrilla warfare. Their scattered units became known as Decoit bands, which spent their time marauding across the region to disrupt the everyday life of the

Decoits were desperate rebels who took refuge in the vast, thick Burmese jungle, from where they launched a campaign of guerrilla warfare. Decoit bands spent their time marauding across the region to disrupt the everyday life of the British. They twice raided Mandalay and set fire to much of it, and British troops were faced with the massive task of pacification, while protecting British interests. Any Decoits who were captured by the British were immediately put to death, and 'It was woe indeed for the soldier who fell into their clutches.'

British. They twice raided Mandalay and set fire to much of it, and British troops were faced with the massive task of pacification, while protecting British interests.

To give an idea of the type of terrain and enemy Major Bromhead encountered, the following is an extract from a first-hand account by Colour Sergeant Edward J. Owen of the Hampshire Regiment:

> We had conquered Mandalay and taken it, but we had not quelled the Burmese, who set to work to worry us, and succeeded amazingly well.
>
> Gangs of Decoits broke into the city, in spite of all our precautions, and killed people, and set fire to places, and scurried off before even their presence was known. The buildings were mostly made of wood and bamboo, and burnt fiercely when they were once alight, especially as there were practically no fire appliances. Sometimes several acres were destroyed before the flames were conquered.
>
> The Decoits used to slip in and out at night, seldom trying their luck in the daytime, for they had a holy dread of British rifles. They were positively merciless, and for some time after the occupation of the city it was unsafe to move about singly. No men were allowed to go outside the walls unless properly armed, and in parties of at least three.
>
> Mandalay was very unhealthy, and I was glad when I was ordered away to chase Decoits, though I should have thought better of it if I had known what the work really meant. For eighteen months I was away from civilisation, marching through a country where no proper roads existed, and thinking that I had done well if an average of ten miles a day had been covered.
>
> Decoit hunting in a hot, dangerous climate was hard work, with very little glory in it. We seldom got the enemy to close quarters, as he was so nimble, and the country so jungly. The robber-murderers had runs like rabbits, and it was almost impossible to follow them. It was woe indeed for the soldier who fell into their clutches.

During the campaign Bromhead's older brother, General Benjamin Parnell Bromhead, received such serious injuries while fighting in the jungle that he had to have his right arm amputated. For his service during the pacification of British Burma Major Bromhead received the Indian General Service Medal, 1854, with *Burma 1885–7* and *Burma 1887–9* clasps.

Major Gonville Bromhead died from typhoid fever in India in 1891 and he was laid to rest at the New Cantonment Cemetery in Allahabad. By the turn of the twenty-first century the cemetery had become neglected and the cross on his grave had fallen backwards off the plinth. Thankfully it has now been restored and a protective metal railing placed around it.

Major Bromhead never married, and according to his great-great-nephew, Brigadier David Bromhead, his main passion was for salmon fishing. In fact, the Bromhead family was very interested in fishing, and in the 1880s his relation, Henry Brougham Bromhead, was the editor of a journal called *The Little Anglers' Annual and Fishing Diary*.

Gonville Bromhead died of enteric fever at Camp Dabhaura in Allahabad, India, on 9 February 1891, in his 46th year, and he was buried in McPherson's Cemetery, which is part of the New Cantonment Cemetery in Allahabad. The inscription on his grave memorial states: 'This stone was erected by his brother officers of both Battalions in token of their esteem.'

A fellow officer wrote:

Major Bromhead VC was beloved by all ranks, and during the thirteen years I served with him I never heard him say an unkind word to or of anyone. He was the quintessence of an English gentleman, gentle, kind, modest to a degree, retiring – the soul of honour – a most perfect character indeed.

He had the misfortune to be deaf, but he was an exceedingly well-read and well-informed man on all subjects, and I never saw a trashy book in his hand. He was a good game shot, and a few years ago quite the best slow bowler in the army.

It will be a long, long day ere his place will be re-filled in the roll of the regiment which had the honour of claiming him.

* * *

114

John Chard never married, but he is said to have had a relationship with a woman called Emily Rowe, who bore a daughter to him at Exeter, believed to have been born on 16 February 1882, who was named Violet Mary. Emily Rowe married Lawson Durant, and had a second daughter, named Irene and born on 6 January 1884. Emily Durant died in 1939. Violet's birth would have been kept secret because of the stigma of illegitimacy at the time, and because of Chard's fame and association with the queen. He left an annuity to Emily and Violet for the duration of Violet's lifetime, and the family have preserved two letters written by Chard to Emily telling her about his trip to Japan. At his funeral it was recorded that an anonymous wreath bearing the inscription 'That day he did his duty' took pride of place beside a tribute from Queen Victoria on the coffin. It is interesting to wonder who might have sent this wreath.

The Victoria Cross awarded to Major John Chard, which is now part of the Lord Ashcroft collection housed at the Imperial War Museum. The coveted medal was established in 1856, and 111 men who fought in the Crimean War became the first recipients. It was during the Crimean campaign that twenty Victoria Crosses were awarded for the first assault on the Great Redan at Sebastopol on 18 June 1855. This was the most ever given for a single action. The eleven awarded for the defence of Rorke's Drift has never been equalled since, and the seven given to Bromhead's 24th Regiment is the most to one unit for a single action in the history of the medal.

This information is taken from letters the author received from a family descendant which state:

> I was particularly interested to read about Lt Chard as he is my great-grandfather. Although you are quite correct in your book when you say he was not married, he had had a relationship with an Emily Rowe who gave birth to a daughter, Violet, on 16 February 1882. Emily Rowe subsequently married a Lawson Durant. Violet Durant (Rowe) was my father's mother.
>
> As well as some letters from John Chard to Emily, Chard left £50 annuity for Emily and her daughter Violet for her lifetime. This money was duly received by my grandmother.
>
> I feel that at Rorke's Drift, Chard was just an ordinary man who kept his head and used common sense and training to good effect.

A second letter states:

> I do have some information which you may find useful. Violet Mary Rowe/Durant (Chard's daughter) was born on 16 February 1882 at Exeter, or so we believe, but my parents think that the year of birth might be suspect. It is possible that Emily, her mother, lied about her birth as she was illegitimate. Violet had a younger sister, Irene Durant, who was born on 6 January 1884, making her just two years younger than Violet. I would also add that although Emily married Lawson Durant, we are not certain that Irene was in fact his child.
>
> The only information I have about Emily Rowe is that she was born on 4 January (but no year), and died in January or February 1939.
>
> My parents have in their possession a couple of letters from John Chard written to Emily, telling her about his trip to Japan.

In January 1880 Chard began service at Devonport, and the 1881 census records him as living with his mother and sister Margaret at 19 Portland Villas in Plymouth. His mother died on 27 July 1885, just after her 70th birthday, and she was buried with her husband and daughter at St Budeaux church.

After the cessation of Cyprus from the Ottoman Empire to become a protectorate of Britain in 1878, Elliot Charles Bovill was appointed as legal adviser to the government, becoming Judicial Commissioner in 1881. John Chard was sent to Cyprus in December 1881, and became friends with him, and his wife, Anna. Elliot was appointed Chief Justice in 1883, and he was knighted for his services in the following year. Chard also became a friend of Judge Middleton in Nicosia. Some of Chard's family papers describe how he was the starter and steward at the Limassol Spring Meeting of 10 and 11 March 1885. He brought back a number of Cypriot antiques which on his death he bequeathed to the art collection at the Brassey Institute in Hastings.*

Chard was appointed regimental major on 17 July 1886, and returned home in March 1887. He was posted to Fulwood Barracks in Preston in May 1887. He became friends with Frank Hollins, 1st Baron of Greyfriars, who lived at Greyfriars Hall on Walker Lane in Fulwood. The baron was also the head of Horrockses, Crewdson and Company, a well-known local cotton manufacturing concern.

The 1891 census records that John Chard lived in a house close to the barracks at 80 Victoria Road in Fulwood (which still exists), and he had a 25-year-old Cypriot servant named George Theodoulie working for him. Some family letters written during his time in Preston have been preserved.

As a point of interest, at the time when Colonel Chard lived in Preston the town was riding high on the achievements of the local football team, Preston North End. They won the 1888–9 English League Championship, which was the first football championship in history, without losing a game, and they won the Football Association Challenge Cup without conceding a goal. They won the Championship again in 1889—90. They were so dominant that that they became known as 'The Invincibles'.

Colonel Chard was posted to Singapore on 14 December 1892, where he was Commanding Royal Engineer for three years, and was promoted lieutenant colonel on 18 January 1893. Sir Elliot had been appointed to the position of Chief Justice of the Straits Settlement in 1892, and when Chard was posted there he lived at Sherwood Cottage in Paterson Road, Singapore. Chard regularly played golf with Sir Elliot, and he had played a round with him the day before he died of cholera in 1893.

On his return to Britain in January 1896, Chard took up his final post as Commanding Royal Engineer at the Perth District. In May that year he presented Queen Victoria with Japanese mementoes he had brought

---

* The author contacted the museum which very kindly checked all their acquisitions for the period 1897–8, and although they still have Cypriot artefacts in their collection, they could not say if any were the ones donated by Colonel Chard.

Colonel John Chard VC pictured wearing a kimono while serving as Commanding Royal Engineer at the Straights Settlement in Singapore from 1892 to 1896.

back from the East especially for her. He was promoted colonel on 8 January 1897.

While in Scotland Chard was diagnosed with cancer of the mouth. In November 1896, he was too ill to visit Balmoral at the request of Queen Victoria, and he underwent an operation in Edinburgh. In March 1897 surgeons had to remove his tongue. He was still able to converse quite well, but his condition became critical. The doctors' prognosis was that the cancer was terminal, and he was placed on sick leave from 8 August 1897. On 11 July 1897, he received the Diamond Jubilee Medal at his residence, 19 Walker Road in Edinburgh.

Chard spent the last days of his life with his brother in the rectory at Hatch Beauchamp Rectory, where many friends, including Queen Victoria, expressed their concern about his condition. After suffering terrible distress towards the end, he died peacefully in his sleep on 1 November 1897, aged 50. He was buried in the churchyard at Hatch

The rectory at Hatch Beauchamp was the home of John's brother, the Revd Charles Edward Chard. John Chard spent his last days there suffering with cancer before he died peacefully in his sleep on 1 November 1897. *(Courtesy of Steve Lee)*

Beauchamp, where a rose-coloured marble-cross headstone marks the spot. Queen Victoria sent a wreath, and there were wreaths from Colonel Edward Bowne VC and the officers of the South Wales Borderers, and from fellow defender, Walter Dunne – and there were tributes from all over the world. For many years the queen's wreath lay beneath a memorial window which was placed in Hatch Beauchamp church.

The report of his funeral stated:

The funeral took place in the beautiful little churchyard of Hatch Beauchamp yesterday in the presence of a large concourse of people, who entirely filled the church, and signs of mourning were everywhere to be seen. The attendance was thoroughly representative not only of the military forces and the gentry of the district, but also of the poor, for the Colonel was beloved by all by whom he was known. This was exemplified by a remark of Sergeant-Major Gibbs, RE, who was present with the deceased immediately after the defence of Rorke's Drift, and who helped to bury the dead after the battle. He stated yesterday that no one could do too much for the gallant Colonel so much was he liked by all who served under him.

The day was in keeping with the sad event, for it was a dull November one, yet quite without rain, and signs of beautiful Autumnal decay surrounded one on every hand and were particularly to be seen in the quiet graveyard, situated as it is among hefty trees. The grave, an ordinary earth one, had been prepared on the south side of the church. It was lined in a most artistic manner with moss and smilax creeper, which were studded with white chrysanthemums, white geraniums, abutilons and violets, while at the head was a large cross of white chrysanthemums. This beautiful work had been carried out by Messrs J Shute (gardener to Major Barrett at Moredon); W Bellringer (gardener to Mrs Raban at Beauchamp Lodge); Walter Durman (gardener to Mrs Hardstall at Hache Court); and Lewis Faulkner (gardener to the Reverend C E Chard of the Rectory).

The wreaths were very numerous and of a most magnificent character, all the wealth of floral beauty having been lavished upon them. Her Majesty the Queen sent a large wreath of bay leaves tied with long streamers of white satin. Attached to it was a card bearing the inscription in Her Majesty's own writing: 'A mark of admiration and regard for a brave soldier from his Sovereign. Victoria RI'. This was placed upon the breastplate of the coffin. The Reverend C E Chard also received most sympathetic private letter from Her Majesty.

Other wreaths were from the Deputy Adjutant-General, RE, on behalf of the Corps of Royal Engineers: 'In sorrow for the loss of their gallant brother officer'; from Colonel Browne [Bourne] and the officers of the Depot, South Wales Borderers, 24th Regiment (the regiment engaged at Rorke's Drift): 'With deep sympathy'; from the officers of the Royal Engineers, Scottish District; Colonel Walter Dunne, AAC, York. The Countess of Camperdown: 'With heartfelt sympathy'; Lady Frere, widow of Sir Bartle Frere, Governor of South Africa at the time of the Zulu campaign: 'In memory of the heroic defence of Rorke's Drift.' An anonymous wreath bore the words: 'In remembrance of Rorke's Drift, 22 January 1879. That day he did his duty'. The Bishop of Bath and Wells sent a beautiful wreath by Mr John Marshall, himself a Crimean veteran, wearing a medal with four clasps. Mr W Bellringer, Hatch: 'With heartfelt sympathy and regret from the servants at Hatch Rectory;

The following is a complete list of the other wreaths that were received. Colonel Bridgman, Malta; Mr G Maudsley-Williams, London; Mr W R W Upjohn, Hastings; Miss Beryl and Coral Montague, Bath; Mr and Mrs Peel; Lady Bovill: 'In loving memory';

120

Mrs Sykes, Ayr; Major and Mrs Whiteside, Preston; Mrs and the Misses Birley, Preston; Mr and Mrs Frank Hollins, Preston; Mr and Mrs Bird, Garstang; Mr and Mrs Calvert, Perth; Major and Mrs Barrett, Moredon; Captain and Mrs Heycock, Cheltenham; Messrs W, A, and C Barrett, Moredon; Mrs Ring, Hatch; the Messrs Ring, Hatch; Mrs Baker, Hatch; Mrs Trevor, St Leonards; the Dean of St Andrews, Perth; the servants of Moredon; Miss Dorothy Barrett, Moredon; Sergeant-Major Selby, RE, and Mrs Selby; Maurice Bovill; Mrs Cuthbert, Perth; Reverend W and Mrs Strong, Somerton; Mrs Barrow; Mr and Mrs Mullins, Weston-super-Mare; Mrs Carland Harrison; Mrs, Miss and Miss Agnes Watson, Perth; Mrs Chard and children, Mount Tamar; Mr and Mrs Napier, Singapore; Lodge of St George, Singapore; Mr L W Reynolds; Major F C Mein; Mr Thomas, Perth; Mrs Farquhar, Perth; Colonel and Mrs C Birch; Captain J B Muir, RE, Clifton; Reverend J E G and Mrs Farmer; Mrs Hyde, Ladysmith; Mrs J Mills; Mrs Treffrey, Cornwall; Mrs Elliot Square, Plymouth; Garland W C Harrison; The Reverend R C and Mrs Lathom-Browne; Mr and Mrs W Marshall; Hon H P and Mrs Gore-Langton, Hatch Park.

The solemn tolling of the bell at half-past two o'clock announced that the funeral cortege had left the Rectory situated about half-a-mile from the church. The coffin was borne on the North Curry parish bier, kindly lent for the occasion, and the procession was entirely a walking one. The coffin had previously reposed in the hall of the Rectory with the Queen's wreath upon it, with the anonymous wreath and that from the Rectory servants at either end. On the table were the deceased's cocked hat and sword, his Victoria Cross and South Africa Medal, the Jubilee Medal recently presented to him by the Queen, and a signed Jubilee portrait of the Sovereign, also presented by Her Majesty. The coffin, made by Mr James Mills of Hatch, was of polished oak, with brass mountings, and it bore the inscription:

JOHN R M CHARD
Born 21st December 1847
Died 1st November 1897

On each side of the coffin walked a deputation of Royal Engineers in full uniform. These included Sergeant-Major Gibbs (Torquay); Sergeant-Major Falkner (Exeter); Sergeant-Instructor Carter (Weston-super-Mare); and Quartermaster Fryer (Bristol).

The following officers of the Royal Engineers attended in uniform – Colonel Mein (Plymouth); Colonel Rogers, Commanding, 1st Battalion, Gloucestershire V R E; Major Bagnold (Exeter); Major Cregan (Cheltenham); Captain Muir (Bristol) and Lieutenant Dibbs (Exeter). Colonel Bell VC, CB, ADC, RE, Commanding Engineer in the Western District, sent to say that unfortunately duty prevented him from attending.

The chief mourners were the Reverend C E Chard and Mrs Chard, of Hatch Rectory (brother and sister-in-law); Major and Mrs Barrett of Moredon (brother-in-law and sister); Mrs Chard of Mount Tamar, Plymouth (sister-in-law, and widow of the late Colonel Wheaton Chard, commanding the 7th Royal Fusiliers); Master W Wheaton Chard (nephew); the Reverend R C Lathom-Browne and Mrs Browne, of Hever, Kent (brother-in-law and sister). Mr Browne will be remembered as a former vicar of North Curry; Captain and Mrs Heycock, of Cheltenham (brother-in-law and sister); Mrs Bond (sister); Mr W Barrett, Mr A G Barrett and Mr C J Chard Barrett (nephews); and Miss Dorothy Barrett (niece).

Among the military men present in addition to those mentioned were Brigadier-General H B Patton CB, commanding the Severn Brigade; General England CB; Major-General Emerson; Colonel Orange and Major Poynton of the Taunton Depot PASLI; Major Smith, late of the Queen's Own Royal West Kent Regiment, and others.

The clergy and ministers were represented by the Dean of St Andrews (a personal friend of the deceased colonel); The Revered Prebendary Buller, vicar of North Curry; the Reverend A H A Smith, vicar of Lyng and chaplain to the West Somerset Yeomanry Cavalry; The Reverend A D Reece, vicar of West Hatch; the Reverend W Rouse, rector of Enmore; the Reverend F C Kinglake, rector of West Monckton; and the Reverend E Curtis, Baptist minister of Hatch.

The Dean of St Andrews conducted the whole of the service. He recited the opening sentences of the burial service as the procession went up the churchyard path, and as the mourners took their places in the sacred edifice Miss Alice Rich, the organist, played the beautiful aria *O Rest in the Lord*. The Dean then proceeded with the service, and read the lesson in an impressive manner. The only hymn sung was *Days and Moments Quickly Flying*, and as the procession left the church Miss Rich played the *Dead March* from *Saul*.

John Chard was buried close to the wall of St John the Baptist Church in Hatch Beauchamp. His younger brother, Charles, who was the rector of the church from 1885 until his death in 1910, is laid to rest behind the Chard grave.

The remainder of the service was said at the graveside, and it closed with the Benediction. At the conclusion of the service the Dean said: 'I have been desired by Mr Chard to return to you, his friends and neighbours, his most sincere thanks for the kindness and sympathy which you have shown on this occasion by your presence here today.'

The numerous assemblage then dispersed, many having previously taken a last look at the grave.

In his will, drawn up at Edinburgh on 14 June 1897, Chard's brother Charles was the sole executor. Newspapers reported:

The will of the late Colonel John Rouse Merriott Chard, the hero of Rorke's Drift, has been proved by his brother, the Reverend Charles Edward Chard, Rector of Hatch Beauchamp in Somerset, who is appointed sole trustee and executor. The testator leaves the picture and book given to him by the Queen, the sword and watch given to him by the people of Plymouth, the sketch by De Neuville, various illuminated addresses, certain pictures of Rorke's Drift, and his Victoria Cross and South Africa Medal, with *1879* clasp; as well as his regimental sword, to his brother, the Rev C E Chard, for his life use only, and on his death to his nephew, William Wheaton Chard of Mount Tamar in Plymouth. He also bequeaths to his brother a life estate in certain stocks and shares, and the moneys at his bankers, and on his death the income is to be divided between his sisters, Margaret Edith Bond and Mary Jane Haycock, and to pass on their death to his nephew, William Wheaton Chard. The residue of his estate goes to his brother. The personalty is sworn at £8617 16s 11d gross, and £8165 net.

The full list of items included:

A picture portrait given to him by Queen Victoria

The sword and watch presented by the people of Plymouth

A colour sketch of himself drawn by Alphonse de Neuville

The illuminated Address

Engravings and photographs of Rorke's Drift, Bromhead and Chard

Books containing letters and newspaper cuttings made up by William Wheaton Chard

The Victoria Cross and South Africa Medal, 1879

His Regimental sword

His property at Moredon to his sister, Charlotte Barrett in North Curry

A gun to J C C Middleton, the son of Judge Middleton of Nicosia, Cyprus

A collection of Cyprus antiques to the art collection at the Brassey Institute in Hastings

A telescope to Humphrey, the son of Frank Hollins of Greyfriars in Preston

A quantity of diamonds in the possession of his sister-in-law, Annie Chard, to his friends, Sir Elliot and Lady Bovill

A miniature Victoria Cross and South Africa Medal, 1879; a gold pencil case; and a plain gold ring 'I shall be wearing when I die' to Lady Bovill

Chapter 9

Life Goes On

Helen Morrison Bromhead never married, and at the time of Gonville's death, his sister Alice Margaret was recorded as a spinster living at 6 Villa de la Reunion in Auteuil, Paris. Janette Gonville married George Hutton-Riddell of Carlton-on-Trent in Nottinghamshire in the 1860s, but she was a widow living back at Thurlby by the time of the 1871 census. Janette may have met her husband through Gonville, because George's brother, Charles, attended Thomas Magnus Grammar School and played on the cricket eleven with Gonville. Janette died on 28 September 1892, aged 56, and is buried at Thurlby. Victoria Gonville (Diamond) had seven children between 1864 and her last child born at Lambeth on 15 August 1881, when she was 48 years old. Victoria died on 8 June 1909, aged 64. Frances Judith (Coates) died on 20 February 1917, aged 92, and Elizabeth Frances (Pocklington) died at Hartley Wintney near Basingstoke on 10 October 1921, aged 74.

Charles James married Alice Marie, the daughter of Thomas Freckleton (1821–57), on 5 October 1876, at St Michael's Church in Paddington, London. They had two sons: Richard Freckleton Gonville was born at Weston-super-Mare on 6 November 1877 and Charles Edward Gonville was born as Secunderabad on 23 December 1882, but he died on 4 October 1890 at the age of 8, and was buried at Thurlby. Charles was appointed major on 1 July 1881, when the regiment became the South Wales Borderers. He was appointed lieutenant colonel on 31 January 1885, brevet colonel on 31 January 1889 and he retired as colonel on 31 January 1891. He was appointed Commander of the Bath (CB) on 3 June 1893. He received the Indian General Service Medal, 1854, with clasp for *Burma 1887–9*. He was colonel of the South Wales Borderers regimental district from 1892 to 1897. He was appointed a Justice of the

Peace for Denbighshire in North Wales. He died on Christmas Eve in 1922, aged 82, and Alice Marie died on 19 October 1932, in her 81st year.

Charles' brother-in-law, George William Freckleton, also saw active service in South Africa. He was commissioned as lieutenant in the 88th Connaught Rangers on 10 November 1877. He saw active service in the 9th Cape Frontier War and in the Zulu War, for which he received the South Africa Medal with *1877–9* clasp. He became captain in 1887, retired from the army in 1892 and died in Bournemouth in 1929.

Benjamin Parnell was appointed lieutenant colonel with the 32nd Sikh Pioneers, Indian Staff Corps in 1885. For his service he received the Indian General Service Medal, 1854, with *Burma 1887–9* clasp. He was also appointed Companion of the Bath (Military). At the time of the 1901 census he was recorded as living in Twickenham with his daughter, Lady Birdwood, and her daughter, Nancy, but he had returned to Thurlby a decade later. His wife died on 8 February 1902 and is buried at Thurlby, where Benjamin has several memorials, one of which states: 'his ashes were committed to the sea'.

In a newspaper interview at Thurlby Hall in January 1934 it was stated under the headline 'Life's Too Slow':

Sir Benjamin Bromhead has become a legendary hero in the Lincolnshire countryside . . . Thurlby Hall, the Bromheads' stronghold for six centuries, was studded with anecdotes built around the remarkable man.

One is that he always gives an ounce of tobacco to a certain newspaper seller in Lincoln when he passes him because he has lost a leg. He once, it is said, slammed the door of his car in the face of a man who tried to congratulate him on his birthday. 'I am too old for congratulations.' He said. I found him reading the newspaper without glasses.

A brief time ago he took his first flight in a slow passenger aeroplane, and he found it too tame. 'I could not see anything in it,' he said, and immediately he returned to the air in a tiny Puss Moth. He was enchanted with this. His ambition now is to make a long flight – 'A couple of continents will do.'

It is preposterous after all this to congratulate such a young man on his great age. Sir Benjamin Bromhead, a descendant of famous soldiers, lost an arm while fighting in India in 1888. He completed my admiration by remarking, 'Do you know my car is not fast enough. I am going to buy one of the new 20hp super cars.'

Another report stated:

> Now Sir Benjamin leads a quiet life by compulsion. He lost an
> arm while fighting. The other is withered at the elbow. He lives on
> his Lincolnshire estate with his nurse, who is also his companion,
> seven servants, and a cat – which has double paws on each leg. The
> entire housekeeping is managed by Sir Benjamin himself, and he
> spends much of his spare time motoring and doing jigsaw puzzles.
> He shows astonishing vitality as a motorist. Often he goes as far
> afield as Wales and Scotland.

Benjamin Parnell had been the Baron Bromhead for sixty-five years
when he died on 1 August 1935, and his obituary in *The Times* stated:

> Colonel, Sir Benjamin Parnell Bromhead, the oldest English
> Baronet [The Scottish baronet, Sir Fitzroy Maclean, was seventeen
> months older], died on Wednesday night at his home, Thurlby Hall
> in Lincolnshire, at the age of 96. He was the head of a family with
> a centuries-long tradition of Army service. His inherited bravery
> made it almost impossible to restrain him in Service days from
> rushing into the thick of the fighting in the Indian Frontier wars.

Sir Benjamin had owned 700 acres of land in Sligo when the local
council acquired it. Cairsfoot was partially destroyed by fire in 2004,
and was subsequently demolished. Several of his letters to Lord and
Lady Birdwood are kept at the Australian War Memorial.

Gonville's Aunt, Anne Fector Bromhead (1812–86), along with her
daughter, Henrietta, pioneered nursing in Lincolnshire, and Bromhead
Nurses were famous for their work. They founded the Bromhead
Institution and the Bromhead Hospital in Lincoln, which is now a
Grade II listed building.

Two of Gonville's nephews fought in the Boer War and are buried
at Thurlby. Charles James' surviving son, Richard Freckleton, became
a major with the 2nd Battalion, Lincolnshire Regiment. Benjamin
Parnell's son, Benjamin Gonville, was commissioned as 2nd lieutenant
with the 3rd Battalion, South Wales Borderers in 1898, being promoted
lieutenant in 1900.

Tension between the two independent Boer republics of Transvaal
and the Orange Free State and British interests in South Africa had been
building up for years, until diplomacy finally broke down. In early
October 1899, 10,000 men from the Indian and Mediterranean garrisons

began to arrive in Natal, and the 1st Army Corps mobilised in England. On 11 October 1899, Boer commando units invaded British territory, laying siege on the garrison towns of Kimberley and Mafeking in Cape Colony, and Ladysmith in Natal.

Fighting on home soil in mounted commando units, in some cases containing three generations of the same family, the Boers were a formidable enemy. With superior firearms and smokeless ammunition, and camouflaged in the drab colours of their ordinary farming clothes, skilled Boer marksmen knew how to conceal themselves in the rocky terrain and snipe from long range, as the British advanced in parade-ground fashion across the open veldt. Then with excellent horsemanship they would leave the scene before the British could react effectively.

British relief forces made a two-pronged advance during which they suffered three serious reverses in mid-December, at Magersfontein and Stromberg in the Cape, and at Colenso in Natal, which came to be known as 'Black Week'. As the Natal Field Force struggled northwards they suffered their worst defeat of the campaign at the notorious Battle of Spion Kop on 24 February 1900, before reaching Ladysmith four days later. Kimberley, under Cecil Rhodes, was retaken at about the same time, and the relief of Mafeking on 17 May 1900, which had been under the leadership of Robert Baden-Powell, caused a frenzy of Imperial hysteria in Britain.

Eventually, Lord Roberts, whose son had been killed in action while winning a posthumous Victoria Cross at Colenso, took over command. His experience turned the tide and British forces entered the Boer capital of Pretoria on 5 June 1900. The British then launched a campaign, mainly in the eastern Transvaal, to track down the Boer commanders, while the Boers adopted guerrilla tactics, attacking isolated outposts, supply convoys and patrols.

In October 1900, Herbert Kitchener took command, and countered Boer strategy by dividing the country into fenced sections, guarded by blockhouses. With his scorched earth policy, the farms of hostile Boers were burned to diminish their chances of refuge. Their families were put in secure compounds, which came to be known notoriously as concentration camps, where the death rate was high. Not surprisingly, the Boers began to lose heart, but sporadic fighting by the 'bitter-enders' continued to keep British troops on alert. Hostilities finally ended officially when a peace treaty was signed on Lord Kitchener's dining table at Vereeniging, on 31 May 1902.

Benjamin Gonville resigned his commission in order to serve in the Boer War, and went to South Africa as a Special Service Officer with various units: the Rhodesia Field Force under General Carrington, on attachment with Thorneycroft's Mounted Infantry, 1901–2, and with A Division of the South African Constabulary. He was awarded the Queen's South Africa Medal with *Cape Colony* and *Orange Free State* clasps; and after joining the South African Constabulary he was awarded the King's South Africa Medal with *1901–2* clasp. Richard sailed to South Africa on the troopship *Goorkhas*, arriving in late January 1902. He saw service in the Bloemfontein region of operations.

Richard married Edith Maud Andrews in 1912, and during the First World War he was on active service on the Western Front with the Royal Berkshire Regiment, being severely wounded in 1917. He retired in 1922 and died at Wellington House at Walmer in Kent on 13 May 1939. His medals sold at auction in 2017. His son, Colonel Robert Benjamin Gonville, was the last commanding officer of the Royal Berkshire Regiment in 1959.

It is reported that following the turn of the century, a Colonel Bromhead, a veteran of the Zulu Wars, was living at a house named Plas-Draw, in Llangynhafal, Ruthin, North Wales. Richard later served in the First World War, and on 15 June 1927, having turned 50 years old, he married a Lancashire lass named Lydia Davey, and they made their home at Plas-Draw.

Local press reports of 30 October 1935 refer to a tragic accident that befell Mrs Lydia Bromhead, aged 45, wife of Major Richard Freckleton Gronville Bromhead of Plas-Draw. She was accidentally shot by a gun which was kept for bird scaring and later died. She was buried at Thurlby.

During the Second World War, Major Bromhead opened his house to receive young evacuees from the Liverpool area. Many of them told how they were 'greeted by the heads of stuffed antelopes, assegai shields, and other assorted exotica'. Major Bromhead died on 16 December 1949, aged 72.

Benjamin Parnell's daughter Janetta Hope Gonville (known as Jenny) was born in India on 3 September 1872. On 5 March 1894, at Lahore cathedral in India, she married the dashing Indian army officer William Riddell, 1st Baron Birdwood (1865–1951), who saw distinguished military service on the North-West frontier of India, in the Second Boer War and during the First World War commanded the ANZAC troops at Gallipoli. He was Commander-in-Chief in India from 1925 to 1930, and visited the cemetery where Jenny's brother, Edward, was buried at Thayetmyo in 1929, and had all the graves cleared and cleaned up.

A keen gardener, Jenny was appointed to the Imperial Order of the Crown of India in 1930, which was an order of chivalry presented to

Gonville Bromhead's niece, Janetta Hope Gonville (known as Jenny), married the 1st Baron Birdwood. Lady Birdwood was appointed to the Imperial Order of the Crown of India in 1930, which was an order of chivalry presented to her as the wife of the Commander-in-Chief in India.

her as the wife of the Commander-in-Chief in India, and her husband became Lord Birdwood of Anzac and Totnes in 1938. During the Second World War Birdwood Castle was hit by bombs and partly destroyed. Jenny died after a short illness at Hampton Court Towers on 14 November 1947, after fifty-three years of devoted marriage, and is buried at Thurlby. There are several pictures of her in the National Portrait Gallery, and a scrapbook she compiled from 1902 to 1939 is held at the Australian War Memorial.

Another daughter, Kathleen Gonville, was born in Bengal in 1878. She married Lieutenant Colonel Robert Edward Archibald Udny-Hamilton (1871–1950) of the Indian army, who became the 11th Lord Belhaven and Stenton, and they had two children. Their daughter Julia Hamilton (1901–71) married Fitzroy Richard Somerset, 4th Baron Raglan, whose great-grandfather commanded the British expeditionary force during the first part of the Crimean War. Kathleen died at Udny Castle in Aberdeenshire in 1935.

Benjamin Parnell's grandson is the last Baron Bromhead to be buried at Thurlby. He was Lieutenant Colonel Sir Benjamin Denis Gonville, who was born on 7 May 1900 in Bengal, India. He was the son of Major Edward Gonville Bromhead (1869–1910) of the 2nd King Edward VII's Own Gurkha Rifles, and his wife, Emily May (formerly Hosking). He was educated at Wellington College.

Benjamin was on active service during the Iraq campaign of 1920; and he was wounded during the campaign in Waziristan from 1922 to 1924. He was back on the North-West Frontier in 1930, where he was Mentioned in Dispatches. He gained the rank of lieutenant colonel while serving with the Frontier Field Force of the Indian army.

Benjamin succeeded as 5th Baron Bromhead on 1 August 1935, and in 1938 he married Nancy Mary, the daughter of Thomas Seon Lough. He was Mentioned in Dispatches while serving in Waziristan in 1937, and he served as commandant of the Zhob Militia in Beluchistan from 1940 to 1943, being appointed Officer of the Order of the British Empire (OBE) in the latter year. He was employed as political agent for the North Waziristan region from 1945 to 1947. He died on 18 May 1981 and is buried at Thurlby.

Brigadier David Bromhead was appointed colonel of the Royal Regiment of Wales in 1994.

* * *

William Wheaton Chard was on active service during the Afghan War of 1878–80, and in 1879 he married Fanny Alexandrina Augusta (formerly Yule, 1855–1922), who came from a distinguished naval family, including Commander John Yule, RN, who fought with Admiral Nelson at Trafalgar in 1805. They settled at Mount Tamar, and had four sons and four daughters. William served in Egypt and rose to the rank of colonel. He commanded the Royal Fusiliers from 1887 until his death on 12 September 1890, aged 48. He had contracted fever while in India and died at the Yule family home at Anderton in Cornwall. He is buried at St Budeaux church, and there is a plaque dedicated to him in the church, which reads:

> In affectionate remembrance of Colonel William Wheaton Chard, late 7th Royal Fusiliers; Eldest son of William Wheaton Chard of Pathe, Somerset and Mount Tamar, Devon. He served for 30 years in the above regiment and commanded the 1st Battalion for 34 years, in Egypt and in India. He took part in the Unbeyla campaign in 1863 (medal), and in the Afghan War 1879–80 (medal). He died 12 September 1890 at Anderton, Cornwall, of disease contracted in India. This memorial is erected by his brother officers who served with him in the regiment, in token of their regard for a good soldier and a steadfast friend.

His son, also named William Wheaton, commanded the 1st Battalion, Royal Fusiliers as a lieutenant colonel during the First World War in 1918.

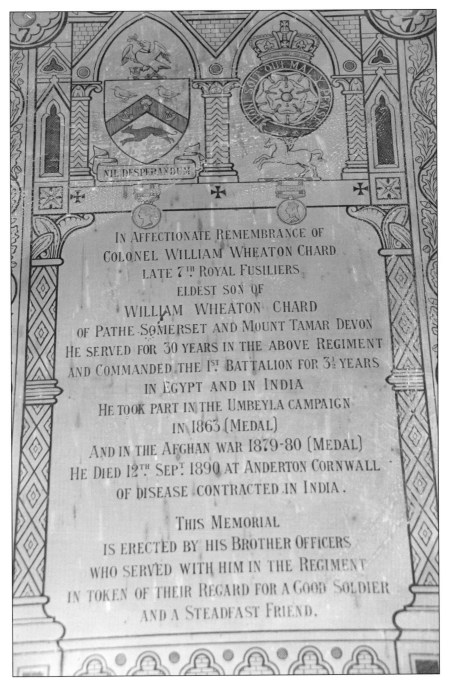

The commemorative plaque at St Budeaux church dedicated to John Chard's brother, William Wheaton. *(Courtesy of Stephen Luscombe)*

Charles Edward was ordained deacon in 1881. He became the vicar at Ashted church in Warwickshire, and the reverend at Hatch Beauchamp in Somerset in 1885. He married a widow named Annie Mildred Raban, the daughter of Arthur and Mary Baker, on 30 November 1886, at All Saints Church in Kensington. The ceremony was conducted by his brother-in-law, the Revd Lathom-Browne. They resided at the rectory in Hatch Beauchamp, and at the time of the 1901 census his step-son, Lieutenant (later Captain) Herbert Trevor Raban (1877–1932) of the Bengal Lancers (Indian Cavalry) was residing with them. Charles was appointed honorary chaplain to the 4th Yeomanry Brigade at Taunton on 4 March 1894. He was the rector of Hatch Beauchamp until his death at 7 Mandeville Place, Marylebone, London, on 12 September 1910, aged 53. He lies buried close to his brother, John, at St John the Baptist Church in Hatch Beauchamp. His obituary described him as 'a well-known hunting parson and a familiar figure with the Taunton Vale foxhounds'.

Sadly, his sister, Jane Brimacombe, died on 2 January 1880, in her 30th year, and she is buried with her parents at St Budeaux church. Margaret Edith appears on the 1881 census as unmarried, and she attended John's funeral unaccompanied; being described as Mrs Bond.

The Chard family grave at St Budeaux church, which contains his parents and one of his sisters. (*Courtesy of Stephen Luscombe*)

Charlotte's husband, Major Barrett, was appointed Sheriff for Somersetshire in 1892.

He died in Taunton on 10 October 1914 and is said to have left the modern equivalent of £52 million in his will; including £50,000 to the Moredon House cook. Their youngest son, Captain Charles John Chard Barrett, served in the Boer War and was killed in action while serving with the Royal Scots Fusiliers at Hooge in Belgium on 14 November 1914. His wife placed a brass plaque dedicated to him in the Church of St Peter and St Paul at North Curry. Charlotte was aged 97 when she died in Kensington on 26 July 1937. She is buried with her husband in the churchyard at North Curry.

Mary Jane and Charles Heycock made their home Pytchley Manor House in Kettering. They had twelve children, only one of them being a girl. At the time of Colonel Chard's funeral they had lived in Cheltenham for about twenty years. Charles became a justice of the peace until his death in 1912. Mary Jane died in North Curry in 1937.

Florence married the Revd Robert Charles Lathom-Browne, the vicar of North Curry, at Taunton on 8 October 1879. To keep John informed of how things were at home while he was away, between 11 February 1879 and 21 August 1880, Florence kept a scrapbook of news cuttings and ephemera concerning the family.

The Revd Browne later moved to St Peter's Church at Hever in Kent, famous for its castle and gardens, where he dedicated the Hever war memorial when it was unveiled on 4 July 1920. He was a member of the Kent Archaeological Society, and as a tennis enthusiast he donated a trophy in his name to the Prince's Club in Brighton in 1925, which is still contested by the Royal Tennis Court Club at Hampton Court Palace. The Revd Browne died on 6 August 1928, and Florence died at Hever in 1933. They are buried in St Peter's Churchyard.

Chapter 10

Memorials and Commemorations

Towards the end of 1879, Annie Elizabeth Foster, the secretary of the Salvation Army in Eccles near Manchester, decided to establish the Ladies' Rorke's Drift Testimonial Fund, to raise money to buy commemorative Bibles to be presented to all the surviving defenders – 'as a small mark of our high appreciation of the splendid defence of Rorke's Drift'. They are a number in the regimental museum at Brecon, and the one presented to Colonel Chard was sold at auction in 2020.

Men of B Company who took part in the defence of Rorke's Drift received an illuminated address from the Mayor of Durban, Mr H.W. Currie, just before they sailed from Durban to Gibraltar in January 1880. It stated:

To the Officers, Non-Commissioned Officers and Men of the 2nd Battalion of HM 24th Regiment.

As the time has now arrived when you must take your departure from this Colony, We, the Mayor, and Town Council, as representing the Burgesses of Durban, Natal, cannot allow you to leave the land whose frontier your heroism has kept inviolate, without delaying your footsteps for a moment upon the shore, while we place upon enduring record this expression of our admiration of your deeds and of our lasting gratitude to you, for the heroic services performed by you in the defence of this Colony when menaced by an invasion of overwhelming numbers of Zulus on the night of 22nd January 1879.

It is not yet a year since, in the shadows of the evening, a Company of your Regiment saw approaching from the slopes of the Buffalo River the darkest cloud of invasion that had ever lowered over the wide frontier of British Dominion in Africa.

The storm which then gathered around you, held in it all the fierce power caught from a recent victory gained over your brethren who had fallen fighting at a vast disadvantage, on the sad and fatal field of Isandhlwana.

Reckless of loss, confident in its numbers and strength, that wild wave of savage invasion burst upon your hastily improvised defences, and surged against the scanty defenders as the sun went down; all through the night, the savage but doubtless foe renewed again and again its attempts to break your line, a line which was weak to all save courage, loyalty and duty. No need for us now to repeat now the story of Rorke's Drift.

As the daylight faded away above the heights of Helpmekaar it left you simple and untried soldiers, holders of an unknown post; when daylight broke again over the Zulu hills, Rorke's Drift had become a name of pride to those who speak the English tongue over the earth, and each and all of that little garrison had become Heroes.

Out of the gloom of a great disaster the star of your victory shone resplendent and Natal, saved by your heroism, dried the tears of her anguish in the glory of your victory.

Take then, Officers, Non-Commissioned Officers and Soldiers of the 2nd 24th Regiment the thanks which we Burgesses of Durban, and Colonists of Natal heartily offer you.

Wherever your future fortunes and destinies of the Empire you serve may call you, be assured you will carry with you the honour, the admiration and the gratitude of those who now bid you FAREWELL!

A stained-glass memorial window dedicated to Major Bromhead was placed in the Church of St Germain at Thurlby. He left his medals to his brother, Charles, who, along with his sister, Alice, were the executors of his estate. He eventually presented them to the Regimental Museum of the South Wales Borderers in Brecon in 1973. The British Stanton and Co. .45 revolver, which had been presented to him by the people of Lincoln, is also at the museum in Brecon, along with a broken shield shaft that he had picked up at Rorke's Drift. His name is inscribed on the colour pole of the 24th Regiment.

There was a number of Zulu War centenary celebrations arranged in Brecon in 1979. Sir Stanley Baker used the male voice choir from his home town of Ferndale for the soundtrack in the film *Zulu!*, when Ivor Emmanuel led the defenders in a rendition of 'Men of Harlech' to

The Gonville Bromhead memorial window which was placed in the Church of St Germain. It gives his year of birth as 1844 not 1845.

try to inspire the men, and the Ferndale Male Voice Choir gave their services in a commemoration concert held at the hall in Penlan School on 14 January 1979; they were accompanied by the band of the Depot at Crickhowell at Brecon. A local lady named Ann Smith sang various operatic arias during the concert. The mayors of Brecknock and Brecon were also in attendance. It was recorded in the centenary booklet:

> The concert programme was varied, to appeal to all tastes, and concluded with 'A Tribute to Rorke's Drift' when junior soldiers dressed in the period costume, re-enacted the battle on the stage, firing large quantities of blank ammunition. The 1812 Overture held nothing to it! We even had a symbolic Zulu to attack the defenders – one of the Ferndale choir who sportingly dressed and blackened up for the part.

On 21 January 1979, the colonel and 3rd and 4th Battalions of the Royal Regiment of Wales (24th/41st Foot), along with the band of the 3rd Battalion, marched from the Brecon Barracks for a commemorative service at Brecon cathedral. They were accompanied by a large contingent of ex-members of the regiment, and sixty direct descendants of those who gained the Victoria Cross at Rorke's Drift and Isandlwana.

The cathedral choirmaster, David Gedge, 'produced a service which I am sure those who attended will never forget'; and the Revd Graham Roblin of the Royal Army Chaplains Department, who had served with the South Wales Borderers in Malaya, preached the sermon 'with sincerity and depth of feeling'.

The 1st Battalion were on operational duties in Northern Ireland and it was business as usual for all ranks. However, they did manage to have a celebration at the Drummad Barracks in Armagh on 22 January. Present on the day was James Faulkner, who acted and co-produced the film *Zulu Dawn*, which was soon to be released in the United Kingdom. The booklet recorded: 'Helping us in our celebrations was Ann Jones (Miss United Kingdom), whose great-grandfather, Private Evan Jones was a survivor of the Rorke's Drift battle. Apart from her more obvious attractions, her charming personality and good humour made many a soldier's day as she visited company bases by helicopter.'

At about the same time as the service in Brecon cathedral, Brigadier and Mrs Charles Cox were able to lay a wreath on behalf of the regiment on the Regimental Memorial at Isandlwana, and later at Rorke's Drift.

A pilgrimage to South Africa had been in the planning since 1973, and after 'much frustration and difficulty' the colonel and a party of members of the Regimental Association took off from Heathrow Airport on 18 May 1979. Also among them was Major and Mrs Edward H. Lane, Ted being the grandson of Rorke's Drift defender Sergeant Henry Gallagher, and Mr and Mrs D.O. Spain, great-niece of Lieutenant Charles Pope, who was killed in action at Isandlwana.

On 20 May they visited the Garrison Church at Fort Napier, where they viewed the dozens of memorials on the walls of the church dedicated to British soldiers who had been killed or died in great numbers whilst serving in that area in years gone by. On 22 May they visited the grave of General Penn-Symons of the 24th Regiment, the first general to be killed during the Boer War; and on the following day they visited Hlobane. After a guided tour of Isandlwana and Rorke's Drift on 24 May, the party prepared for the commemorations which had been organised for the following day. The booklet states:

At last the great day had arrived and we got on the bus for Isandlwana, arriving just in time to sort ourselves out, find the seats allotted to us close to the 24th Regiment memorial and beneath the flag which we had brought out with us of the Royal Regiment of Wales as it proudly flew in the strong breeze alongside the flags of the Republic of South Africa and KwaZulu.

The celebrations began with a banner parade led by our own party with the two banners of the Brecon branch and our Comrades Association which had been brought out for that purpose. This was followed by choral items sung by the Amazwi Kazulu choir, a performance by some 150 Zulu warriors, dressed in the regimental regalia that was worn in the battle (we closed our eyes to the odd gym shoe, football sock and cigarette); carrying knobkerries, shields and assegais. Shouting their traditional war cry 'Usutu' and chanting the royal salute 'Bayete' they encouraged the Zulu king, HM Zwelithini Goodwill Ka Bhekuzulu and his chief minister, Chief Gatsha Buthelezi to join them in their dancing. A memorial plaque was unveiled and an address was given by the guest of honour, Dr, the Honourable P G J Koornhof, minister of plural relations following a short religious service. The function concluded with a wreath-laying ceremony when the colonel of the regiment laid a wreath on the 24th Regiment memorial.

The crowds were immense, as were the Zulu ladies attending King Goodwill and Chief Buthelezi, and one could not but feel the excitement and festival spirit generated by the Zulus in the audience. But to us the huge Isandlwana Hill towering 800 feet

140

above us somehow dominated the scene and reminded us of that fearsome battle one hundred years ago.

The ceremony at Rorke's Drift was a much smaller affair taking place as it did roughly within the same perimeter as the battle 100 years ago. A covered dais had been erected on which sat the King of the Zulus and the chief minister with their wives and princesses, the administrator of Natal, The Honourable W W B Havemann and Bishop L E Diamini of the Evangelical Lutheran Church.

The actual ceremony consisted of a short religious service conducted by the bishop and accompanied by the Amazwi Kazulu Choir, with whom we joined in singing the hymns, by choral items from the choir, a short speech by the King and address by the administrator of Natal, following which he unveiled the memorial. As the graves of the Zulus who were killed are in three different locations around the perimeter it was not possible for Mr Havemann to unveil each at the same time, so ex-members of the 24th Regiment, Lt-Colonel Jack Adams, Bill Breakspeare and George Scott were asked to do this for him at the same time as he unveiled the main memorial; a thoughtful and nice idea.

Finally, the colonel of the regiment laid a wreath on our own memorial, and the chief minister of the Zulus, the British military attaché, the French Ambassador, and other representatives of those regiments involved laid theirs on the main memorial.

Thus ended a day which will forever remain in the minds of those fortunate enough to be there.

* * *

In addition to Colonel Chard's grave at St John the Baptist Church at Hatch Beauchamp, a stained-glass memorial window was placed in the south wall of the chancel.

A brass plaque mounted on wood memorial on the south wall of St Michael's Church in Othery states:

In loving memory of the three sons of William Wheaton CHARD, of Pathe House, Somerset, and Mount Tamar, Devon: Colonel William Wheaton Chard; he served for 30 years abroad in the Royal Fusiliers and commanded the 1st Batt: in Egypt and in India, Born 24th Dec 1841, died 12th Sept 1890, buried at St Budeaux, Devon. Colonel John Rouse Merriott Chard, V.C., R.E. The hero of Rorke's Drift; born 21st Dec 1847, died 1st Nov. 1897, buried at

141

The John Chard memorial window at Hatch Beauchamp church. The wreath that was sent to his funeral by Queen Victoria was placed beneath the memorial and it remained there for many years afterwards.

> Hatch Beauchamp. The Rev Charles Edward Chard, B.A. Rector of Hatch Beauchamp, Somerset, for 25 years; born 4th Dec 1856, died 12th Sept 1910, buried at Hatch Beauchamp.

On 2 November 1898, a bronze bust memorial of Colonel Chard was unveiled in Taunton Shire Hall, by the Commander-in-Chief, and excess funds were contributed to Taunton Hospital as part of an endowment for a Soldier's Bed. It was reported in newspapers:

> It will be satisfactory to admirers of the hero of Rorke's Drift to know that the requisite sum for the Chard memorial bust and soldier's bed (£1,000) has now been collected, and that the County of Somerset will have at its disposal forever in the county hospital at Taunton a free bed for a soldier (born in the county, or with certain residential qualifications), his wife, widow or child.

A brass memorial to the three Chard brothers was placed in St Michael's Church in Othery. *(Courtesy of Steve Lee)*

On the day after the first anniversary of John Chard's death, 2 November 1898, a bronze bust was unveiled at the Shire Hall in Taunton. It was created by Edgar George Papworth junior, who was popular during the late Victorian period, and was copied from a marble bust which had been in the possession of Major Barrett and Chard's sister, Charlotte. It is now in the collection of the Somerset Military Museum housed in Taunton Castle. *(Courtesy of Steve Lee)*

In Plymouth there is a plaque at the YMCA Sports Centre at Pennycross, and a road bollard bearing his name is situated at Hoe seafront in Plymouth, which recognises famous people associated with Plymouth, and Chard Road in St Budeaux, Plymouth, was named after him.

A brass plaque in his honour was placed at Rochester cathedral as 'A tribute from his fellow officers of the Royal Engineers'. A brass memorial plaque has been placed in the North Quire Aisle in Jesus Chapel at Rochester cathedral, which reads: 'The Hero of Rorke's Drift remembered after his death by his mess mates'. His name appears on the 'For Valour' board at the Royal Engineers Museum in Chatham. The museum also holds his officer's sword, a water bottle and a Zulu shield, assegai and knobkerrie – taken by Chard at Ulundi.

A Territorial Army Centre in Swansea has a 'John Chard VC House'. Chard Street in Nottingham was named after him, and there are other streets in the area named in association with the Zulu War, although there is no Bromhead Street.

The John Chard-Dekarasie Medal in sliver was awarded to all ranks of the South African Union Defence Forces from 1952 to 2003 for twenty years' long and efficient service, with the John Chard Medal in bronze being awarded for twelve years' service.

In 1979 the *Royal Engineers Journal* reported:

The Defence of Rorke's Drift
22 January 1879
The Commemoration of the Centenary
It is said that fortune favours the brave; that was certainly the case at Hatch Beauchamp in Somerset on Sunday, 21 January 1979. On that day many serving and retired members of the Corps of Royal Engineers, led by the Chief Royal Engineer, Lieutenant-General Sir David Willison, KCB OBEMC, and others joined together to commemorate the defence of Rorke's Drift and to remember in particular Lieutenant (later Colonel) J R M Chard RE, who was awarded the Victoria Cross for his part in the action. Despite the appalling weather which gripped the country as a whole, the day was fine and sunny, and by contemporary standards warm.

The ceremony was a culmination of months of planning. It was inspired by the desire of Mrs Dorothy Phillips, a niece of Colonel Chard, to present to the Corps certain relics connected with her

TO THE MEMORY OF
COLONEL J.R.M.CHARD,
V.C., R.E.,
RORKE'S DRIFT 22ND JAN.1879.
BORN 21ST DEC.1847. DIED 1ST NOV. 1897.
A TRIBUTE FROM HIS BROTHER OFFICERS
OF THE ROYAL ENGINEERS.

The Royal Engineers brass plate memorial dedicated to Colonel Chard which was unveiled in the north wall of the north quire aisle at Rochester cathedral. *(Courtesy of Steve Lee)*

famous uncle. Originally Mrs Phillips, whose 94th birthday would have coincided with the anniversary, was to have made the presentation herself, but very sadly she died in March 1978. It was left to her son, Donald Phillips, to fulfil her wishes. On behalf of the Corps Major-General R C A Edge CB MBE; a retired colonel-commandant; formed a committee to plan and organise the commemoration.

As Colonel Chard is buried in the churchyard of the Church of St John the Baptist at Hatch Beauchamp his grave was to be the focus of the events. A further family connection was that at the time of Colonel Chard's death the Rector of this church was his brother. Commander and Mrs Barry Nation very kindly offered the use of their nearby home, Hatch Court, for the parade.

It was here in front of the impressive Georgian mansion, looking out over a wide sweep of gravel and lawn, that the Chief Royal Engineers was received with a General Salute at 11:00 am on 21 January 1979. On the right were the Royal Engineers Aldershot band and the Corps of Drums of the Royal Monmouthshire Royal Engineers (Militia) resplendent in scarlet. Next to them were over a hundred members of the Royal Engineers Association from South Wales, Taunton and Plymouth, together with members of the Royal British Legion led by fifteen standards. Then came contingents from the Army Apprentices College Chepstow, 100 Field Squadron The Royal Monmouthshire Engineers (Militia), and the Somerset Army Cadet Force. The parade was commanded by Major J W Quin, RE, from the Army Apprentices College. There were many spectators, including a large number of distinguished guests who were seated on the steps below the imposing portico of Hatch Court.

After the General Salute the Chief Royal Engineer inspected the parade and spoke to many members of the Association. Mr Donald Phillips then presented to the Chief Royal Engineer a splendid marble bust of Colonel Chard and the sword which he carried at Rorke's Drift. In his speech Mr Phillips emphasised Colonel Chard's qualities of courage, calmness, resolution and modesty. He said that his family thought it only right that these valued possessions, which had been in their care for nearly a hundred years, should be made available to a wider public through the Royal Engineers Museum. Lieutenant-General, Sir David Willison accepted the bust and sword and thanked Mr Phillips and his family for their great generosity in presenting them to the Corps. He said that Colonel Chard's deeds were a very good illustration of the fact that Sappers are soldiers first and engineer afterwards. The heroic defence of Rorke's Drift had altered the whole course of the Zulu War, redeeming in a single night the British Army's earlier disastrous defeat at Isandlwana. The Chief Royal Engineer also said that he had exchanged greetings with the Royal Regiment of Wales, who were holding their own celebrations in Brecon.

To the strains of 'Wings' and with a proud 'swing' the parade then marched off to the church, where the rector of Hatch Beauchamp, the Reverend K B Edwards, B Sc; assisted by the Reverend J C R Webb, FCA, CF, conducted the appropriate and dignified memorial service. The lesson was read by Lieutenant-Colonel (Retd) W W M Chard, late of the Royal Regiment of Fusiliers, and a collection was taken for the Charles Johnson Hospital, Ngutu, Zululand. The singing was led by the North Curry Choral Society, who had very kindly volunteered their services. After the service the parade formed up in a hollow square about the plain marble headstone.

The buglers of the Royal Monmouthshire Engineers (Militia) sounded the Last Post and the Royal Engineers Association Standards were dipped. The sounding of Reveille ended the two minutes silence. Wreaths were then laid upon the grave of Colonel Chard by Lieutenant-Colonel W W M Chard on behalf of the family, by the Chief Royal Engineer on behalf of the Corps, by Her Majesty's Lieutenant for Somerset on behalf of the County of Somerset, by Captain W Bailey RE, on behalf of 5 Field Squadron (in which Colonel Chard was serving at the time of Rorke's Drift), by the Chairman of the Royal Engineers Association on behalf of the Association, and by Colonel Welchman DSO on behalf of the Royal Regiment of Wales. This simple yet moving ceremony in the country churchyard on a sunny winter's day was a fitting tribute to the officer of whom the Chief Royal Engineer said that his deeds stand out even in the illustrious company of the Sapper officers and soldiers who have won forty-six Victoria Crosses for deeds of great valour and gallantry.

All those on parade then returned to the village hall for lunch. The guests of the Corps, who included Her Majesty's Lieutenant for Somerset and Mrs Luttrell, the Chairman of the Somerset County Council, and Mrs Leonard Williams, Colonel, the Right Honourable E D L du Cann PC MP and Mrs du Cann, the Lord Mayor and Lady Mayoress of Plymouth; the Mayoress of Taunton; and members of the family of Colonel Chard had lunch at Hatch Court. After lunch there was an opportunity to inspect an excellent display of items connected with Rorke's Drift, including the sword of honour presented to Colonel Chard by the City of Plymouth. The display had been prepared by the curator of Taunton Museum.

The Corps is indebted to Commander and Mrs Nation for offering the use of their splendid house and grounds for the ceremony.

It was a great delight to all those who had been involved in planning the ceremony that General Edge, who had unfortunately suffered a stroke in December, had recovered sufficiently to attend. General Edge was responsible for the concept of the ceremony and its success was very largely due to his drive and enthusiasm.

147

During the 1979 centenary celebrations, the chief Royal Engineer lays a wreath at the grave of John Rouse Merriott Chard VC at Hatch Beauchamp.

The location of Chard's Victoria Cross had remained a mystery for many years. In 1972, what was described as his South Africa Medal and a cast copy of his VC was offered for auction in London. Sir Stanley Baker, who had portrayed Chard in the film *Zulu!*, purchased the set of medals. It was offered for auction again in 1996, and one of the most extraordinary stories in the history of the Victoria Cross began to unfold. Prompted by the mystery surrounding the whereabouts of the original medal, the auctioneers decided to send it to the Royal Armoury in Leeds to be examined. The tests revealed it to be identical to all

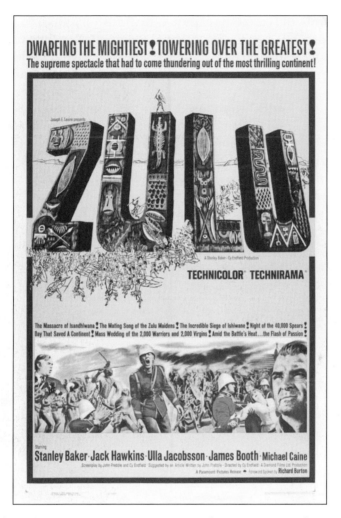

In 1964 the defence of Rorke's Drift was brought once again to the attention of the public by the showing of the epic motion picture *Zulu!* which starred the popular hard-man Welsh actor Stanley Baker and introduced Michael Caine to the cinema-going public. In later years they were both knighted for their contribution to the industry. Although the film does contain some glaring factual mistakes, such as Colour Sergeant Bourne, played by Nigel Green, wearing his medals before he had actually received them, it became one of the most popular war films ever made. There have been rumours over the years that a new version of the film has been considered, but apart from the fact that the subject matter of Britain's colonial past has become frowned upon in modern times – at least by some people – even with all the technical advances it is unlikely that anyone will re-capture the atmosphere of the battle in such a way that producer Cy Endfield and his crew managed to do.

VCs cast from the cascobels captured by British forces in the East, and therefore proved to be the VC originally presented to John Chard. The medal is now displayed on rotation at the Lord Ashcroft Gallery, as part of the 'Extraordinary Heroes' exhibition at the Imperial War Museum in London.

In 1964, Cy Endfield produced the motion picture *Zulu!* based on the action at Rorke's Drift. Starring Sir Stanley Baker as Chard and Sir Michael Caine as Bromhead, and launching the latter's career, this atmospheric film brought the battle back into the public eye, has been the initial inspiration for hundreds of enthusiasts, including the author, and is still being shown regularly on television to this day.

John's great-nephew, Lieutenant Colonel Michael Chard, stated during the centenary of the defence of Rorke's Drift in 1879: 'All my family are Royal Regiment of Fusiliers and he was the black sheep because he became a sapper – but he ended up doing rather well.'

Memorials to the Bromhead Family at the Church of St Germain

Benjamin Bromhead, 7 March 1702

Here lies the body of Benjamin Bromhead esq'r of Thurlby who died March 7th 1702.

Edward Bromhead Edward esq'r, 4 October 1718

Here lieth the body's of Edward Bromhead esq'r and Anthony his youngest son who departed this life April 10th 1718 aged 34 years. Mr Anth'y 2 years. Edward Bromhead was the son of Benjamin Bromhead esq'r of Thurlby & Rebecca his wife also the body of his wife Anne Bromhead.

Benjamin Bromhead, 23 June 1782

Here lieth the body of Benjamin Bromhead late of the City of Lincoln esq who departed this life the 23rd day of June 1782 aged 77 years 'disce mori' he was the son of Edward Bromhead esq'r of Thurlby & Anne Bromhead.

And Frances his wife only daughter of William Gonville esq'r of Alford Lincolnshire, she died Jan'ry 9th 1801 aged 71 years.

In memory also of their grand-daughter Catherine Ffrench Bromhead daughter of their only son Major General Sir Gonville Bromhead Baronet and the honourable Dame Jane Bromhead his wife she died Dec'r 15th 1796 aged 5 years Edward, Anne & Eliza children of Benjamin Bromhead & Frances. His wife died young.

Boardman Bromhead, 7 December 1804

In memory of Boardman Bromhead esq eldest son to the above mentioned Benjamin Bromhead esq'r and Frances his wife only daughter of William Gonville esq'r of Alford Lincolnshire he died Dec'r 7th 1804 aged 77 years. She died Jan'ry 9th 1801 aged 71 years.

Lieutenant General Gonville Bromhead BART, 18 May 1822, grave

Lieut General Sir Gonville Bromhead Bart, the son of Bordman Bromhead and Frances Gonville his wife, born at Lincoln 1758 buried at Thurlby 1822, and Frances Gonville his wife.

Edward Bromhead, 9 January 1869

In memoriam Edward Bromhead Captain 76th Regiment, eldest son of Major Sir Edmund de Gonville Bromhead Bart and Judith Christine Wood his wife born 21st March 1832 died at Thyetmyo Burmah 9th January 1869.

Sir Edward Ffrench Bromhead, 14 March 1855

'The dead shall be raised' Sir Edward FFrench Bromhead, Bart born March XXVI MDCCLXXXIX – died March XIV MDCCCLV.

Major Sir Edmund de Gonville Bromhead, 25 October 1870

Major Sir Edmund de Gonville Bromhead Bart Son of Lieut General Sir Gonville Bromhead Bart and the Honourable Jane Ffrench his wife born 22 January 1791 died 25th October 1870 Served in the French War 1813–14–15 Present at the Battle of Waterloo.

Judith Christine Bromhead, 12 January 1873

To the glory of God and in memory of Judith Christine, Lady Bromhead born 11th September 1803 died 12th January 1873.

Major Sir Edmund de Gonville, Bromhead, Bart, 25 October 1875 and the Honourable Jane Ffrench, his wife, grave

Born 22 January 1791 – died 25 October 1875. Served in the French War, 1813–14–15. Present at the battle of Waterloo.

Charles Edward Gonville Bromhead, 4 October 1890, aged 8

To the glory of God and in loving memory of Charles Edward Gonville son of Colonel C J Bromhead 24th Reg't born 23rd Dec'r 1882 died 4th Oct'r 1890.

Janetta Gonville Bromhead, 28 September 1892

Janetta Gonville Daughter of Sir Edmund de Gonville Bromhead Bart of Thurlby and Judith Christine his wife and widow of George Hatton-Riddell Esq're of Carlton-on-Trent born July 4th 1836 died Sept 28th 1892.

Hannah Bromhead, 8 February 1902

In Loving memory of Hannah Wife of Colonel Sir Benjamin Bromhead BART C.B. of Thurlby died 8th February 1902.

Edward Gonville Bromhead, 18 December 1910

In memoriam Edward Gonville Bromhead Major, King Edward's Own Gurkha Rifles, eldest son of Colonel Sir Benjamin Bromhead, Bart C.B. and Hannah his wife born the 2nd September 1869 died the 18th December 1910 at Aijal Assam.

Alice Margaret Bromhead, 4 November 1920

RIP In Loving Memory of Alice Margaret Daughter of Sir Edmund de Gonville Bromhead born March 12th 1834 died Nov 4th 1920.

Charles James Bromhead, 24 December 1922

In Memory of Colonel Charles James Bromhead C.B. 24th Reg't born 15th Sept 1840 died 24th Dec 1922.

Colonel Charles James Bromhead, 24 December 1922, grave

Colonel Charles James Bromhead CB, 24th Regiment. Born 15 September 1840 – Died 24 December 1922, and Alice Marie, his wife, daughter of Thomas Freckleton, died 19 October 1932, in her 81st year.

Adeliza Pocklington, 16 August 1932

In Loving Memory of Adeliza The beloved wife of Frederick Pocklington, who fell asleep 16th Aug 1932 aged 82 years The Lord gave and the Lord hath taken away. Blessed be the name of the Lord.

Alice Marie Bromhead, 19 October 1932

Alice Marie his wife Daughter of Thomas Freckleton Esq'r died 19th October 1932 in her 81st year.

Colonel Sir Benjamin Parnell Bromhead, 31 July 1935

In loving memory of Colonel Sir Benjamin Parnell Bromhead C.B 4th Baronet of Thurlby son of Major Sir Edmund de Gonville Bromhead B't born 22nd Oct 1838.

Lydia Bromhead, 30 October 1935

In memory of Lydia beloved wife of Major R F G Bromhead daughter of W J Davey esq'r/of Maes Mynan Flintshire died 30th Oct 1935.

Major Benjamin Gonville Bromhead, 13 May 1936

In loving memory of Major Benjamin Gonville Bromhead the Royal Berkshire Regt, 2nd son of Colonel Sir B.P. Bromhead C.B 4th Baronet born 19th August 1876 died 13th May 1936.

Janetta Hope Gonville Birdwood, 14 November 1947

Sacred to the memory of Janetta Hope Gonville Birdwood member of the order of the Crown of India dearly beloved and devoted wife for over fifty-three years of Field-Marshall Lord Birdwood of Anzac and of Totnes in the County of Devon.

Major Richard Freckleton Gonv Bromhead, 16 December 1949

And of her husband Major Richard Freckleton Gonville Bromhead son of Colonel C J Bromhead C.B. of Plas-Draw, N Wales died 16th Dec 1949.

Emily May Bromhead, 22 November 1956

In loving memory of Emily May wife of the late Major Edward Gonville Bromhead of Thurlby Lincolnshire eldest daughter of the late Edward Hosking I.C.S. and Annette his wife born 12th October 1876 died 22nd November 1956 – her ashes were placed here.

James Gonville Stewart Smith, 8 October 1958, aged 2 days

James Gonville Stewart Smith 6th Oct 1958 8th Oct 1958.

Edith Maud Bromhead, 26 March 1975

Also of his wife Edith Maud born 14th December 1884 died 26th March 1975.

Lieutenant Colonel Sir Benjamin Denis Bromhead, 18 May 1981

In Memory of Lt Col. Sir Benjamin Denis Gonville Bromhead O.B.E 5th Baronet of Thurlby. Born 7th May 1900 Died 18th May 1981.

Lieutenant Chard's Official Report on the Defence of Rorke's Drift

THE ZULU WAR
MADIERA, Monday.

The following has been received here from Cape Town:-
Lord Chelmsford has issued the following general order:-

The Lieutenant-General commanding Her Majesty's Forces in South Africa has much satisfaction in publishing the subjoining official report of the gallant defence of Rorke's Drift Post made on January 22 and 23. The Lieutenant-General feels sure that the gallant conduct of the garrison will receive most ample recognition, and trusts the example set by a few brave men, and the success attended their noble efforts, will be taken to heart by all under his command. The odds against them were nearly thirty to one; but taking advantage of the material which lay to hand, and hastily constructing with it such cover as was possible, this heroic little garrison was able to resist during the space of twelve hours the determined attacks made upon them, and, further, inflicting heavy loss on the enemy, the killed alone being more than three times their number.

RORKE'S DRIFT, January 25.
'My Lord – I have the honour to report that on the 22nd instant I was left in command at Rorke's Drift by Major Spalding, who went to Helpmekaar in order to hurry forward a company of the 24th Regiment. I was specially ordered to protect the ponts. At 3:15pm that day I was watching at the ponts when two men came towards us from Zululand at the gallop. They shouted out and were taken across the river; and I was

then informed by one of them – Lieutenant Adendorff of Commandant Lonsdale's regiment, who afterwards remained to assist in the defence – of the disaster befallen at the Isandlwana camp, and that the Zulus were advancing upon Rorke's Drift. The other, a Carbineer, rode on to take the news forward to Helpmekaar.

Almost immediately afterwards I received a message from Lieutenant Bromhead – commander of the company of the 24th Regiment at the camp near the commissariat stores – asking me to come up at once. I gave instructions to strike tents, and to put all stores into the wagon, while I instantly made my way to the commissariat store, and there found that a note had been received from the Third Column, stating that the enemy was advancing in force against our post, which we were to strengthen and hold at all costs. Lieutenant Bromhead was already most actively engaged loop-holing and barricading the store-building and hospital, and also in connecting the defences of the two buildings walls constructed of mealie-bags and wagons. I held a hurried consultation with him and Mr Dalton, of the commissariat – who was actively superintending the work of defence, and whom I cannot sufficiently thank for his most valuable services – and I entirely approved all his arrangements. I then went round our position down to the ponts, and brought up along with their guard one sergeant and six men, the gear, wagon &c. I desire here to mention for approval the offer of these pont guards, Daniels and Sergeant Millne, of the 3rd Buffs, who, with their comrades, volunteered to moor the ponts out in the middle of the stream, and there to defend them from the decks, with a few men to assist.

We arrived back at our post at 3:30pm, and, shortly after, an officer with some of Durnford's Horse came in and asked orders from me. I requested him to send a detachment to observe the ponts and drift, and to throw out vedettes in the direction of the enemy, in order to check their advance as much as possible, his men falling back on the post when forced to retire, and thereafter to assist in the defence. I next requested Lieutenant Bromhead to station his men, and, having seen every man thoroughly knew his post, the rest of the work went quickly on.

At 4:20pm, the sound of firing was heard behind the hill to our south. The officer of Durnford's Horse returned, reporting that the enemy was now close upon us. His men, he told me, would not obey orders, but were going off towards Helpmekaar, and I myself saw them in retreat, numbering apparently about one hundred, going in that direction. About the same time Captain Stephenson's detachment of the Natal Native Contingent left us – as did that officer himself. I saw that our line of defence was too extended for the small number of men now left, and at once commenced an inner entrenchment of biscuit boxes, out of which we had soon completed a wall two boxes high.

About 4:30pm, five hundred or six hundred of the enemy came suddenly in sight around the hill to our south. They advanced at a run against our south wall, but were met by a well-sustained fire; yet, not withstanding heavy loss, they continued to advance to within fifty yards of the wall, when their leading men encountered such a hot fire from our front, with a cross one from the store, that they were checked. Taking advantage, however, of the cover afforded by the cook-house, and the ovens, they kept up thence heavy musketry volleys; the greater number, however, without stopping at all, moved on towards the left round the hospital, and thence made a rush toward our north-west wall and our breastwork of mealie bags. After a short but desperate struggle those assailants were driven back with very heavy loss into the bush around our works.

The main body of the enemy close behind had meantime lined the ledge of rocks, and filled some caves overlooking us at a distance of a hundred yards to the south, from whence they kept up a constant fire. Another body, advancing somewhat more to the left than those who first attacked us, occupied a garden in the hollows of the road and also the bush beyond it in great numbers, taking especial advantage of the bush, which we had no time to cut down. The enemy were thus able to advance close to our works, and in this part soon held one whole side of the wall, while we on the other kept back a series of desperate assaults which were made on a line extending from the hospital all along the wall as far as the bush. But each attack was most splendidly met and repulsed by our men, with the bayonet, Corporal Ferdinand Schiess, of the Natal Native Contingent, greatly distinguished himself by conspicuous gallantry. The fire from the rock behind our post, though badly directed, took us completely in reverse, and was so heavy that we suffered very severely, and at six o'clock was finally forced to retire behind the entrenchment of biscuit boxes.

All this time the enemy had been attempting to force the hospital, and shortly afterwards did set fire to the roof. The garrison of the hospital defended the place room by room, our men bringing out all the sick who could be moved before they retired. Privates John Williams, Henry Hook, Robert Jones and William Jones, of the 24th Regiment, were the last four men to leave, holding the doorway against the Zulus with bayonets, their ammunition being quite expended. From want of interior communication and the smoke of the burning house, it was found impossible to carry off all the sick, and, with most heartfelt sorrow and regret, we could not save a few poor fellows from a terrible fate. Seeing the hospital burning, and the desperate attempts being made by the enemy to fire the roof of our stores, we now converted two mealie-bag heaps into a sort of redoubt, which gave a second line of fire all along, Assistant Commissary Walter Dunne working hard at this though much exposed; thus rendering most valuable assistance.

Darkness then came on. We were completely surrounded, and, after several furious attempts had been gallantly repulsed, we were eventually forced to retire to the middle and then to the inner wall of our kraal on the east of the position we first had. We were sustaining throughout all this a desultory fire, kept up all night, and several assaults were attempted, but always repulsed with vigour, the attacks continuing until after midnight, our men firing with the greatest coolness, not wasting a single shot. The light afforded by the burning hospital proved a great advantage.

At four o'clock on the morning of 23 January firing ceased; and at daybreak the enemy were passing out of sight over the hill to our south-west. We then patrolled the ground, collecting arms from dead bodies of the Zulus, and strengthening the position as much as possible. We were still removing thatch from the roof of the store, when about seven o'clock, a large body of the enemy once more appeared upon the hills to the south-west. I now sent a friendly kaffir, who had come in shortly before, with a note to the officer commanding at Helpmekaar, asking help. About eight o'clock, however, the British Third Column appeared, and at sight of this the enemy, who had been gradually advancing towards us, commenced falling back as our troops approached.

I consider the enemy which attacked us to have numbered about three thousand; we killed about three hundred and fifty. Of the steadiness and gallant behaviour of my whole garrison I cannot speak too highly. I wish especially to bring to your notice the conduct of Lieutenant Gonville Bromhead, of the 2/24th Regiment, and the splendid behaviour of his Company, B, 2/24th. Of Surgeon James Reynolds in regard of his constant attention to our wounded under fire, assisting them where they fell. Of Acting Commissary Officer James Dalton, to whose energy much of our defences were due, and who was severely wounded while gallantly assisting in the fight. Assistant-Commissary Walter Dunne, Acting Storekeeper. Colour-Sergeant Frank Bourne, 2/24th; Lance-Sergeant Thomas Williams, 2/24th, wounded dangerously; Sergeant Joseph Windridge; Corporal Ferdinand Schiess, Natal Native Contingent, wounded; Private Joseph Williams, 2/24th; Private William

Jones 2/24th; Private Michael McMahon, Army Hospital Corps; Private Robert Jones, 2/24th; Private Henry Hook, 2/24th; and Private William Roy, 2/24th.

The following is the list of killed: Sergeant Robert Maxfield, Privates John Scanlon, Garret Hayden, Robert Adams, Thomas Cole, John Fagan, James Chick and Joseph Williams, all of the 2/24th Regiment; Privates Edward Nicholas, William Horrigan and James Jenkins, 1/24th; Mr Louis Byrne, Commissariat Department; Trooper Sydney Hunter, Natal Mounted Police; Corporal Michael Anderson, Natal Native Cavalry; a private of the NNC. Total: Fifteen, and Twelve wounded, of who two have since died; Sergeant Thomas Williams, 2/24th; and Private William Beckett, 1/24th.

(Signed) JOHN R M CHARD, Lieutenant, RE.
To Colonel Glyn, CB, Commanding, 3rd Column

Rorke's Drift Defenders Who are Known to have Fought with Major Chard at Ulundi

Charles Robson

Charles John Robson was born on 7 January 1855, at 7 Ebury Mews in Belgravia, London, the son of George Robson, a coachman, and his first wife, Ann (formerly Dieper). He had five older sisters. In 1871 they lived at 16 Bloomsbury Street in Westminster, and his father was working as an ostler (stableman).

Charles left his job working with his father as a groom, and enlisted into the Corps of Royal Engineers at Bow Street Police Court, on 30 April 1873, suggesting that he chose a stretch with Her Majesty's army, as opposed to a stretch at Her Majesty's pleasure. He was described as being 5ft 5in tall, and weighing 9 stone 7lb. He had a fresh complexion, grey eyes and brown hair. He had several scars on his neck and between his shoulder blades and his muscular development was average. 12046 Driver Robson was sent to Aldershot, being posted to 'B' troop (Equipment) RE Train. He spent three days in jail at Aldershot in January 1874 for a misdemeanour which is unrecorded, and this would be the only blemish on his army career, and he was in hospital on several occasions suffering with a variety of ailments. In October 1874 his mother fell down a flight of stairs which left her paralysed, and she died a month later.

When Lieutenant John Chard joined the company on 18 April 1876, Charles was detailed as his batman and groom. He received good conduct pay of 1*d*. a day from 13 September 1876. On 2 December 1878, he and his officer accompanied the 5th company as they boarded the

SS *Walmer Castle* bound for active service in South Africa. They arrived in Durban on 4 January 1879, to be greeted by a torrential downpour in which they had to unload hundreds of tons of stores and equipment. Lieutenant Chard and Driver Robson, a corporal and three sappers, were ordered to go up to Rorke's Drift post to repair the pontoon bridge across the Buffalo River. A small mule train was organised on which the men and their equipment were loaded. Chard rode on horseback with Charles on his spare mount.

On the morning of 22 January, the engineers rode to Isandlwana, where they saw Zulus on the distant hills. Charles and his officer rode back to Rorke's Drift, leaving the other men at the base camp. During the defence he placed himself behind the stone kraal at the eastern end of the defences where he could fire at the Zulus who were trying to ransack the Engineers' wagon. He told Chard that during the fighting 'I was protecting our things.'

Charles and Chard remained at Rorke's Drift for several weeks to work on a more permanent fortification of the garrison. On 4 July 1879, they were in the British square at the Battle of Ulundi, for the final devastating defeat of the Zulus. Following the cessation of hostilities the 5th Company moved to Saint Paul's Mission, where they were occupied in building another fortified position. They embarked aboard the SS *Eagle* and arrived in Portsmouth on 2 October. They were met as heroes, and Charles accompanied his officer on many official engagements, including a trip to Balmoral for an audience with Queen Victoria.

The *Royal Engineers Journal* for 1 November 1879, recorded: 'Major Chard was accompanied by his military servant in full regimentals and the appearance of this soldierly young fellow bearing an armful of Zulu assegais and other trophies of the campaign excited much interest.'

He transferred to the 7th Field Company at Chatham in February 1880. However, when the 7th Company left for Natal in 1881, he decided to leave the army and discharge to the reserve from the 11th Field Company on 20 June 1881. However, in September 1881, he began a new job at the Chatham barracks as a civilian groom and general servant to Captain C.H. Gordon RE. He accompanied his officer to Cork, and when his officer returned to Chatham in July 1882 they parted company. He was re-called to the Colours on 2 August 1882 and posted to Aldershot as 'batman' to Lieutenant Maude. He received 2*d*. good conduct pay from that date, and on 13 November 1882, he re-engaged to serve a further twelve years. He received his final discharge on 30 April 1894.

Charles met Jane Elizabeth Farrand in Aldershot, and they married at Hale Parish Church in Surrey, on 13 May 1883. John Chard VC attended the wedding. He and Jane both gave their address as Heath End in Hale, and by 1891 they had moved to 8 Perowne Street in Aldershot, and it was there on 22 June 1891, that their only child, Annie Lilian, was born. The family moved to Orchard Road in Dorking, and by 1901 they had moved to Ceres Road in Plumstead, before settling at 43 Swingate Street in Plumstead, where he kept a chicken house, grew a grapevine and enjoyed smoking his variety of pipes. Charles and Jane worked in the Royal Arsenal during the First World War, and in 1917 Annie, then Mrs Peter Ewart, gave them a grandson, Edwin Peter, who remembered his 'kind, solidly-built' grandfather with great respect.

Charles Robson died on 19 July 1933, at St Nicholas's Hospital in Plumstead, the cause of death being 'cerebral embolism'. He was aged 78, and he had been married to Jane for fifty years. He was buried in an unmarked common grave in Woolwich Old Cemetery. A hand-carved wooden marker plaque was placed at the grave site on 22 January 1993, and in 1999 a more permanent memorial plaque was placed at the grave by the Royal Engineers Association.

His South Africa Medal and the Holy Bible presented to him by the Ladies' Rorke's Drift Testimonial Fund were sold at auction in 2017.

Arthur Howard

Arthur Howard was born on 2 May 1851, at Eynsford (pronounced Ainsford), near Swanley in Kent. He was the second son in a family of five children to William Howard, an agricultural labourer, and his wife, Maria (formerly Tucker). All the Howard children were educated at the Eynsford village school.

Arthur began his working life as an agricultural labourer before becoming a groom, but by the beginning of 1871 he was unemployed. Consequently, on 28 April 1871, he enlisted in the Royal Regiment of Artillery at Woolwich Barracks in London. He was described as being 5ft and 6¾ in tall, with a fresh complexion, hazel eyes and brown hair. His chest measurement was 34in, and he weighed 140lb. His muscular development was good and he had no distinctive marks.

He was posted to the 14th Brigade at Woolwich, where 2077 Gunner Howard transferred to the 15th Brigade, being posted to Newcastle upon Tyne on 20 August 1872. He was admitted to hospital for ten days in May 1873, suffering with primary syphilis. He was posted back to Woolwich on 5 May 1874, where he was back in hospital from 22 July until 14 August, being treated for ulcers on the left ankle. He was admitted to hospital with the same complaint on 9 January 1875 and discharged on 15 February 1875. On 17 April of that year he was posted to Newlodge in Ireland. He transferred back to the 14th Brigade on 29 April 1877 and on 1 August 1877 he transferred to the 5th Brigade, where he became the servant and batman to Major Arthur Harness.

The unit received orders for active service in South Africa and embarked on the troopship *Dublin Castle* on 9 January 1878. They arrived at King Williamstown on 11 February 1878, to find that much of the heavy baggage had been ransacked, and Gunner Howard was annoyed to find that his two sets of servant's clothes had been stolen, along with a clock belonging to Major Harness. The unit saw active service in the 9th Cape Frontier War, and on 2 November the battery was given orders to move to Greytown. They then moved to Helpmekaar, followed by the order to move up to Rorke's Drift, where Arthur was admitted to the hospital on 18 January suffering with fever.

On 7 February 1879, he wrote a letter to his family from Helpmekaar describing the events which was printed in the *Daily Telegraph*, on 25 March 1879, apparently to his dissatisfaction.

Arthur developed a good relationship with Major Harness. In a letter the major joked: 'Arthur Howard's correspondence is so large that I tell him he must provide separate mail arrangements, and that no government can stand the pressure he puts upon it.' By June 1879 Major Harness and Gunner Howard were camped on the banks of the Upoko River, and they were present at the Battle of Ulundi on 4 July, for the final defeat of the Zulus. Harness describes Arthur as 'always anxious to have a clothes-washing, in order, as he calls it, that we may start clean'. In a letter dated 7 September 1879, he hinted to his sister that he wanted Arthur to remain as his servant on his return home, by saying:

> Arthur Howard is with me here. I have not mentioned to him my hope of getting leave, but if successful I intend telling him and getting him a passage home on a troopship if he likes to come. I have not made up my mind which is best; I shall send him to his friends of course on landing in England, I don't suppose you want him roaming about the village and garden.

On 14 October 1879 they boarded the *Edinburgh Castle* and arrived in Plymouth on 14 November 1879. Major Harness and Gunner Howard were posted to Hillsborough Barracks at Nether Hallam in Sheffield, and then to the Cadets Academy on Woolwich Common in 1882.

Arthur had met a pantry maid called Frances Bird in Sheffield, and he found accommodation for her at 3 Woolwich Common. They married at the register office in Woolwich, on 24 May 1882. They had one child, who was known as Elsie, born in 1883, before Frances died of pneumonia in 1889. Leaving Elsie with his sister in Sheffield, Arthur returned to Woolwich, from where he was discharged at his own request on 30 May 1890, with a pension of 11*d*. a day. His character was described as 'exemplary'.

He obtained lodgings at 11 Adelphi Street in Nether Hallam, Sheffield, and found employment as a book-keeper's clerk. By 1901 Arthur and Elsie had moved back to Woolwich, where he obtained employment as an ammunition case examiner at the Royal Arsenal factory, and took lodgings at 1 Parry Place in Plumstead. As his sight and general health gradually deteriorated with age, he retired from his job at the Royal Arsenal and took employment as a night watchman. He eventually retired for good and survived on his pension and savings.

On 14 February 1930, the *Daily Mirror* published a report that it had been announced in Australian newspapers that he had died in Sydney, after complaining of an old assegai wound received in the historic Drift fight. Arthur expressed great surprise when he was informed of the story. The report went on to say: 'Although he is blind, he is an active man, and takes a keen interest in present day affairs.' Arthur added:

I was at Ulundi too, where we beat the Zulu Armies in forty minutes. I never received a wound of any sort from an assegai, or from anything for that matter. How Sydney Art Gallery can have a picture of me leaving the burning hospital carrying another man over my shoulder is more than I can understand. It certainly cannot be a picture of me. It was as much as I could do to leave the building myself, without carrying anyone else. I think the Australian report must be incorrect in the name.

The man who had died in Australia was actually named Howard English, who claimed for many years to have been a defender of Rorke's Drift, and stated that he had been wounded during the battle. He said that he appears in the Alphonse de Neuville picture as one of the central figures carrying a wounded man from the hospital, along with Henry Lugg.

Arthur Howard died on 15 July 1935, aged 84, at St Alfege Hospital, Vanbrugh Hill, Greenwich, London, the cause of his death being reported as senility. His home address at that time was his lodgings at

7 Harton Street in Deptford, London. He was buried in an unmarked grave in Brockley Cemetery in Lewisham, London (plot Y, grave 614), which had been purchased by his landlord, Walter Tanner. A new headstone was unveiled at the grave in 2012, and his medals were sold at auction in 2019.

Frederick Millne

Frederick Augustus Millne was born on 18 February 1854, at 2 Suffolk Place, Holly Street, Hackney. He was the only child of David George Millne and his wife, Mary Ann (formerly Slate). Mary died in 1857, and within a year David married her sister, Frederick's aunt, Louisa Marie, and they had three children. Fred was reasonably well educated and when he left school he became a clerk.

Fred enlisted into the 2nd Battalion, 3rd Regiment (The Buffs), at Lambeth, on 4 June 1872. 2260 Private Millne was 5ft 5½in tall, with a chest measurement of 34½in. He had a fair complexion, grey eyes and brown hair. It was noted that he had his own initials tattooed on his left forearm. He gave his age as 18 years and 2 months and his religion as Church of England. Promotions came fast, and Fred was promoted corporal on 24 February 1873, lance sergeant on 1 April 1876 and sergeant on 6 July of the same year. He had received a second class certificate of education on 1 March 1876.

In 1876 the 2nd Battalion, 3rd Regiment, received orders for active service in South Africa, and he and his unit set sail from Dublin aboard the troopship *St Lawrence*. The passage was an uncomfortable affair, and on 8 November 1876, the ship struck a reef about 90 miles north of Cape Town. They were forced to abandon ship before it sank, with no loss of life, but nine mountain guns, 50 tons of gunpowder and 1,000lb worth of government rations went down with her. Some newspapers listed Sergeant Millne as having been 'lost', so he held the dubious honour of being one of the very few men to read his own obituary after the shipwreck.

On the outbreak of the Zulu War, the 3rd Buffs were attached to the 1st Column, under Colonel Pearson, 3rd Buffs, which was to cross the river border at the Lower Drift. However, Sergeant Millne probably became attached to Lieutenant Newnham-Davis' unit of Mounted Infantry which was detached from the battalion on scouting and reconnaissance duties, and he must have remained at Rorke's Drift when the unit moved on to Isandlwana, maintaining the ponts and waiting for a party of Royal Engineers to arrive.

166

In his official report Lieutenant Chard stated: 'I desire here to mention for approval the offer of these pont guards, Daniels and Sergeant Millne, of the 3rd Buffs, who, with their comrades, volunteered to moor the ponts out in the middle of the stream, and there to defend them from the decks, with a few men to assist.' However, as the Revd Smith stated: 'Our defensive force was too small for any to be spared, and these men subsequently did good service within the fort.'

Lieutenant Chard also requested Sergeant Millne to post himself in the storehouse, where he was to protect two caskets of rum, with strict orders to shoot any man who tried to touch them. A trooper of the Natal Carbineers named J.P. Symons stated:

The men spoke very highly of Chard, and another man named Millne. He ought to get the Victoria Cross. For when the men were distracted with thirst and parched with dust from the thatch and smoke, they went to breach a cask of rum, but this man stood upon it and threatened to shoot any man who touched it.

The 2nd Battalion, East Kent Regiment, formed part of the British square which inflicted the final crushing defeat of the Zulu army at Ulundi on 4 July 1879. For his service Sergeant Millne received the South Africa Medal with *1879* clasp. Fred was promoted to colour sergeant on 1 October 1879, but he reverted to sergeant at his own request in 1882, being promoted back to colour sergeant on 11 January 1883. He served at Singapore and Hong Kong, where he won $40,000 on the lottery. He purchased his discharge on 15 December 1883, and gained employment as an instructor with the Shanghai Municipal Police.

On returning to England, Fred lived with his aunt-cum-step-mother, Louisa, and her family, at 1 Camden Villas in Sebastopol Road, Edmonton, London; which placed him in an emotional dilemma when he became involved with his own cousin and half-sister, Catherine, who was thirteen years his junior, and they married at Edmonton parish church, on 2 April 1889.

Fred entered into a business partnership with Stephen White as joint proprietors of a grocery store in Dale Road, Matlock. It is listed in *Kelly's* 1891 directory as 'White and Millne, wholesale and retail family grocers and tea dealers, wine and spirit merchants, and mineral water manufacturers.' Fred and Catherine had a daughter named Catherine in 1890, and the 1891 census shows Frederick and his family living at The Beehive. It is uncertain what happened to the business, which only lasted for two years, but it seems that the parting of Frederick and Stephen White was not amicable, and nothing was left of Fred's winnings.

Fred moved to Manchester in 1893, where he gained employment as assistant labour master at the Crumpsall workhouse, before becoming the caretaker at Birley Street Board School in Hulme. The family lodged at the school for a while, and here George Frederick was born in 1893. Four girls were also born in Manchester but three of them died very young, the only survivor being Ada Rorke, her second Christian name reflecting the fact that she was born on 22 January 1902.

At the outbreak of the First World War in 1914, Fred, then aged 60, volunteered for active service with several training battalions of the Lancashire Fusiliers, retaining his old rank of colour sergeant, and he had rose to regimental sergeant major with the Devonshire Regiment, the unit from which he took his discharge at the age of 65. His son also served in the First World War.

In retirement he became the caretaker at the Princess Road School in Moss Side, where he was described as 'A sturdy gentleman with a small pointed beard.'

Fred died of pneumonia at his home, 5 Lofas Street, Moss Side, on 5 June 1924, aged 71, and he was buried in an unmarked grave at the Southern Cemetery, Manchester (non-Conformist, section H, grave 483). His campaign medal and a commemorative Bible were sold at a Sotheby's auction in 1990, and on 8 July 2001, a service of commemoration and re-dedication was held at his grave.

Little is known about Mr Daniells, the civilian ferryman who was one of the men who volunteered to defend the ponts in mid-river with Sergeant Millne, other than he is believed to have died in South Africa.

Surgeon James Reynolds VC

James Henry Reynolds was born at Kingstown (now Dun Laughaire), Ireland, on 3 February 1844, the son of Laurence Reynolds, a merchant and Justice of the Peace, of Dalyston House, Granard, County Longford, where he had been born in 1843. He had an older brother named Thomas James. James was educated at Castle Knock, and at Trinity College, Dublin, from where he graduated Bachelor of Medicine and Bachelor of Surgery in 1867.

Prior to the Crimean War medical officers and orderlies were 'regimental', in that medical officers were appointed to each regiment and it was their duty to provide a hospital and keep an eye on the continuing health of the troops in the regiment not just at the theatre of war. However, during the Crimean campaign the Medical Staff Corps was established, which became the Army Hospital Corps (men only) in the following year, and later was officered from the Army Medical Department.

Dr Reynolds entered the Medical Staff Corps as assistant surgeon on 31 March 1868, and in this capacity he was appointed to the 36th (Herefordshire) Regiment on 24 March 1869. He received a commendation for his efficient service during an outbreak of cholera in the regiment in India.

In 1873 a co-ordinated medical service was set up, and a qualifying doctor needed to be single, aged over 21 and much more trained and qualified. Having been placed on the Medical Staff in 1870, Dr Reynolds was appointed surgeon in the Army Medical Service in 1873.

When the 1st Battalion, 24th Regiment, sailed to South Africa in 1874, he went with them as part of the medical team. He took part in the campaign in Griqualand West in 1875, and during the 9th Cape Frontier War, he was stationed at the Impetu depot with the 24th Regiment when the garrison was besieged for several weeks until relief came in January 1878. He was appointed for service with the British troops preparing for hostilities against the Zulus, and on 22 January 1879 he was on medical duties at Rorke's Drift. He was helped by a servant named William Pearce, who was aged about 27 and born at Devonport in Plymouth.

Dr Reynolds' account of the action at Rorke's Drift was published as an appendix to the *Report of the Army Medical Department* in 1878:

At 1:30 a large body of natives marched over the slope of Isandlwana in our direction, their purpose evidently being to examine ravines and ruined kraals for hiding fugitives. These men we took to be our native contingent. Soon afterwards appeared four horsemen on the Natal side of the river galloping in the direction of our post, one of them was a regular soldier, and feeling they might possibly be messengers for additional medical assistance, I hurried down to the hospital as they rode up. They looked awfully scared, and I was at once startled to find one of them was riding Surgeon-Major Shepherd's pony. They shouted frantically 'The camp at Isandlwana has been taken by the enemy and all our men in it massacred, that no power could stand against the enormous number of the Zulus, and the only chance for us all was in immediate flight.' Lieutenant Bromhead, Acting-Commissary Dalton, and myself, forthwith consulted together, Lieutenant Chard not having as yet joined us from the pontoon, and we quickly decided that with barricades well placed around our present position a stand could best be made where we were. Just at this period Mr. Dalton's energies were invaluable. Without the smallest delay, he called upon his men to carry the mealie sacks here and there for defences. Lieutenant Chard (R.E.) arrived as this work was in progress, and gave many useful orders as regards the lines of defence. He approved also of the hospital being taken in, and between the hospital orderlies, convalescent patients (eight or ten) and myself, we loopholed the building and made a continuation of the commissariat defences round it. The hospital however, occupied a wretched position, having a garden and shrubbery close by, which afterwards proved so favourable to the enemy; but comparing our prospects with that of the Isandlwana affair, we felt that the mealie barriers might afford us a moderately fair chance.

At about 3.30 the enemy made their first appearance in a large crowd on the hospital side of our post, coming on in skirmishing order at a slow slinging run. We opened fire on them from the hospital at 600 yards, and although the bullets ploughed through their midst and knocked over many, there was no check or alteration made in their approach. As they got nearer they became more scattered, but the bulk of them rushed for the hospital and the garden in front of it.

We found ourselves quickly surrounded by the enemy with their strong force holding the garden and shrubbery. From all sides but especially the latter places, they poured on us a continuous fire, to which our men replied as quickly as they could reload their rifles. Again and again the Zulus pressed forward and retreated, until at last they forced themselves so daringly, and in such numbers, as to climb over the mealie sacks in front of the hospital, and drove the defenders from there behind an entrenchment of biscuit boxes, hastily formed with much judgement and forethought by Lieutenant Chard. A heavy fire from behind it was resumed with renewed confidence, and with little confusion or delay, checking successfully the natives, and permitting a semi flank fire from another part of the laager to play on them destructively. At this time too, the loopholes in the hospital were made great use of. It was however, only temporary, as, after a short respite, they came on again with renewed vigour. Some of them gained the hospital veranda, and there got hand to hand with our men defending the doors.

Once they were driven back from here, but other soon pressed forward in their stead, and having occupied the veranda in larger numbers than before, pushed their way right into the hospital, where confusion on our side naturally followed. Everyone tried to escape as best they could, and owing to the rooms not communicating with one another, the difficulties were insurmountable. Private Hook, 2/24th Regiment, who was acting as hospital cook, and Private Connolly, 2/24th Regiment, a patient in hospital, made their way into the open at the back of the hospital by breaking a hole in the wall. Most of the patients escaped through a small window looking into what may be styled the neutral ground. Those who madly tried to get off by leaving the front of the hospital were all killed with the exception of Gunner Howard.

The only men actually killed in the hospital were three, excluding a kaffir under treatment for compound fracture of the femur. The names were Sergeant Maxfield, Private Jenkins, both unable to assist in their escape, being debilitated by fever, and Private Adams, who was well able to move about, but could not be persuaded to leave his temporary refuge in a small room. The engagement continued more or less until about 7 o'clock p.m. and then, when we were beginning to consider our situation as rather hopeless, the fire from our opponents appreciably slackened giving us some time for reflection.

Lieutenant Chard here again shined in resource. Anticipating the Zulus making one more united dash for the fort, and possibly gaining entrance, he converted an immense stack of mealies standing in the middle of our enclosure, and originally cone fashioned, into a comparatively safe place for a last retreat. Just as it was completed, smoke from the hospital appeared and shortly burst into flames. During the whole night following desultory fire was carried on by the enemy, and several feigned attacks were made, but nothing of a continued or determined effort was again attempted by them. About 6 o'clock a.m., we found, after careful reconnoitring, that all the Zulus with the exception of a couple of stragglers had left our immediate vicinity, and soon afterwards a large body of men were seen at a distance marching towards us.

I do not think it possible that men could have behaved better than did the 2/24th and the Army Hospital Corps (three), who were particularly forward during the whole attack.

Dr Reynolds' award of Victoria Cross was announced in the *London Gazette* of 17 June 1879, and he was promoted to surgeon major, dated 23 January 1879. He remained at Rorke's Drift after the battle, and Henry Harford wrote:

> I shall not easily forget one particular night when Doctor Reynolds and I met in the dark having literally been washed out of our sleeping place, and mooched about, endeavouring to find a more sheltered spot. Suddenly we hit on the idea of lying down under the eaves of B Company's [storehouse] roof, so coiled ourselves up in our soaking-wet blankets, thanking our stars that at all events there would be no river running under us, when presently swish came about half a ton of water clean on top of us – B Company were emptying their tarpaulin!

According to the Records of Service Ledger of the 1st/24th Regiment, Dr Reynolds received his Victoria Cross from Colonel Richard Glyn of the 24th Regiment during a parade of the troops at Pinetown on 26 August 1879; along with Lieutenant Edward Browne of the 24th Regiment for gallantry at Khambula on 29 March 1879.

Dr Reynolds was at the decisive Battle of Ulundi to witness the defeat of the Zulus, and he arrived back in England on board the *Eagle* on 2 October 1879. For his service he was awarded the South Africa Medal with *1877–8–9* clasp. In July 1879, he was awarded the British Medical Association's gold medal, and he was elected honorary fellow of the Royal College of Physicians, Ireland, an honorary doctor of law, Dublin. On 17 October 1879, he and John Chard were guests of honour at a dinner held at the Wanderers Club, Pall Mall, London, 'In recognition of their splendid defence of Rorke's Drift.'

In 1880 he was appointed senior medical officer for the expedition to aid Captain Charles Boycott during the Irish Land War, and while stationed at Richmond Barracks in Dublin he married Elizabeth Mary McCormick, the daughter of a medical doctor named George McCormick, at Glenealy church in County Wicklow, on 22 September 1880. They lived at 5 Usher's Island in Dublin. A son named George Cormac was born on 3 August 1881. He was accidentally shot and killed while serving as a private with the Loyal North Lancashire Regiment on 14 January 1916. Percival was born on 9 January 1884. He was killed in action while serving as a private with the Royal Dublin Fusiliers on 13 November 1916. Henry Laurence was born on 30 June 1885. He served as a private with several units during the First World War. He survived the conflict, but died of tuberculosis in Liverpool in 1935.

His wife was aged only 30 when she died on 8 December 1886. In 1891 he was living at Cheriton Cliffs, St Paul's Parish, Sandgate, at Hythe in Kent, with four children, George, Percy, Henry and Lily, who had all been born in Ireland. He also had a daughter named Elizabeth.

Dr Reynolds was promoted to lieutenant colonel on 1 April 1887 and to brigade surgeon lieutenant colonel on 25 December 1892. He retired on 8 January 1896, and while on the retired list he was employed as senior medical officer at the Royal Army Clothing Factory at Pimlico in London. He retired this post in May 1905. According to the *Naval and Military Magazine* for 1899, he was at that time medical officer for the 1st Cadet Battalion, King's Royal Rifle Corps.

A keen sportsman, Dr Reynolds was a member of the Army and Navy Club from 1890 until his death. On 9 November 1929, he and John Fielding were guests of honour as the two senior Victoria Cross holders at a dinner hosted by the Prince of Wales in the Royal Gallery at the House of Lords.

The 1901 census records Dr Reynolds as living alone at 156 Cambridge Street in Belgravia, London, and he was living at the Rubens Hotel in Westminster when he became ill and was admitted to the Empire Nursing Home in Victoria, London. He died of pleurisy and influenza on 4 March 1932, aged 88, and he was buried in St Mary's Roman Catholic Cemetery at Kensal Rise in London. The granite cross memorial which marks his grave became blackened and had subsided badly, so it was cleaned and re-set in 1991. His medals are with the Royal Army Medical Corps Museum in Aldershot.

At the time of the death of Dr Reynolds, Walter G. Spencer sent some personal recollections of him which were published in the *British Medical Journal*:

When Colonel Reynolds was in charge of the Pimlico Clothing Department he frequently sent workers to Westminster Hospital for treatment, and later he came to me about his health, the last time at the beginning of 1929. Then a cancer, for which a grave operation would previously have been called for, disappeared in about ten days under radium. Colonel Reynolds was thus able to walk at the head of the VCs at the thanksgiving ceremony and to be present at the dinner in the House of Lords. Our conversations often returned to Rorke's Drift, and from notes I jotted down I have picked-out a few of his reminiscences which I have not noticed in print.

There were 36 patients in the hospital, most in different stages of typhoid fever. No preparations had been made for the defence of the station. Reynolds was senior officer, having been already six years in South Africa; Bromhead and Chard were young subalterns just come out from England; Dalton, an army non-commissioned officer, who had re-joined, had had experience in methods of defence employed by the Boers. When fugitives from Isandlwana reached Rorke's Drift it was first proposed to evacuate the place, but Reynolds declared that to be impossible. Even if the convoy could cross the river the ascent of the opposite bank was so long and steep that the Zulus would certainly catch it up. It was Dalton who arranged the defence with mealie bags.

When the Zulus came into view there appeared horsemen in scarlet and the cry was that the cavalry were returning; but Reynolds pointed out that the riders were not rising in their saddles but sat on the horses as the natives did. Coming nearer, the Zulu impi drew up and ceremoniously took snuff, heralding a charge to the uttermost. A few Zulus got into the garden and into the hospital before two patients in bed could be got within the laager, and a third lost his head, took a wrong turning, and was also killed. The remaining 33 cases were saved and survived the subsequent stench.

A number of items which Surgeon Reynolds had used at Rorke's Drift were auctioned at Spinks in 2001. They included two Gladstone bags engraved with his initials, a travelling wooden medicine chest containing unused ointment tubes and glass bottles, and two leather pocket cases containing the surgical instruments he used in the field. The lot included his revolver, an eighteenth-century pocket watch he had been given by his grandfather, a silver medal which had been presented to him by the Royal Welsh Fusiliers and dress miniatures of his Victoria Cross and South Africa campaign medal.

Commissary Walter Dunne

Walter Alphonsus Dunne was born on 10 February 1853, at 28 Victoria Street in Cork, Ireland. He was the third son of six in the family of twelve children born in Cork between 1845 and 1865 to James Dunne and his wife, Margaret (formerly Creedon). His father was the secretary of the Country Club at 80 South Mall in Cork, and later of St Stephen's Green in Cork. The family were devout Roman Catholic, and Walter was baptised at St Finbarr's South Catholic Church in Cork. He was educated at Trinity College in Dublin.

Dunne joined the Control Department as Sub-Assistant Commissary (2nd Lieutenant) on 9 April 1873, and served with the Commissariat

Department in Dublin until October 1877. He was posted to South Africa, where he saw active service with the 1st Battalion, 24th Regiment, during the 9th Cape Frontier War of 1878, and in the campaign against the rebellious chief Sekhukhune in the north-east of Transvaal, who was defying all attempts to prize him from his mountain stronghold. At the end of 1878, Assistant Commissary Dunne received orders to go to Helpmekaar in Natal where a force was being assembled for the invasion of Zululand, and he arrived exhausted after riding a hundred miles across country to take up his duties as Senior Commissary with the 3rd Central Column.

Commissary Dunne was Mentioned in Dispatches for his service during the defence of Rorke's Drift, and although Lord Chelmsford recommended that Dunne should be awarded the Victoria Cross it was not granted. Major Chard stated that Commissary Dunne had supervised the erection of the original defences and was later made responsible for building the inner defences, including the mealie-bag redoubt meant as a last rallying point. When building the redoubt, Dunne, a tall man, encouraged the exhausted soldiers while standing on the growing pile of bags high above the defences, drawing fire on himself and ignoring any danger.

Dunne took part in the re-invasion as Deputy Commissary of Supplies with the Flying Column, and he was in the square which destroyed the Zulu army at the Battle of Ulundi on 4 July 1879. He was in further action during the renewed Sekhukhune Expedition, taking part in the successful assault on his stronghold in November 1879, for which he was Mentioned in Dispatches.

Two days after the battle Dunne wrote a letter to a friend named Lieutenant Waneford describing the events at Rorke's Drift, and in February 1892, the *Corps Journal*, later known as *The Waggoner*, published the third chapter containing his detailed account of the invasion of Zululand and the defence of Rorke's Drift under the title *Reminiscences of Campaigning in South Africa, 1877–81*, from which the following extract is taken:

The force that was to invade Zululand in three columns from three different points on the border, under command of Lord Chelmsford, numbered 12,000 men, including the Native contingent, but Cetewayo's army was known to be about 30,000 strong, well-drilled, organised in regiments and held under strict discipline.

I was attached to number 3 column, commanded by Colonel Glynn CB, under the personal supervision of Lord Chelmsford, who accompanied it, and was instructed to form a supply depot at Rorke's Drift, the site of a Swedish mission station on the banks of the River Buffalo, 12 miles from Helpmekaar. The house and school of the mission, which had been abandoned, were utilised as a hospital and store respectively.

The strength of number 3 column was over 2000 whites and 2500 natives, composed as follows: One battery of Royal Artillery, N5 RA; one company of Royal Engineers; 1st and 2nd battalions of the 24th Regiment; one squadron of mounted infantry; one squadron of Natal Mounted Police; the Natal Carabiniers; Newcastle Mounted Rifles; Buffalo Border Guard; and the 3rd Regiment of the Natal Native Contingent under European officers. The transport comprised 1500 oxen, 70 mules, 220 wagons and 82 carts.

The quantity of supplies to be stored was very large and my work was very arduous; the staff placed at my disposal for supply duties being very inadequate, but I did not then understand the magnitude of the task before us. An Acting Commissariat Officer, Assistant Commissary Dalton; a civilian clerk, Mr Byrne, and Cpl Attwood of the Army Service Corps were all the assistants I had at first. I mention their names as they all took a gallant part of the defence of Rorke's Drift Post and are now no more. To these were subsequently added Lt Griffith, of the 24th Regiment, a most promising young officer, and a sergeant and three privates as issuers, etc.

The once quiet mission station was now a busy scene; heavily-laden ox wagons constantly came and went, accompanied by the usual yelling, whip cracking, and bellowing; poles of corn bags, biscuit boxes, etc, rose up; detachments of troops were continually arriving and pitching their tents – all the bustle of a large camp and depot was apparent.

On 10 January 1879, the first portion of the column crossed the river and encamped on the Zulu side, and for the next ten days was engaged in road making. On the 20th the remainder of the column crossed, with the exception of the small garrison left to guard the Depot. The camps were struck and a general advance was made to Isandlwana, about 12 miles distant, where a fresh camp was formed. On that day we said goodbye to friends and comrades, so many of whom we were destined never to meet again in this world – all of them, both officers and men, as fine fellows as the British Army had ever numbered in its ranks. Our post at Rorke's Drift seemed silent and lonely after they had left; but we expected to join them soon and to hear of some fierce but successful fight with the enemy. Alas, for human hopes and expectations!

Before daylight on 22 January, Lord Chelmsford advanced in force from Isandlwana, leaving his camp there in charge of Lt-Col Pulleine, of the 24th Regiment, who had under his command about 800 of all ranks, including five companies of the 1st/24th and one company of the 2nd/24th. Colonel Durnford RE, arrived at the camp later on the same morning with about 500 of the Native contingent and took over the command. What followed at the camp was learned by putting together the accounts given by the few survivors and from the Zulus themselves after the war.

Early in the morning reports were brought in of bodies of the enemy being in sight. The troops turned out to meet them about a mile or two from the camp, but were soon obliged to fall back, for fresh regiments of the enemy were continually arriving on the scene. About 11:00am a force of 20,000 Zulus advanced simultaneously to the attack and gradually surrounded the defending force, developing the movement with great swiftness and bravery, undaunted by their heavy losses. The Native contingent gave way before their determined assault and fled, thus exposing the rear and flank of the British force, whose ammunition was nearly all expended, while they found themselves unable to obtain a fresh supply, as they were cut off from the camp. A desperate hand-to-hand fight now ensued. The Zulus suffered enormous losses, but numbers prevailed. Surrounded on all sides by crowds of the enemy the small British force was finally overwhelmed, and very very few escaped from the dreadful melee.

How Melvill and Coghill of the 24th tried to save the colours, and how they were overtaken and killed in the river is well known. How groups of men formed back-to-back and fell to a man where they stood was shown only too well by their corpses when the battlefield was revisited.

On that ill-fated day 51 officer and 766 non-commissioned officers and men, including regulars, police and volunteers were killed. The 24th suffered most, having lost 21 officers and 433 men. Twelve days' supplies for the column and the transport fell into the hands of the Zulus; besides two guns, hundreds of rifles and large quantities of ammunition. It was one of the most complete disasters that had ever occurred to a British force.

In the meantime we at Rorke's Drift were all unconscious of the tragedy which was being enacted only twelve miles away.

The story of the engagement at Rorke's Drift has already been graphically told by the gallant Chard; but there are probably many readers of the Journal who have never read it.

The little garrison consisted of one company of the 2nd 24th Regiment under Lieutenant G Bromhead, and a number of details, regulars, police and volunteers, making a total of 138 officers, non-commissioned officers and men, besides 300 of the Natal Native Contingent under an officer named Stephenson. They were variously employed on their different duties on that morning. Lt Chard RE, who commanded the post, was down at the river repairing the pont which had got out of order; poor young Griffith, too eager for fighting to remain at Rorke's Drift, where there seemed to be no prospect of seeing any, had asked permission to ride out to Isandlwana and left the night before – never more to return!

Bromhead and I were resting after luncheon under an awning which we had formed by propping-up a tarpaulin with tent poles; everything was peaceful and quiet, when suddenly, we noticed at some distance across the river a large number of mounted natives approaching, preceded by a lot of women and children and oxen. We were going down to find out what they were, but had not gone many steps when we were called back by one of the men who said that a mounted orderly wished to see the officer in command. Turning back at once we met a mounted man in his shirt sleeves riding hurriedly towards us. His first words were, 'The camp is taken by the Zulus!' When I heard the words a strange feeling, which I cannot account for, came over me that I had heard this somewhere before. Though we could not realise it fully at first, we soon gathered the truth that a great disaster had befallen that portion of number 3 column which was left to defend the camp at Isandlwana, and that the Zulus, flushed with victory, were advancing to attack our post.

Dalton, as brave a soldier as ever lived, had joined us, and hearing the terrible news said, 'Now, we must make a defence!' It was his suggestion which decided us to form a breastwork of bags and grain, boxes of biscuits, and everything that would help to stop a bullet or keep a man out. An ox-wagon, and even barrels of rum and lime juice were pressed into the service.

Bromhead at once ordered the men to fall in, outposts were thrown out, tents were struck, ammunition was served out, and the work of putting up the barricade was begun by all hands. Other preparations were also made. A water barrel was filled and brought inside, and several boxes of ammunition were opened and placed in convenient places. It was well for us that we had the help of the 300 natives at this juncture, otherwise the work could not have been accomplished in time. Chard now came up from the river and heartily superintended the progression of the fortification, making many improvements. The men knew what was before them – a struggle for life – but they one and all displayed the greatest coolness, though some of them were very young soldiers. On all faces there was a look of determination which showed that they meant to 'do or die'.

In about two hours a wall breast high had been made nearly all around, taking in the hospital and store. When I went to look at the progress of the former place, I saw that the weakest point for there was nothing but a plank to close the opening at one part; but before anything could be done to strengthen it a shot was fired. Turning round, I saw one of the outposts running back, and at the same moment a single Zulu appeared, standing out against the sky on top of a high hill which rose up about 100 yards in the rear of the store.

Immediately they heard the shot our 300 natives took up their assegais and made off towards Helpmekaar, followed by their officer! Chard, seeing that we could not now hold the original line, immediately had the space curtailed by drawing a row of biscuit boxes, two high, across the middle. This probably saved us later from destruction for it afforded shelter for the men when they were obliged to retreat on the hospital being taken.

Very soon the Zulus appeared round the foot of the hill in a black mass, coming on without a sound at a steady trot. The men on that side, without waiting for any word of command, opened fire on them at once at about 800 yards range and dropped many of the foremost, causing the remainder to swerve away to their left and thus round to the front of our position. Soon they were all round us, and all sides of the square became hotly engaged. The store, which had been loop-holed, afforded shelter for some of the men, who were able to do great execution on that side, but the heaviest attack was made on the hospital, which was soon captured after a very stubborn resistance on the part of the few men defending it, who were forced back by numbers, fighting all the time with their bayonets. Pts Williams, Hook, and R and W Jones, of the 24th, greatly distinguished themselves in their efforts to save the sick. Those of the sick who were able to move escaped by running back to the second line of boxes, but some of the poor fellows were stabbed to death with assegais in their beds.

All this had not occurred without loss on both sides, numbers of the Zulus having fallen, and on our side Pte Cole (Old King Cole) and another man of the 24th had been shot dead, and three or four wounded. The doctor, Surgeon Reynolds, was busy attending the wounded as they fell. Early in the fight Mr Byrne was shot through the head, and later Dalton, when first standing at full height, received a bullet in the chest, but the wound fortunately did not prove fatal.

About five o'clock some of us who were on the lookout for help from Helpmekaar, noticed a cloud of dust some miles away, and we felt little doubt that the two companies of the 24th quartered there were coming to our aid. The news passed round like wildfire, putting new spirits into all, and was welcomed with loud cheers, which must have astonished the Zulus. But the dust was dispersed by the wind and the longed for help never came.

As darkness came on we saw that the hospital had been set on fire, but this proved fortunate, for the blaze gave light for the greater part of the night, thus enabling the men to take better aim. Several times the foremost Zulus rushed right up to the barricade, but were always driven back with heavy loss; many being stopped by only the bayonet. The men behaved with splendid coolness and bravery. It was a soldiers' battle, each man fighting for their own hand; and well did they avenge the slaughter of their comrades at Isandlwana.

However, the position was a desperate one and our chance of escape seemed slight indeed, so Chard decided to form a sort of redoubt of mealie bags, where a last stand could be made. We laboured at this till we dropped with exhaustion, but succeeded in building it up to about eight feet high on the outside, and here the wounded were brought for protection. It was hard work, for the bags of mealies weighed 200 pounds each. Overhead the small birds, disturbed from their nests by the turmoil and the smoke, few hither and thither confusedly.

As the night wore on the attack slackened from time to time, all firing ceased for the moment and a profound silence reigned, broken only by the words of command by the Zulu leaders, which sounded strangely close. How we longed to know what they said! Every man was then on the alert, straining eyes and ears to detect the rush which was sure to follow, only to be checked each time by a withering volley. Luckily the supply of ammunition was plentiful and it was served out as required; the chaplain, the Reverend George Smith, being very active in helping to distribute it.

Towards morning there was a longer pause than usual, causing us to wonder what devilment the Zulus could be planning; but when the pale dawn, glimmering to the east, lit up the scene they had disappeared! Without a sound to betray their movements they had gone – beaten, carrying their wounded with them, all except a few whose case was hopeless. Then the garrison gave vent to their feelings in ringing British cheers, while the hearts of all gave gratitude to God for their escape from what seemed certain death.

The scene we beheld was a strange and sad one! On one side stood the blackened walls and still smoking ruins of the hospital. Around it and in front of that side of the barricade lay the bodies of Zulus in rows, as if literally mown down, showing how brave had been the assault and how unerring the fire which laid them low. Inside, were our own dead comrades – stark and cold, one still kneeling in a natural position against the wall – while the wounded excited pity by their sufferings, patiently borne. The ground was strewn with trampled grain which had run from the bags pierced by bullet or assegai, and every face was black with smoke and sweat of toil and battle.

No words of mine can do justice to the gallant soldiers who kept overwhelming numbers of those brave savages at bay all through the afternoon and the long hours of the night with a steadiness which has never been surpassed. I am glad to say several of them in due time were awarded the Victoria Cross, but every private present deserved a special reward. Our casualties were seventeen killed and ten wounded.

We could not believe that the Zulus would quietly accept their defeat, so we set to work to repair, as far as possible, the damage that had been done during the fight, and to prepare for another attack. One party proceeded to tear down the thatch from the roof of the store, which might easily be set alight; another collected and destroyed the muskets and assegais strewn about the ground, while a third had the painful task of decently laying out our dead in a corner of the enclosure. We walked round the scene of the fighting, finding everywhere dead Zulus – all 'ring kop' that is, married men, who alone wear a black ring woven into the hair of the head.

While this was going on a pale white face suddenly appeared like a ghost from some small out-buildings, where the Commissariat ovens had been established. 'Who and what is it?' we asked. To our intense astonishment it proved to belong to a man of the Artillery, who, in some unexplained manner, had been out all night while the fight had been raging round him, and who, strange to say, had escaped the notice of the Zulus. Just then one of the apparently dead Zulus rose up, fired his musket at us and *walked* away. We were too surprised for the moment to do anything to stop him and though a couple of shots were fired after him, he got away round the base of the hill.

After 7:00am our attention was drawn to a large column of men advancing towards us some miles off in Zululand. We all scanned them anxiously, fearing that they might be a fresh body of the enemy, and we felt, and said to each other, that in that case our doom was sealed. Even at that distance there was something strangely silent and solemn about them which depressed our hearts. In time, suspense was turned into relief when, through glasses, we could descry the familiar red jackets of the infantry, and then once more the little garrison burst forth into wild cheering, while many helmets were waved aloft, for there could be no doubt that this was the column returning under Lord Chelmsford. But they, seeing in the distance the smoke still rising up from the ruins of the hospital, feared that the post had been captured, and that the signalling which they saw was a ruse of the enemy.

Approaching cautiously at first, a mounted officer, when re-assured, galloped up and anxiously enquired if any of the men from the camp at Isandlwana had escaped and joined us. Sadly we answered 'No'. Overcome by emotion at the terrible certainty conveyed by the short word, he bent down to his horse's neck trying in vain to stifle the sobs which broke from the overcharged heart. No wonder his grief mastered him, for he had passed during the night by that camp where hundreds of his brave comrades lay slaughtered, and the hope that some portion might have fought their way through was crushed forever.

Lord Chelmsford next rode up. No one could envy him then, for in defeat, as in success, all thoughts centre on the commander. His first words were, 'I thank you all for your gallant defence'. Then the main body of the column began to arrive – Strange arrival! No train of wagons to park – no tents to pitch – weary and sad they looked from fatigue, hunger and anxiety. Fortunately it was that we were able to provide them with food, for they had been without any for 18 hours.

They had no change of clothes, no blankets, no greatcoats, no cooking utensils, except what we could lend them. Empty sacks suddenly became most valuable, slit open at the bottom, and with holes made for the arms, they were worn by the men in lieu of greatcoats, and under different circumstances it would have been laughable to see British soldiers gravely mounting guard in such a costume; But one sees strange things on active service.

The day after the fight our dead were buried near the foot of the hill, not far from the spot where they nobly fell. The little cemetery was afterwards enclosed by a wall and a monument erected, on which was recorded their names and how they died fighting for 'Queen and Country'. For the bodies of the Zulus two huge excavations were made in front of the hospital and therein were interred 351 corpses.

Death has already thinned the ranks of the survivors of the little band that fought at Rorke's Drift. Bromhead, who was beloved by his regiment; Dalton, the lion-hearted; and Corporal Attwood, who received the Distinguished Conduct Medal, having since passed away.

The garrison having been increased to 800 men and strengthened by two guns, the remainder of the column left next day *en route* to Pietermaritzburg, whither Lord Chelmsford proceeded direct to telegraph home for reinforcements, and to make arrangements for a fresh advance on their arrival.

Mr Dunne remained in South Africa, where he was stationed in the Transvaal. When the Boer uprising began in 1880, he was again involved in a siege, this time by Boer commando units at the garrison town of Potchefstroom, a flashpoint of discontent. The 200 defenders, including women and children, had to survive behind a makeshift perimeter in an area about 30 paces square, their only protection against the elements being a few bell tents. Commissary Dunne sat on the parapet each Sunday reading the Roman Catholic service to the people of that faith. They held out under constant fire for three months until sickness and starvation forced them into dignified surrender in March 1881.

The ordeal affected Dunne's health and on returning to Natal he was nursed back to strength by friends, including Winifred, the daughter of John Bird, CMG, Treasurer of Natal, and they became engaged. After five years of active service in South Africa, Walter returned to England in April 1882, to be stationed at Aldershot. On his return to England in 1885 he and Winifred were married at Bath on 23 July of that year.

Just four months later Dunne sailed for active service in north-east Africa, taking part in the decisive victory over Egyptian forces at Tel-el-Kebir on 13 September 1882. He returned to England, and in February 1885 he was posted back to north Africa to join the British forces station at the Red Sea port of Saukin in the Sudan, and he was present during the British advance against Dervish warriors at Hasheen on 19 March 1885.

Dunne was transferred as a lieutenant colonel to the Army Service Corps on the establishment of that unit in 1888, serving on Mauritius, 1887–9, and he was DAAG of the Southern District, 1892–5. He was appointed Commander of the Bath for distinguished service in 1896, and was promoted colonel in 1897, becoming HAAG of the North-East District at York, a position he held until 1899. From January 1900 he was Assistant Quartermaster General at Army Headquarters in Aldershot, representing the War Office on the Army Medical Advisory Board. He was considered for promotion to major general in 1905, and in the same year he was appointed Director of Supplies and Transport at Gibraltar, from where he retired from military service in February 1908.

Dunne was active in various public undertakings. While stationed at York he was president of the York Catholic Association, and he was a supporter of the Catholic Soldiers' Club in London. He sent a wreath to the funeral of Colonel Chard in 1897 on behalf of the Association.

Colonel Dunne died at the English Convent Home in Rome, on 2 July 1908, aged 55, and he was buried at the Verano Cemetery at Lazio in Rome. The letter he wrote from Rorke's Drift was sold at auction in 2014, and is now in the Museum of the Royal Welsh at Brecon.

The Revd George Smith

George Smith was born at Docking, Norfolk, on 8 January 1845, the son of William and Frances Smith, and he was at college in Canterbury before going to South Africa as a lay missionary in 1870. He was ordained deacon in 1871 and priest in 1872. He was a tall man with a great red beard, and he was appointed to St John's Parish, based at the Estcourt Mission in Natal, where he became well-known as a hard-working man. He served as a volunteer during the Langalibalele Rebellion, and in 1878 he was appointed acting chaplain to the volunteers. It was in this capacity that he took part in the Zulu War.

On 22 January 1879, he was going about his duties at Rorke's Drift when it was reported that there was possible action at Isandlwana, so, in the company of Surgeon Reynolds and the Revd Witt, he decided to go on a reconnaissance to the top of Oscarberg Hill to try to get a clearer view of what was happening. They saw a number of colonials returning from enemy territory on the Zululand side of the river, so Surgeon Reynolds went back to the mission station in case they required medical assistance. The two clerics watched a large number of natives moving slowly up from the Natal bank of the river at such a leisurely pace that they believed them to be colonial troops. However, the increasing force was within rifle range when they saw that the two men on horseback leading them were not Europeans, but had black faces. When they realised that the oncoming mass was a Zulu *impi*, they climbed hastily back down the hill to report the danger to the officers.

During the ferocious Zulu onslaughts the Revd Smith spent his time moving along the barricade, apparently with the aid of a native servant, handing out cartridges from his hat, as well as reproving the curses of the hard-fighting soldiers and stopping to give spiritual consolation to the wounded.

Colonel Harford was with the column that arrived at Rorke's Drift on the morning of 23 January, and stated: 'The part which the Reverend Smith played in the defence, and the splendid example he set throughout that terrible night, ought to have earned for him the VC. I noticed that directly Mr Smith showed himself, he received an ovation from the men.'

The Revd Smith served throughout the Zulu War, his deeds and reputation earning him the nickname 'Ammunition Smith', and he was in the British square at Ulundi to witness the final defeat of the Zulus. He visited the devastated battlefield at Isandlwana, and said many prayers for the soldiers who had been massacred, and held a short service at the bodies of Lieutenants Coghill and Melvill, who had lost their lives while trying to save the queen's colour of their battalion from falling into enemy hands, and would many years later be awarded the Victoria Cross. In November 1879, he was one of several clergymen who visited the site, with a view to establishing a mission church in remembrance of the dead. This became the Zululand Memorial Church.

A correspondent of one of the Natal papers relates the following story of the Revd G. Smith, a hero of Rorke's Drift:

Mr. Smith, it is well known, without taking any part in the actual fight, administered very efficient aid in serving out ammunition.

One of the Soldiers was in high spirits at the prospect of a brush with the enemy.

'Hand me some cartridges,' he said, with a frightful oath, 'and let us give the beggars —— as they are coming.' Mr. Smith handed over some cartridges, and said in a solemn voice, 'There they are, my man; don't swear at the enemy, but fire low!'

'T.2' of *Truth* relates the same anecdote, which he heard from one of the officers recently returned from Africa. His report of the action at Rorke's Drift dated 3 February 1879 was published in the *Royal Army Chaplains' Department Journal* for July 1936:

About three o'clock p.m. or shortly after, several mounted men arrived from Isandlwana and reported the terrible disaster which had occurred. Lieutenant Bromhead, commanding the company (B) of the 2nd/24th Regiment, at once struck his camp and sent down for Lieutenant Chard R.E. (who was engaged with some half dozen men at the ponts on the river) to come up and direct the preparations for defence, as in the absence of Major Spalding the command of the post devolved upon him.

The windows and doors of the hospital were blocked up with mattresses, etc., and loopholes made through the walls both of the hospital and the storehouse. A wall of mealies and other grain bags was made, enclosing the front of the hospital and running along the ledge of the rocky terrace to the stone wall of the kraal, which has been described as coming from the far end of the storehouse at right angles to the front of that building, down to the edge of these rocks.

A praiseworthy effort was made to remove the worst cases in hospital to a place of safety. Two wagons were brought up after some delay, and the patients were being brought out when it was feared that the Zulus were so close upon us that any attempt to take them away would only result in their falling into enemy hands.

So the two wagons were at once utilised to form part of the defensive wall connecting the right hand front corner of the storehouse with the left hand back corner of the hospital, also used as barricades underneath and upon the wagons. A barricade filling up the small space between the left front corner of the storehouse and the stone wall of the kraal before referred to. And the blocking up of the gates of the kraal itself, made the outer defence works complete. The men worked with a will and were much encouraged by the unremitting exertions of both the military officers, the medical officer [Reynolds] and Assistant Commissary Dalton, all of whom not merely directed but engaged most energetically in the construction of the barricades. The water cart, in the mean-time, had been hastily filled and brought within the enclosure.

The pontmen Daniells and Sergeant Millne (3rd Buffs) offered to moor the ponts in the middle of the stream and defend them from their decks with a few men. But our defensive force was too small for any to be spared, and these men subsequently did good service within the fort.

About 4:30 p.m. the Zulus came in sight round the right hand end of the large hill in our rear. Only about twenty at first appeared advancing in open order. Their numbers were speedily augmented and their line extended quite across the neck of land from hill to hill. A great number of Dongas in their line of approach, a stream with steep banks, the garden with all its trees and surroundings, gave them great facilities for getting near to us unseen. The garden must have been occupied, for one unfortunate Contingent Corporal, whose heart must have failed him when he saw the enemy and heard the firing, got over the parapet and tried to make his escape on foot, but a bullet from the garden struck him, and he fell dead within a hundred and fifty yards of our front wall.

An officer of the same Corps, who had charge of the three hundred and fifty natives before referred to, was more fortunate; being mounted, he made good his escape and 'lives to fight another day'.

But the enemy are upon us now and are pouring over the right shoulder of the hill in a dense mass, and on they come, making straight for the connecting wall between the storehouse and the hospital, and then make a desperate attempt to scale the barricade in front of that building, but here too, they are repulsed, and they disperse and find cover amongst the bushes and behind the stone wall below the terrace. The others have found shelter amongst numerous banks, ditches and bushes, and behind a square Kaffir house and large brick ovens, all at the rear of our storehouse. One of the mounted chiefs was shot by private Dunbar (2nd/24th), who also killed eight of the enemy with as many consecutive shots as they came round the ledge of the hill. As fresh bodies of Zulus arrive, they take possession of the elevated ledge of rocks overlooking our buildings and barricades at the back, and all the caves and crevices are quickly filled, and from these the enemy pour down a continuous fire upon us.

A whisper passes around amongst the men: 'Poor old King Cole is killed!' He was at the front wall: a bullet passed through his head, and then struck the next man upon the bridge of the nose, but the latter was not seriously hurt. Mr. Dalton who is a tall man, was continually going along the barricades, fearlessly exposing himself and cheering the men, and using his own rifle most effectively. A Zulu ran up near the barricade. Mr. Dalton called out 'Pot that fellow' and himself aimed over the parapet at another, when his rifle dropped and he turned round, quite pale, and said that he had been shot. The doctor was by his side at once, and found that a bullet had passed quite through above the right shoulder. Unable any longer to use his rifle (although he did not cease to direct the fire of the men who were near him) he handed it to Mr Byrne, who used it as well.

Presently, Corporal C Scammel (Natal Native Contingent), who was near Mr Byrne, was shot through the shoulder and back. He crawled a short distance and handed the remainder of his cartridges to Lieutenant Chard, and then expressed the desire for a drink of water. Byrne at once fetched it, but whilst giving it to him, he was shot through the head and fell dead instantly.

The garden and the road – having the stone wall and thick belt of bush as a screen from the fire of our defences – were now occupied by a large force of the enemy, they rushed up to the front barricade, and soon occupied one side, whilst we held the other; they seized hold of the bayonets of our men and in two instances succeeded in wresting them off the rifles, but the two bold perpetrators were instantly shot. One fellow fired at Corporal Schiess of the Natal Native Contingent (a Swiss by birth and a hospital patient), the charge blowing his hat off. He instantly jumped upon the parapet and bayoneted the man, regained his place, and shot another, and then, repeating his former exploit, climbed upon the sacks and bayoneted a third. A bullet struck him on the instep early in the fight, but he would not allow that his wound was sufficient reason for leaving his post, yet he has suffered most acutely from it since.

Our men at the front wall had the enemy hand-to-hand and were besides being fired upon very heavily from the sacks and caves above us in our rear. Five of our men were here shot dead in a very short space of time, so at 6 p.m. the order was given for them to retire to our entrenchment of biscuit boxes, from which such a heavy fire was sent along the front of the hospital that, although scores of Zulus jumped over the mealie bags to get into the building, nearly every man perished in that fatal leap; but they rushed to their death like demons, yelling out their war cry of 'Usuto! Usuto!' Shortly after, they succeeded in setting the roof of the hospital on fire at its further end. As long as we held the front wall, the Zulus failed in their repeated attempts to get into the far end room of the hospital, Lieutenant Bromhead having several times driven them back with a bayonet charge.

When we had retired to the entrenchment and the hospital had been set on fire, a terrible struggle awaited the brave fellows who were defending it from within. Private Joseph Williams fired from a small window at the far end of the hospital. Next morning fourteen warriors were found dead beneath it, besides others along his line of fire. When their ammunition was expended, he and his companions kept the door with their bayonets, but an entrance was subsequently forced and, he, poor fellow was seized by the hands, dragged out and killed before the eyes of the others. His surviving companions were Private John Williams and two patients. Whilst the Zulus were dragging out their late brave comrade, they succeeded in making a hole in the partition with an axe and got into another room, where they were joined by Private Henry Hook, and he and Williams – turn about, one keeping off the enemy, the other working – succeeded in cutting holes into the next adjoining rooms. One poor fellow (Jenkins), venturing through one of these was also seized and dragged away, but the others escaped through the window looking into the enclosure towards the storehouse and running the gauntlet of the enemy's fire, most of them got safely within the retrenchment. Trooper Hunter (Natal Native Contingent) a very tall young man who was a patient in the hospital, was not so fortunate, but fell before he could reach the goal.

In another ward, Privates William Jones and Robert Jones defended their post until six of the seven patients in it had been removed. The seventh, Sergeant Maxfield, who was ill with fever and delirious. Private Robert Jones went back to try to carry him out, but the room was full of Zulus and the poor fellow was dead. The native of Umlunga's tribe, who had been shot through the thigh at Sihayo's kraal was lying unable to move. He said that he was not afraid of the Zulus but wanted a gun. When the end room in which he lay was forced, Private Hooke heard the Zulus talking with him; next day his charred remains were found amongst the ruins.

Corporal Mayer (Natal Native Contingent), who had been wounded under the knee with an assegai at Sihayo's kraal, Bombadier Lewis (R.A.), whose leg and thigh were much swollen from a wagon accident, and trooper R.S. Green (N.M.P.) also a patient, all got out of the little end window within the enclosure. The window being high up, and the Zulus already within the room behind them, each man had a fall in escaping and then had to crawl (for none of them could walk) through the enemy's fire inside the entrenchment. Whilst doing this, Green was struck in the thigh with a spent bullet. Some escaped from the front of the hospital and ran round to the right to the retrenchment, but two of the three were assegaid as they attempted it.

Whilst the hospital was being thus gallantly defended, Lieutenant Chard and Assistant Commissary Dalton, with two or three men, succeeded in converting the two large pyramids of sacks of mealies into an oblong and lofty redoubt, and, under heavy fire, blocking up the intervening space between the two with sacks from the top of each, leaving a hollow in the centre for the security of the wounded and giving another admirable and elevated line of fire all round. About this time the men were obliged to fall back from the outer middle, and then to the inner wall of the kraal forming our left defence.

The Zulus do not appear to have thrown their assegais at all, using them solely for stabbing purposes.

Corporal William Allan and Private Fred Hitch behaved splendidly. They were badly wounded early in the morning but, incapacitated from firing themselves, never ceased going round and serving out ammunition from the reserve to the fighting men.

The light from the burning hospital was of the greatest service to our men, lighting up the scene for hundreds of yards around, but before 10pm it had burned itself out. The rushes and heavy fire of the enemy did not slacken till past midnight, and from that time until daylight a desultory fire was kept up by them from the caves above us in our rear and from the bush and garden in front.

At last daylight dawned, and the enemy retired round the shoulder of the hill by which they had approached. Whilst some remained at their posts others of our men were sent out to patrol and returned with about one hundred rifles and guns and some four hundred assegais left by the enemy on the field, and round our walls, and especially in front of the hospital, the dead Zulus lay piled up in heaps. About three hundred and fifty were subsequently buried by us. They must have carried off nearly all their wounded with them.

Whilst all behaved so gallantly, it is hardly possible to notice other exceptional instances, although all their comrades bore testimony to such in the conduct of Colour-Sergeant Bourne (2nd/24th Regiment), Sergeant Williams (2nd/24th), and Privates McMahon (A.H.C.) and Roy (1st/24th).

It was certainly of the utmost strategical importance that this place should not be taken. Perhaps the safety of the remainder of the Column, and of this part of the Colony, depended on it.

After a period at home, the Revd Smith served under Sir Garnet Wolseley in his north-east Africa campaigns from 1882 to 1887. He took part in the Battle of Tel-el-Kebir in Egypt on 13 September 1882, and in the Battle of El Teb in the Sudan on 29 February 1884, when the British defeated a mass army of fanatical Dervish warriors. For his service he received the Queen's Medal for Egypt and the Khedive's Bronze Star.

He was 2nd class chaplain at various military stations at home and abroad from 1887 until gaining an appointment as 1st class chaplain on 16 February 1900, including a spell of duty as chaplain at Fulwood Garrison Church in Preston, from about 1897 to 1903. He retired in 1905.

It would seem the Revd Smith was a well-known character, with many friends, who knew him as 'Daddy Smith', because of his great bushy beard. He was visited in Preston by Colonel Chard, and the Revd Smith went to see Chard in Somerset. Both meetings were during the last months of Chard's life, and his former comrade may have wanted his spiritual consolation.

The Revd Smith chose to take a room at the Sumners Hotel, across the road from the barrack gates, where the manager remembered him as being very popular in the hotel, and staff made sure their 'favourite guest' was always looked after. It has been said that the famous painting of the defence of Rorke's Drift by Alphonse de Neuville once hung in the hotel, which was of particular interest because the names of several of the defenders had been written in by George Smith himself. On his retirement in 1905 he continued to reside at the hotel, although he visited South Africa and Australia frequently and was away a considerable time.

As a note of interest, in 1910 some ghostly figures were said to have been seen in the barracks, and the Revd Smith became so interested in the matter that he said prayers in the rooms and even got in touch with the Psychical Society in London.

In 1918 the Revd Smith became ill with bronchial trouble, and after being confined to his hotel room for six months, he died during the night of 26/27 November 1918, aged 63. His death was only a few days after the armistice which ended the First World War, so his funeral was a small military parade, and among the floral tributes was one from the officers of the South Wales Borderers – 'In Memory of Rorke's Drift'. He was buried in the New Hall Lane Cemetery, and a monument was erected in memory of one of the heroes of Rorke's Drift – 'Who was a brave and modest Christian gentleman'.

In July 2009, Bible and ammunition box representations were placed among a floral tribute to the Revd George Smith at Miller Park in Preston, along with helmets commemorating the eleven VCs gained in the battle.

Corporal Frederich Schiess VC

Ferdinand Christian Schiess, usually known as Frederich, was born at Bergedorf, Canton Berne, Switzerland, on 7 April 1856, the son of Niclaus Schiess, who worked as a stone cutter, and his wife Anna (formerly Ruchti). His father was known locally as 'Bernese Schiess'. Their parents having died while they were young, Ferdinand, and his sister, Anna Marie, were brought up at the Municipal Orphanage at Herisau in Canton Apenzell.

'Friederich', as he became known, left the orphanage at the age of 15. The Franco-Prussian War began in 1870, so he joined General Bourbaki's French Legions. In 1877 he boarded the *Adele* at Hamburg bound for South Africa, arriving at East London on 21 August 1877. He was a strong, stocky young man, and was able to find work as a general labourer.

Schiess served with distinction as a volunteer in the Cape Frontier War, and when colonial forces were being mustered for the campaign against the Zulus, Colonel Anthony Durnford of the Royal Engineers appointed him a corporal in the 2nd Battalion, 3rd Regiment, Natal Native Contingent, under Commandant Robert Lonsdale.

Commandant George Hamilton-Browne, an Irish colonial adventurer of the 3rd Natal Native Contingent, which was Schiess' unit, stated: '[They were] a motley crowd, a few of them old soldiers and ex-clerks, the majority of them runaway sailors, ex-navvies, and East London boatmen. They were an awfully tough crowd, but they looked a hard-fighting lot and though their language was strong, and they were evidently very rough, they looked very ready . . .' This unit was intended to be used as scouts for the advancing British army. On the outbreak of hostilities there had been no time to train the men in the use of firearms, and due to loyalty fears expressed by some Natal colonists no guns were issued to the ordinary natives. Only the African officers and ten NCOs from each company received Enfield percussion rifles. All other ranks were required to carry their traditional weapons of spears and shields. They had no uniform and remained dressed in their traditional native attire. The only item which distinguished them from Zulu warriors was a red rag, known as a pugree, wrapped around their foreheads.

Lieutenant Chard reported:

> Corporal Schiess, Natal Native Contingent, who was a patient in the Hospital with a wound in the foot, which caused him great pain, behaved with the greatest coolness and gallantry throughout the attack, and at this time [the retreat to the biscuit boxes] creeping out a short distance along the wall we had abandoned, and slowly raised himself, to get a shot at some of the enemy who had been particularly annoying, his hat was blown off by a shot from a Zulu on the other side of the wall. He immediately jumped up, bayoneted the Zulu, and shot a second, and bayoneted a third who came to their assistance, and then returned to his place.

The Revd Smith stated:

> One fellow fired at Corporal Schiess of the Natal Native Contingent, the charge blowing his hat off. He instantly jumped upon the parapet and bayonetted the man, regained his place and shot another, and then, repeating his former exploit, climbed upon the sacks and bayonetted a third. A bullet struck him on the instep early in the fight, but he would not allow that his wound was sufficient reason for leaving his post, yet he has suffered most acutely from it since.

Private Hitch noted:

> There was a certain space of about nine yards where the barricade was uncompleted. It was, of course, the weakest link in the chain,

and the Zulus were not long in discovering this fact. In this position eight of us, Bromhead, Nichols (Nicholson) Fagan, Cole, Dalton, Schiess, Williams and myself – made a stand, and it was here, I think, that the hardest work was done.

Henry Harford stated: 'Some of the men of the 24th told me that he fought like a tiger. At one time, when some Zulus actually managed to clutch hold of his bayonet, he got it out of their hands, and springing over the parapet bayoneted some six or seven straight away.'

Captain William Penn-Symons recorded: 'Corporal Schiess, they said, "fought like a tiger." He could not restrain himself, but more than once dashed over the barricade, bayoneted a Zulu, and got back in again.'

Surgeon Reynolds was a first-hand witness to the fighting at the compound in front of the hospital veranda when it was at its fiercest, and later stated: 'It would be difficult to pick out the heroes from our garrison, but Corporal Schiess of the Natal Native Contingent (a Swede by birth) came under my notice as the most deserving of praise and recommendation.'

Eventually, Major Chard was asked to provide a statement concerning Schiess' bravery, which he did in a letter dated 22 October 1879. The letter formed the basis of his Victoria Cross citation:

I have the honour in accordance with instructions from the Field Marshal, Commander-in-Chief, to forward for your approval this my application for the decoration of the Victoria Cross on behalf of Corporal Schiess, late Natal Native Contingent, in recognition of his gallant conduct on 22nd–23rd Jany last at Rorke's Drift.

This man, who had been wounded in the attack on Sihayo's Kraal a few days before, was a patient at Rorke's Drift on the 22nd Jany 1879, and in spite of his wound (in the foot) he particularly attracted my notice by his activity and devoted gallantry throughout the defence. Amongst many acts of his I may mention one I myself witnessed – after we had retired to our inner line of defence. The Zulus occupied the wall of mealie bags we had abandoned. Corporal Schiess without any order, crept out along this wall a few feet, to dislodge one in particular of the enemy who was shooting better than usual; on his raising himself to get a shot, the Zulu who was close to him on the other side of the wall, fired knocking off his hat. Cpl Schiess immediately jumped on the wall and bayoneted the Zulu, and in less time than I take to write it, shot a second and bayoneted a third, and then came back to the cover of the inner defence again.

Corporal Schiess became the first man serving with South African forces under British command to be awarded the Victoria Cross, when his VC citation, the last for the defence of Rorke's Drift, appeared in the *London Gazette* of 29 November 1879:

> For conspicuous gallantry in the defence of Rorke's Drift post on the night of 22 January 1879, when, in spite of his having been wounded in the foot a few days previously, greatly distinguished himself when the Garrison were repulsing, with the bayonet, a series of desperate assaults made by the Zulus, and displayed great activity and devoted gallantry throughout the defence.

Schiess suffered most acutely from his wounded foot after the defence, but he served throughout the Zulu War, and he was with the British square at Ulundi on 4 July 1879, to witness the final defeat of the Zulu army. For his services in the campaign he also received the South Africa Medal with *1877–8–9* clasp.

Schiess received his Victoria Cross from Sir Garnet Wolseley at a special parade of the troops in garrison in Pietermaritzburg, on 3 February 1880.

When the Natal Native Contingent was disbanded, Schiess joined C Troop of Baker's Horse on 24 January 1880, for service in the Basuto Gun War, and he discharged on 12 April 1881. When he left Baker's Horse he went back to civilian life and gained employment in the telegraph office at Durban.

Schiess then went to Allahabad in India, where he gained employment in a jeweller's shop and was a volunteer serving with the East Indian Railway. A report in the 'Military Intelligence' column concerning the Homeward Mail from the East dated 10 January 1884, states:

> The Duke of Connaught at Allahabad – On arrival of the special train at Allahabad on 1 December with their Royal Highnesses the Duke and Duchess of Connaught (after being presented to the nobilities of the Station), the Duke proceeded to inspect the guard of honour composed of a very strong muster of the E I R Volunteers (East Indian Railway). Glancing over the men his quick eye detected one little fellow, Volunteer F C Schiess VC, in the ranks, on whose breast hung the Victoria Cross. With that readiness and good feeling

so general with the members of the Royal Family, he at once stepped up to him and kindly with interest enquired where and how had he earned the distinguished decoration. The gallant little fellow answered: 'At Rorke's Drift in South Africa,' such being actually the case. Unfortunately, poor Schiess, having his rifle at the present, was unable to grasp the ready hand extended to him by the Duke.

By the latter months of 1884 Schiess was unemployed and had become destitute. He spent most of his time writing neat and eligible letters desperately trying to gain some kind of government work in Natal, the colony he had fought so bravely to defend. Towards the end of the year he was found in tragic circumstances on the streets of Cape Town suffering from the effects of exposure to the elements and malnutrition. The Royal Navy offered him a trip to England on the *Serapis*, the cost of his rations being paid for by a public fund. Sadly, his health deteriorated and he died on board ship off the coast of Angola, West Africa. He was only 28 years old. The ship's log recorded: 'Sunday, 14 December 1884, 10:20am. Departed this life Mr F C Schiess VC, aged 28. 5:10pm. Stopped. Committed to the deep the remains of the late Mr Schiess VC. 5:15pm Proceeded. He was buried about 1,376 kilometres north-east of St Helena in the South Atlantic Ocean. (Latitude 13.00 south - Longitude 07.24 west).'

Schiess' Victoria Cross is believed to have been found on his person, and according to the National Army Museum in London it arrived there from the Ministry of Defence in about 1958. They also suggested that it would probably have been taken to the predecessors of the Ministry of Defence after being taken from him. The whereabouts of his South Africa Medal are not known. He may well have sold it, or even thrown it away because of its association with the country he had helped to defend and could not offer him work of any kind. The fact that he held on to his Victoria Cross when in such desperate circumstances is another indication of his gallantry. For that he received a 5-minute burial service.

There is a bronze plaque dedicated to Schiess at the Rorke's Drift Memorial Museum in Natal. A plaque is dedicated to him at the home of the VC Trust at Ashworth Barracks in Doncaster. He is one of the men awarded the Victoria Cross who has no known grave and is commemorated on a plaque at the Union Jack Club in London.

A strange note appears at the back of a page in Captain Penn-Symons' report held at the Brecon Museum, which states: 'I saw Corp Schiess in Nov 1891, in Allahabad, India. He had been working in a jeweller's shop, and was just going to Australia. Being afraid to lose his Victoria

Cross, he has sent it on ahead by registered post to his destination.' However, it would seem that Penn-Symons wrote a hurried note and the date should have been November 1883; Penn-Symons was in India in 1883, and Schiess never went to Australia.

The 'Personalia' column in the *Natal Witness* for 2 November 1899 states:

> Cpl Schiess, Natal Native Forces, was at Rorke's Drift in January 1879.
>
> P G Crow asks 'Where is he now?'
>
> A response two days later says: 'A correspondent writes that he remembers reading years ago both in the *Witness* and the *Advertiser* of Corporal Schiess (of Rorke's Drift fame) dying in India destitute.

A further reply two days afterwards says:

> A correspondent writes: I see information is asked on the whereabouts of the late Corporal Schiess. Immediately after the Zulu War he joined the Telegraph Service as a linesman and was stationed at Durban. He left after being decorated with the VC. He went through the Basuto War later, and returned to Durban invalided and destitute. He was (if memory serves me correctly) sent to England in one of HM transports and died either at Netley or Haslar Hospital. The Hon. Mr Jameson was, I think, the means of his being sent home. I have a good photo given me by Schiess. Should anyone care for a copy I will get it re-taken.

Research Sources by Chapter

Introduction

Bancroft, James W., *Rorke's Drift: The Zulu War, 1879*, 1988
Bancroft, James W., *The Zulu War VCs: Victoria Crosses of the Anglo-Zulu War, 1879*, 2018
Chard, Lieutenant John, his official report dated 25 January 1879, TNA, WO 32/7737
London Gazette, 19 February 1806, 2 May, 17 June, 18 November and 2 December 1879
Morris, Donald, 'War on the Veld', *British Empire Magazine*, 1971

Chapter 1

Ancestry.com
Annual Biography and Obituary for the Year 1823
Biographical History of Gonville and Caius College, 1349–1897 (4 vols), 1897
Bracken, Charles William, *A History of Plymouth and Her Neighbours*, 1931
Bromhead, Lieutenant Colonel, Sir Benjamin Denis, 5th Baronet
Bromhead, David de Gonville
Burke's Peerage
census returns, 1841–1921
Daily Telegraph, 7 March 1879, letter from the Revd Henry Calverley
Devon Archives and Local Studies Service
FamilySearch
Guide to the Church of St Michael in Othery
History of St George's Lodge Number 112, Exeter Freemasons
Journal of the Society for Army Historical Research, 'The "Royal Military Academy" of Lewis Lochee', Autumn 1992
Lincolnshire Archives

Lincolnshire Local Studies at Lincoln Central Library
London Gazette, 19 February 1806
New Oxford Dictionary of National Biography, 2004
Plymouth Historical Society
Plymouth Register Office
Plymouth and West Devon Record Office
Pring, James Hurley, *A Memoir of Thomas Chard DD, Suffragan Bishop, and the Last Abbot of Forde Abbey*, 1864
Regimental Museum of the Royal Welsh
Reid, Stuart, *Battles of the Scottish Lowlands*, 2004
St Budeaux church, Plymouth, monumental inscriptions
St Germain's Church, Thurlby, monumental inscriptions
St Michael's Church, Othery, monumental inscriptions
Somerset Archives and Local Studies
Tiverton Gazette and East Devon Herald, 7 October 1879
Western Morning News
Woodham-Smith, Cecil and Woodham, Charles, *The Great Hunger, Ireland 1845–1849*, 1962

Chapter 2

Ancestry.com
Bancroft, James W., *Victoria Crosses of the Crimean War: The Men Behind the Medals*, 2017
Bromhead, Lieutenant Colonel, Sir Benjamin Denis, 5th Baronet, letters
Bromhead, David de Gonville
Burke's Peerage
Cannon, Richard, *Historical Records of the 7th or Royal Fusiliers. Now known as the Royal Fusiliers (City of London) Regiment, 1685–1903*, 1903
census returns, 1841–1921
Daily Telegraph, 7 March 1879, letter from the Revd Henry Calverley
Devon Archives and Local Studies Service
FamilySearch
FIBIS (Families in British India Society)
King's Own Royal Regiment Museum at Lancaster
Life magazine, 11 October 1879
Lincolnshire Archives
Lincolnshire Local Studies at Lincoln Central Library
Magnus Church of England Academy History
'Newark Magnus'
New Oxford Dictionary of National Biography, 2004

Plymouth Historical Society
Plymouth Register Office
Plymouth and West Devon Record Office
Regimental Museum of the Royal Welsh
St Budeaux church, Plymouth, monumental inscriptions
St Germain's Church, Thurlby, monumental inscriptions
St Michael's Church, Othery, monumental inscriptions
Wimbledon Society

Chapter 3

Bancroft, James W., *Peril in Paradise: The Andaman Islands Victoria Crosses*, 2017
Bancroft, James W., *The Zulu War VCs: Victoria Crosses of the Anglo-Zulu War, 1879*, 2018
FIBIS (Families in British India Society)
Hartlepool Mail, 26 February 1879
Hicks, Jim, 'White Man's Grave', *British Empire Magazine*, 1971
History of St George's Lodge Number 112, Exeter Freemasons
Paton, G., Glennie, F., Penn-Symons, W., *Historical Records of the 24th Regiment*, 1892
Porter, Whitworth and Watson, Charles Moore, *History of the Corps of Royal Engineers*, 1889
TNA, WO 76/233/6, WO 76/235/9

Chapter 4

Bancroft, James W., *The Zulu War VCs: Victoria Crosses of the Anglo-Zulu War, 1879*, 2018
Bennett, Lieutenant Colonel Ian H.W., *Rorke's Drift: The Story of the Commissaries (Two Parts)*, 1978
Cantlie, Lieutenant General, Sir Neil, *A History of the Army Medical Department*, 1974
Coghill VC, Lieutenant Neville Josiah Aylmer, diary held at the National Army Museum
Crealock, Major John North, *The Frontier War Journal of Major John Crealock*, 1878
Dunne, Commissary Walter Alphonsus, 'Reminiscences of Campaigning in South Africa, 1877–81' (Third Chapter), *Journal of the Army Service Corps*, February 1892

Gardner, Captain Alan, statement written from the 14th Hussars Camp at Rorke's Drift on 26 January 1879

Jackson, F.W. David, *Hill of the Sphinx: The Battle of Isandlwana*, 2004

Laband, John, *Fight Us in the Open: The Anglo-Zulu War Through Zulu Eyes*, 1985

Lugg, Harry Camp, *A Natal Family Looks Back*, 1970, including a letter from Harry Lugg published in the *North Devon Herald Supplement*, 24 April 1879

Lytton, David, 'The Struggle for the Cape', *British Empire Magazine*, 1971

MacKinnon, J.P. and Shadbolt, S.H., *The South African Campaign of 1879*, 1880

Maxwell, Lieutenant John, 2nd/3rd NNC, 'Reminiscences of the Zulu War', in the Christmas 1879 number of the *Natal Witness*

Morris, Donald, 'War on the Veld', *British Empire Magazine*, 1971

Paton, G., Glennie, F., Penn-Symons, W., *Historical Records of the 24th Regiment*, 1892

Smith-Dorrien, General Horace, *Memories of Forty-Eight Years Service*, 1925

South Wales Borderers publication, *Historical Records of the 2nd Battalion, 24th Regiment for the Campaign in South Africa, 1877–78–79, Embracing the Kaffir and Zulu Wars*, 1882

Stafford, Captain Walter H., *Recollections of the Battle of Isandlwana*, January 1938

Sydney Daily Telegraph, 16 December 1907, 'Rorke's Drift and Majuba: Reminiscences of Mr James Page'

TNA, War Office papers, including *The Narrative of the Field Operations Connected with the Zulu War of 1879*, 1881

Tulloch, Major General Alexander Bruce, *Recollections of Forty Years' Service*, 1903

Wassall, Samuel, 'The Last Stand of the 24th at Isandula', *London Magazine*, 31/38

Wood VC, General Sir Evelyn *From Midshipman to Field-Marshal*, 1906

Chapter 5

Bancroft, James W., *The Defenders of Rorke's Drift*, forthcoming 2022

Bancroft, James W., *Rorke's Drift: The Zulu War, 1879*, 1988

Bancroft, James W., *The Zulu War VCs: Victoria Crosses of the Anglo-Zulu War, 1879*, 2018

Baynham-Jones, Alun, and Stevenson, Lee, *Rorke's Drift – By Those Who Were There*, 2004

Bennett, Lieutenant Colonel Ian H.W., *Rorke's Drift: The Story of the Commissaries (Two Parts)*, 1978

Bonhams auctioneer catalogue for 17 December 2020

Cambrian Newspaper in Swansea, 13 June 1879; this publication re-produced interviews of wounded soldiers when they returned to Netley Military Hospital from South Africa, including Rorke's Drift defenders Fred Hitch, John Lyons and John Waters

Chard, Lieutenant John, an account submitted to Her Majesty Queen Victoria at Windsor Castle, 21 February 1880, Royal Archives, Windsor

Chard, Lieutenant John, his official report dated 25 January 1879, TNA, WO 32/7737

Dunne, Lieutenant Colonel Walter Alphonsus, 'Reminiscences of Campaigning in South Africa, 1877–81' (Third Chapter), *Journal of the Army Service Corps*, February 1892

Hayes, Drummer Patrick, 'Survivor Recalls Epic of Rorke's Drift', *News of the World*, March 1939

Hitch, Private Frederick, eyewitness account held in the Regimental Archives of the South Wales Borderers at Brecon, and reproduced in Norman Holme, *The Silver Wreath*, 1979

Hook, Private Alfred Henry, his account published in *Strand Magazine*, June 1891

Hook, Private Alfred Henry, 'How They Held Rorke's Drift', *Royal Magazine*, February 1905

Lane, Edward 'Ted', private letter concerning his grandfather, Sergeant Henry Gallagher, and his part in the Defence of Rorke's Drift, 15 May 1994

The Listener, 30 December 1936, '"I Was There": Rorke's Drift, 1879 by Lieutenant-Colonel Frank Bourne'

London Gazette, 19 February 1806, 2 May, 17 June, 18 November and 2 December 1879

Lugg, Bryn, private letters dated 19 May 1990 and 29 July 1991

Lugg, Harry Camp, *A Natal Family Looks Back*, 1970, including a letter from Harry Lugg published in the *North Devon Herald Supplement*, 24 April 1879

Maxwell, Lieutenant John, 2nd/3rd NNC, 'Reminiscences of the Zulu War', in the Christmas 1879 number of the *Natal Witness*

Melbourne Argus, 21 April 1897, 'The Defence of Rorke's Drift by an Old Soldier'; the identity of this man is not certain but the details provided in the narrative suggest that it may have been Corporal

John Wilson of the Natal Native Contingent, or certainly someone who was more informed than most concerning the events at Rorke's Drift on 22 January 1879

Monmouth Free Press, 15 April 1879

Porter, Whitworth and Watson, Charles Moore, *History of the Corps of Royal Engineers*, 1889

Reynolds, Surgeon James Henry, account in the Appendix to the Report of the Army Medical Department, 1878

Savage, Private Edward, *Manchester Weekly Post*, 19 July 1879

Smith, Revd George, account dated 3 February 1879, published in the *Journal of the Royal Army Chaplains' Department*, July 1936

Smith-Dorrien, General Horace, *Memories of Forty-Eight Years Service*, 1925

Stevenson, Lee, 'The Noble Sapper on the Box: Charles Robson RE', *Royal Engineers Journal*, August 1995

Western Mail, 22 January 1929

Wood, Private Caleb, his account in the *Ilkeston Pioneer*, 26 December 1913

Chapter 6

Bancroft, James W., *The Zulu War VCs: Victoria Crosses of the Anglo-Zulu War, 1879*, 2018

Forbes, Archibald, letter to General Wolseley at Landman's Drift concerning the Battle of Ulundi, 5 July 1879

Harford, Colonel Henry, *The Zulu War Journal of Col. Henry Harford, CB*, ed. Daphne Child, 1978

Laband, John, *The Battle of Ulundi*, 1998

Prior, Melton, report on the Battle of Ulundi contributed to the *Times of Natal*, 26 August 1879

Record of Service Ledger for the 2nd/24th Regiment

Wood VC, General Sir Evelyn, *From Midshipman to Field-Marshal*, 1906

Chapter 7

Bancroft, James W., *The Chronological Roll of the Victoria Cross*, published privately

Bancroft, James W., *Victoria Crosses of the Crimean War: The Men Behind the Medals*, 2017

Bancroft, James W., *The Zulu War VCs: Victoria Crosses of the Anglo-Zulu War, 1879*, 2018

Bonhams auctioneer catalogue, 17 December 2020

Creagh VC, General Sir O'Moore and Humphris, Miss H.M., *The VC and DSO*, 1924

Lummis VC Files compiled on behalf of the Military Historical Society

Newark Advertiser, 12 March 1879

Porter, Whitworth and Watson, Charles Moore, *History of the Corps of Royal Engineers*, 1889

Stevenson, Lee, 'The Noble Sapper on the Box: Charles Robson RE', *Royal Engineers Journal*, August 1995

The Times, 18 October 1879

Tiverton Gazette and East Devon Herald, 7 October 1879

Truth periodical, 1891

Victoria Cross and George Cross Association

Wilkins, Philip A., *The History of the Victoria Cross*, 1904

World periodical, 18 February 1891

Chapter 8

Bancroft, James W., *Deeds of Valour: A Victorian Military and Naval History Trilogy*, 1994

Bancroft, James W., *The Zulu War VCs: Victoria Crosses of the Anglo-Zulu War, 1879*, 2018

Hicks, Jim, 'Enlarging the Jewel', *British Empire Magazine*, 1971

London Magazine, an account of the Burma campaign by Colour Sergeant Edward J. Owen of the Hampshire Regiment

Paton, G., Glennie, F., Penn-Symons, W., *Historical Records of the 24th Regiment*, 1892

Porter, Whitworth and Watson, Charles Moore, *History of the Corps of Royal Engineers*, 1889

Chapter 9

Ancestry.com

Bromhead, Lieutenant Colonel, Sir Benjamin Denis, 5th Baronet, letters

Burke's Peerage

Cannon, Richard, *Historical Records of the 7th or Royal Fusiliers. Now known as the Royal Fusiliers (City of London) Regiment, 1685–1903*, 1903

census returns, 1841–1921

Denbighshire Archives

Devon Archives and Local Studies Service
Daily Express, 11 January 1934
FamilySearch
Gardner, Brian, 'The Boer War', *British Empire Magazine*, 1971
Lincolnshire Archives
Lincolnshire Local Studies at Lincoln Central Library
Newark Advertiser, 18 February 1891
Plymouth Historical Society
Plymouth Register Office
Plymouth and West Devon Record Office
Ruthin Local History Society
St Peter and St Paul Church in North Curry, monumental inscriptions
TNA, WO 76/233/6, WO 76/235/9
Wales Online, 28 March 2013

Chapter 10

Bonhams auctioneer catalogue, 17 December 2020
Men of Harlech: Zulu War Centenary 1879–1979, 1979
Royal Engineers Journal, Special Centenary Edition for June 1979, 'The Defence of Rorke's Drift, 22 January 1879. The Commemoration of the Centenary'

Appendix I

Bromhead, Lieutenant Colonel, Sir Benjamin Denis, 5th Baronet
St Germain's Church, Thurlby, monumental inscriptions

Appendix III

Bancroft, James W., *The Defenders of Rorke's Drift*, forthcoming 2022
Bancroft, James W., *Rorke's Drift: The Zulu War, 1879*, 1988
Bancroft, James W., *The Zulu War VCs: Victoria Crosses of the Anglo-Zulu War, 1879*, 2018
Dunne, Commissary Walter Alphonsus, 'Reminiscences of Campaigning in South Africa, 1877–81', *Journal of the Army Service Corps*, February 1892
Lummis, William, *Padre George Smith of Rorke's Drift*, 1978
Natal Mercury, 24 January 1879

Reynolds, Surgeon James Henry, account in the Appendix to the Report of the Army Medical Department, 1878, Royal Army Medical Corps Museum at Aldershot

Smith, Revd George, account dated 3 February 1879, published in the *Journal of the Royal Army Chaplains' Department Journal*, July 1936, Royal Army Chaplains' Department Museum at Aldershot

Smith, Revd George, 'The Defence of Rorke's Drift by an Eyewitness', published in the *Natal Mercury*, 7 April 1879

Stevenson, Lee, 'The Noble Sapper on the Box: Charles Robson RE', *The Royal Engineers Journal*, August 1995

Stevenson, Lee, *The Rorke's Drift Doctor: James Henry Reynolds VC, and the Defence of Rorke's Drift, 22nd/23rd January 1879*, 2002

Bibliography and Main Research Sources

Ancestry.com

Annual Biography and Obituary for the Years 1821 to 1837 (21 vols)

Army and Navy Gazette, 1891

Atkinson, C.T., *The South Wales Borderers, 24ᵗʰ Foot, 1689–1937*, 1937

Attwood, Corporal Francis, six letters written while he was on active service in South Africa, from November 1878 to December 1879, including one dated 25 January 1879, giving his account of the action at Rorke's Drift

Bancroft, James W., *Deeds of Valour: A Victorian Military and Naval History Trilogy*, 1994

Bancroft, James W., *Peril in Paradise: The Andaman Islands Victoria Crosses*, 2017

Bancroft, James W., *Rorke's Drift: The Zulu War, 1879*, 1988

Bancroft, James W., *The Rorke's Drift Men*, 2010

Bancroft, James W., *Victoria Crosses of the Crimean War: The Men Behind the Medals*, 2017

Bancroft, James W., *The Zulu War VCs: Victoria Crosses of the Anglo-Zulu War, 1879*, 2018

Bancroft, James W., *The Assault on the Great Redan at Sebastopol: The Most Victoria Crosses for a Single Action*, 2022

Bannister, Lieutenant George Stanhope, letter to his father dated 27 January 1879, in the Regimental Archive of the South Wales Borderers in Brecon

Baynham-Jones, Alun and Stevenson, Lee, *Rorke's Drift – By Those Who Were There*, 2004

Bath Chronicle and Weekly Gazette, 9 December 1886 and 22 September 1910

Bennett, Lieutenant Colonel Ian H.W., *Rorke's Drift: The Story of the Commissaries (Two Parts)*, 1978

Biographical History of Gonville and Caius College, 1349–1897 (4 vols), 1897

Bonhams auctioneer catalogues (various)

Bracken, Charles William, *A History of Plymouth and Her Neighbours*, 1931

British Medical Journal, 1911 and 1932

British Army Muster and Pay Rolls held at TNA

Britten, James and Boulger, George Simonds, *A Biographical Index of British and Irish Botanists*, 1893

Bromhead, Lieutenant Colonel, Sir Benjamin Denis, 5th Baronet, letters

Bromhead, David de Gonville

Brown, Brigadier General W. Baker, *The History of the Corps of Royal Engineers*, 1952

Burke's Peerage

Cambrian Newspaper in Swansea, 13 June 1879; this publication re-produced interviews of the wounded soldiers when they returned to Netley Military Hospital from South Africa, including Rorke's Drift defenders Fred Hitch, John Lyons and John Waters

Cannon, Richard, *Historical Records of the 7th or Royal Fusiliers. Now known as the Royal Fusiliers (City of London) Regiment, 1685–1903*, 1903

Cantlie, Lieutenant General, Sir Neil, *A History of the Army Medical Department*, 1974

Cartlidge, Mrs Jill, private letters concerning John Chard dated 2 October 1999 and 26 January 2000

census returns, 1841–1921

Chard, Lieutenant John, an account submitted to Her Majesty Queen Victoria at Windsor Castle, 21 February 1880, Royal Archives, Windsor

Chard, Lieutenant John, his official report dated 25 January 1879, TNA, WO 32/7737

Coghill, Lieutenant Neville Josiah Aylmer, his diary held at the National Army Museum

Creagh VC, General, Sir O'Moore and Humphris, Miss H.M., *The VC and DSO*, 1924

Crealock, Major John North, *The Frontier War Journal of Major John Crealock*, 1878

Daily Express, 11 January 1934

Daily Telegraph, 7 March 1879, letter from the Revd Henry Calverley

Denbighshire Archives

Devon Archives and Local Studies Service

Dunne, Lieutenant Colonel Walter Alphonsus, 'Reminiscences of Campaigning in South Africa, 1877–81' (Third Chapter), February 1892

Dunning, Robert, *A History of the County of Somerset*, 2004

Durnford, Lieutenant Colonel E. (ed.), *A Soldier's Life and Work in South Africa, 1872 to 1879. A Memoir of the Late Colonel A W Durnford, Royal Engineers*, 1882

Emery, Frank, *The Red Soldier*, 1977

Evans, Gunner Abraham, letter in the *Free Press of Monmouthshire*, 18 April 1913

FamilySearch

FIBIS (Families in British India Society)

Forbes, Archibald, letter to General Wolseley at Landman's Drift concerning the Battle of Ulundi, 5 July 1879

Forbes, Archibald, 'A War Correspondent's Reminiscences', published in *Advance Australia Journal*, 26 January 1897

Gardner, Captain Alan, statement written from the 14th Hussars Camp at Rorke's Drift, 26 January 1879

Gardner, Brian, 'The Boer War', *British Empire Magazine*, 1971

Glover, Michael, *Rorke's Drift: A Victorian Epic*, 1975

Guardian, 5 March 1879

Guide to the Church of St Michael in Othery

Harford, Colonel Henry, *The Zulu War Journal of Col. Henry Harford, CB*, ed. Daphne Child, 1978

Hartlepool Mail, 26 February 1879

Hayes, Drummer Patrick, 'Survivor Recalls Epic of Rorke's Drift', *News of the World*, March 1939

Hicks, Jim, 'Enlarging the Jewel', *British Empire Magazine*, 1971

Hicks, Jim, 'White Man's Grave', *British Empire Magazine*, 1971

History of St George's Lodge Number 112, Exeter Freemasons

Hitch, Private Frederick, eyewitness account held in the Regimental Archives of the South Wales Borderers at Brecon, and reproduced in Norman Holme, *The Silver Wreath*, 1979

Holt, H.P., *The Mounted Police of Natal. With an introduction by Major-General Sir J G Dartnell KCB, the Founder of the Corps*, 1913

Hook, Private Alfred Henry, his account published in the *Strand Magazine*, June 1891

Hook, Private Alfred Henry, 'How They Held Rorke's Drift', *Royal Magazine*, February 1905

Ian Knight's Anglo-Zulu History Group

Illustrated London News, 22 November 1879 and 21 February 1891

Imperial War Museum in London

Jackson, F.W. David, *Hill of the Sphinx: The Battle of Isandlwana*, 2004

Journal of the Army Service Corps, February 1892

Journal of the Society for Army Historical Research

King's Own Royal Regiment Museum at Lancaster

Knight, Ian James, *Zulu Rising: The Epic Story of Isandlwana and Rorke's Drift*, 2010

Laband, John, *The Battle of Ulundi*, 1998

Laband, John, *The Eight Zulu Kings from Shaka to Goodwill Zwelithini*, 2018

Laband, John, *Fight Us in the Open: The Anglo-Zulu War Through Zulu Eyes*, 1985

Lane, Edward 'Ted', private letter concerning his grandfather, Sergeant Henry Gallagher, and his part in the defence of Rorke's Drift, 15 May 1994

Life magazine, 11 October 1879

Lincolnshire Family History Society

Lincolnshire Local Studies at Lincoln Central Library

The Listener, 30 December 1936, '"I Was There": Rorke's Drift, 1879 by Lieut-Colonel F Bourne'

London Gazette, 19 February 1806, 2 May, 17 June, 18 November and 2 December 1879

London Magazine, an account of the Burma campaign by Colour Sergeant Edward J. Owen of the Hampshire Regiment

Lugg, Bryn, private letters dated 19 May 1990 and 29 July 1991

Lugg, Harry Camp, *A Natal Family Looks Back*, 1970, including a letter from Harry Lugg published in the *North Devon Herald Supplement*, 24 April 1879

Lummis VC Files compiled on behalf of the Military Historical Society

Lummis, William, *Padre George Smith of Rorke's Drift*, 1978

Lyons, Corporal

Lytton, David, 'The Struggle for the Cape', *British Empire Magazine*, 1971

MacKinnon, J.P., and Shadbolt, S.H., *The South African Campaign of 1879*, 1880 Magnus Church of England Academy History

Manchester Evening Chronicle, 2 December 1905 and 9 February 1911

Maxwell, Lieutenant John, 2nd/3rd NNC, 'Reminiscences of the Zulu War', in the Christmas 1879 number of the *Natal Witness*

Melbourne Argus, 21 April 1897, 'The Defence of Rorke's Drift by an Old Soldier'; the identity of this man is not known but the details provided in the narrative suggest that it may have been Corporal John Wilson (John B. Welson) or someone who was extremely well-informed about the events at Rorke's Drift on 22 January 1879

Men of Harlech: Zulu War Centenary 1879–1979, 1979

Mitford, Bertram, *Through the Zulu Country*, 1983

Monmouth Free Press, 15 April 1879
Morris, Donald, 'War on the Veld', *British Empire Magazine*, 1971
Museum of Freemasonry
Natal Mercury, 24 January 1879
National Army Museum in London
National Library of Ireland
Newark Advertiser, 12 March 1879 and 18 February 1891
'Newark Magnus'
New Oxford Dictionary of National Biography, 2004
Norris-Newman, Charles L., *In Zululand with the British Throughout the Zulu War of 1879*, 1880
Paton, G., Glennie, F., Penn-Symons, W., *Historical Records of the 24th Regiment*, 1892
Plymouth Historical Society
Plymouth Register Office
Plymouth and West Devon Record Office
Porter, Lieutenant Reginald de Costa, his diary of the Zulu War
Porter, Whitworth, and Watson, Charles Moore, *History of the Corps of Royal Engineers*, 1889
Pring, James Hurley, *A Memoir of Thomas Chard DD, Suffragan Bishop, and the Last Abbot of Forde Abbey*, 1864
Prior, Melton, report on the Battle of Ulundi contributed to the *Times of Natal*, 9 September 1879
Record of Service Ledger for the 2nd/24th Regiment
Red Earth, Royal Engineers Museum Publication, 1996
Regimental Museum of the Royal Welsh at Brecon
Reid, Stuart, *Battles of the Scottish Lowlands*, 2004
Reynolds, Surgeon James Henry, account in the Appendix to the Report of the Army Medical Department, 1878
Ritter, E.A., *Shaka Zulu: the Rise of the Zulu Kingdom*, 1955
rorke'sdriftvc.com, discussion forum (now inactive)
Royal Engineers Journals, 1879 and 1897; and a special centenary edition for June 1979, *The Defence of Rorke's Drift, 22 January 1879. The Commemoration of the Centenary*
Royal Engineers Museum at Chatham
Royal Magazine, February 1905
Ruthin Local History Society
St Budeaux church, Plymouth, monumental inscriptions
St Germain's Church, Thurlby, monumental inscriptions
St Michael's Church, Othery, monumental inscriptions
St Peter and St Paul Church, North Curry, monumental inscriptions

Samuelson, R.C.A., *Long Long Ago*, 1929

Savage, Private Edward, *Manchester Weekly Post*, 19 July 1879

Septans, Brevet Lieutenant Colonel Albert, *English Military Expeditions in Africa, Volume 1: Ashanti, 1873–74; Zulus, 1878–79*, 1896

Singapore Free Press, 25 March 1893, 18 September 1894, 10 November 1897

Singapore Mid-Day Herald, 18 November 1897

Smith, Revd George, account dated 3 February 1879, published in the *Journal of the Royal Army Chaplains' Department*, for July 1936

Smith, Revd George, 'The Defence of Rorke's Drift by an Eyewitness', published in the *Natal Mercury*, 7 April 1879

Smith-Dorrien, General Horace, *Memories of Forty-Eight Years Service*, 1925

Somerset Archives and Local Studies

Somerset County Gazette, 6 November 1879

South African Military History Society

South Wales Borderers Publication, *Historical Records of the 2nd Battalion, 24th Regiment for the Campaign in South Africa, 1877–78–79, Embracing the Kaffir and Zulu Wars*, 1882

Stafford, Captain Walter H., *Recollections of the Battle of Isandlwana*, January 1938

Straits Times, 16 November 1892

Stevenson, Lee, 'The Noble Sapper on the Box: Charles Robson RE', *Royal Engineers Journal*, August 1995

Stoke St Mary records

Sydney Daily Telegraph, 16 December 1907, 'Rorke's Drift and Majuba: Reminiscences of Mr James Page'

Symons, J.P., *My Reminiscences of the Zulu War*, 1879 (Campbell Collections, University of KwaZulu-Natal)

Thornton, Neil, *Rorke's Drift: A New Perspective*, 2016

The Times, 18 October 1879 and 2 August 1935

Tiverton Gazette and East Devon Herald, 7 October 1879

TNA, Records of the Bromhead Institution for Nurses and the Bromhead Nursing Home, Lincoln, 1864–1950

TNA, War Office Papers, including *The Narrative of the Field Operations Connected with the Zulu War of 1879*, 1881, WO 76/233/6, WO 76/235/9

Truth periodical, 1891

Tulloch, Major General Alexander Bruce, *Recollections of Forty Years' Service*, 1903

Victoria Cross and George Cross Association

Victorian Military History Society Journal, Soldiers of the Queen, various

Wales Online for 28 March 2013

War Office Army Lists

Wassall, Samuel, 'The Last Stand of the 24th at Isandula', *London Magazine*, 31/38

Western Mail, 22 January 1929

Western Morning News

Wilkins, Philip A., *The History of the Victoria Cross*, 1904

Wilson, John Marius, *The Imperial Gazetteer of England and Wales*, 1870–2

Wimbledon Society

Wood, Private Caleb, his account in the *Ilkeston Pioneer*, 26 December 1913

Wood VC, General Sir Evelyn, *From Midshipman to Field-Marshal*, 1906

Woodham-Smith, Cecil and Woodham, Charles, *The Great Hunger, Ireland 1845–1849*, 1962

World periodical, 18 February 1891

Zulu War 1878–1879: Notes on the Zulu War, manuscript diary by an unknown soldier of the 5th Field Company, Royal Engineers, 1879

Index